Public Enemies:
The Mayor,
the Mob, and the
Crime That Was

GEORGE WALSH

Public Enemies: The Mayor, the Mob, and the Crime That Was

W· W· Norton & Company· New York· London

Copyright © 1980 by George Walsh
Published simultaneously in Canada by George J. McLeod Limited,
Toronto. Printed in the United States of America.
First Edition

Library of Congress Cataloging in Publication Data
Walsh, George, 1931–
  Public enemies.
  Notes: p.
  Includes index.
  1. O'Dwyer, William, 1890–1964. 2. Costello, Frank.
3. Corruption (in politics)—New York (City) 4. New
York (City)—Politics and goverment—1945–1951.
5. New York (City)—Mayors—Biography. 6. Crime and
criminals—New York (City)—Biography. I. Title.
F128.5.W23 1980   974.7'1'040924 [B] 79–17943
ISBN 0-393-01306-5
1 2 3 4 5 6 7 8 9 0

For Joan, Grail, and Simon.
Once more, with feeling.

Contents

Prologue   XI

PART ONE

1942 : Friendship   1

PART TWO

1890-1941 : Beginnings   35

PART THREE

1943-1945 : Interregnum   101

PART FOUR

1946-1950 : Mayoralty   131

PART FIVE

1951 : Investigation   187

PART SIX

1952-1973 : Aftermath   225

Notes   251

Index   263

Acknowledgment

THE CONNECTION between William O'Dwyer and Frank Costello, which culminated in their televised appearances before the Kefauver Committee in 1951, is the subject of this book. *Public Enemies* has been almost entirely researched through the Report of the Special Committee to Investigate Organized Crime, U.S. Senate (19 vols.), and through a careful sifting of material in relevant books, periodicals, and newspapers—as cited in the Notes section. Those persons still living who were closest to O'Dwyer would not be interviewed for Public Enemies, and this I deeply regret. As for the key mobsters in the evolving Syndicate, all but Meyer Lansky are dead.

It often seemed to me, when I was writing this book, that

the criminals—so homicidally single-minded in their quest for riches and respectibility—were not quite real. But they were real, and today, following the thoughtful example of Frank Costello, their successors have pervaded large segments of the American business and entertainment scene. But *Public Enemies* is about the past, the Crime That Was, and I hope it sheds light on the associations that frequently exist between politics and crime. As William O'Dwyer once admitted: "There are things you have to do politically, if you want cooperation." Sad to sad, he was eminently correct.

Prologue

IN DECEMBER OF 1942, William O'Dwyer, the immigrant Irishman known as Bill-O to the hundreds of thousands of New Yorkers who had backed him in his unsuccessful mayoral race against Fiorello LaGuardia the year before, paid an impromptu visit to the lavish Central Park West apartment of Frank Costello. Himself an immigrant (his mother had brought him to this country from Italy as a four-year-old), Costello was known to even greater numbers of Americans as the prime minister of the underworld. Precisely what was discussed during this meeting is a matter of conjecture, although the participants provided some interesting explanations. But the implications of the visit, to Bill-O's detractors at least, were clear. The smiling, gregarious O'Dwyer, the crusading Brooklyn district attorney who had broken up Murder Inc.—the enforcement arm of the National Crime Syndicate—and who had used his new-found fame to run as the Democratic candidate for mayor, was setting the stage for a second mayoral bid. To win, he needed the help of the impassive, close-mouthed Frank Costello, the man uniquely qualified to provide him with the money, political clout, and votes to make his ambition a reality. This is the story of that alliance, of its rise, its flowering, and its fall.

Public Enemies: The Mayor, the Mob, and the Crime That Was

PART ONE

1942:
Friendship

1

BILL-O'S RISE in the world was a Horatio-Alger success story: his record, on the surface, exemplary. Coming to New York in 1910 at the age of twenty, he arrived well after the massive wave of Irish immigration that began in the 1820s, crested at mid-century, and continued until the 1870s. O'Dwyer was an educated man, the son of schoolteachers, and he was determined to make his mark in his new country. First he took a series of laborer's jobs: coal-passer, hod-carrier, plasterer's apprentice. Then he progressed to bartending, mixing drinks in the city's great hotels. It was the decade before World War I, and New York—typified by its opulent Fifth Avenue—was for the well-to-do a magical place. Vanderbilt, Astor, and Frick Renaissance palaces; marble oyster bars and rococo dining rooms in the deluxe hotels; sporty Pierce Arrows and spindly Model T's; fashionable women in high-waisted, flaring skirts, wearing flowered and feathered hats; confident men in bowlers, celluoid collars, and ubiquitous vests.

O'Dwyer enjoyed reminiscing about those days. He would tell of the rainy night he was tending bar in the Plaza, the room almost empty, while three of the town's most eminent personalities—Arnold Daly the actor, John McGraw the coach of the Giants, Jim Corbett the fighter—chinned away the hours together. The waiter was serving the group round after round; Corbett's drinks were nonalcoholic. "Suddenly there was a hullabaloo," O'Dwyer would say. "Daly is up and shouting at the top of his lungs, and John McGraw is eyeing him belligerently, and Jim Corbett the pugilist"—here he would smile at the memory of the unlikely peacemaker— "stretches out his hands and cries, 'Gentlemen, gentlemen!....' "

By 1917, O'Dwyer was a New York City policeman. One of his best friends in the department was Matty Culhane— "one of the sweetest, gentlest men who ever lived, six-feet-two, and loose." Culhane's beat was the Brooklyn waterfront, where the Kid Cheese gang ruled. When the gang was not stealing on the docks, it specialized in luring cops into tenements and beating them up. One day the Kid Cheese boys tried the gambit on Culhane. "But hidden in his pocket is the short billy, not the long one, and a murderous weapon, and in about seven minutes there is a considerable pile of young men lying in the street and crumpled in the doorway. . . ."

While still a policeman, O'Dwyer earned his law degree. He resigned from the force shortly before his admission to the bar, in 1925, at the age of thirty-five. Seven years later, in the aftermath of the scandals surrounding the James J. Walker administration, a reform mayor appointed Bill-O a magistrate, and his public career was launched. From 1939 to 1941, as Brooklyn's district attorney, his prosecution of Murder Inc. earned him city-wide respect, giving him the mayoralty nomination. Though his challenge to the entrenched La-Guardia failed, he was determined to try again for the office.

The reason for their meeting that December night in 1942, both Bill-O and Costello would contend, was an "investigation" O'Dwyer was conducting into contract fraud at Wright Field in Dayton, Ohio. On leave of absence as Brooklyn district attorney, he was serving—during the early months of World War II—as a major in the procurement arm of the army air force, with orders to "keep Wright Field clear" of profiteers. An anonymous letter, sent to the district attorney's office and forwarded to him, Bill-O insisted, charged that a certain "Joe Baker," a friend of Costello's, was cheating the air force. James J. Moran, the hulking O'Dwyer political confidante who had run the district attorney's office for him during the Murder Inc. investigation, had arranged the meeting:

"O'Dwyer wanted to know if there was some way he could get ahold of Costello," Moran said, "and I said I thought there was. And I got ahold of Michael Kennedy and made the arrangements."

"Kennedy was a Tammany Hall political leader?" Moran was asked.

"He was *the* leader."

"And why would you reach Costello through Michael Kennedy?"

"At the time the newspapers were filled with stories that Costello and Kennedy were bosom companions, that they met at the Waldorf and that they met here, there, and everywhere, and it was only natural that I would seek the person I thought could arrange the appointment. . . ."

"What was discussed with Costello?"

"That I don't know."

"Weren't you in the room?"

"O'Dwyer and Costello were the two that conferred."

"They went to one side of the room?"

"Yes."

"And you didn't hear any of the conversation?"

"No."

Several others were in Costello's apartment that December evening. One of them was Bert Stand, Tammany Hall's secretary for a decade and one of the three or four most powerful figures in that Manhattan-based political machine—the Democratic organization that traditionally controlled New York City.

"You say you went up to the apartment with Kennedy?" Stand would be asked.

"I met Mr. Kennedy at the New York Athletic Club, and that is at Fifty-ninth Street," Stand replied, "and we walked up from there to Mr. Costello's home at Sixty-third Street."

"For what purpose?"

"I just met him and he says, 'Come on. We are going up to Frank Costello's house.' "

"Was there any discussion after your arrival?"

"No, it was just one of those cocktail affairs. We were having a drink, and there was a little tray of hors d'oeuvres, and we were talking generally—punching the bag, you might say."

"Did O'Dwyer have any separate conversation with Costello?"

"I could not say."

"Was there any talk about who would be the Democratic nominee for mayor in 1945?"

"I couldn't say there was. There may have been. If there

was, I paid no attention to it."

"Costello had at that time a bad reputation, had he not?"

"I guess he has had a bad reputation all through the years," Stand said.

"Wouldn't there be a natural tendency to shun people with bad reputations, rather than fraternize with them?"

"I was not going to give the leader advice. Mr. Kennedy asked me to go and I went."

Costello's rise in the world, like O'Dwyer's, was also rags-to-riches—though far from exemplary. Growing up in poverty on the streets of East Harlem before World War I, he was one of the hundreds of thousands of Italian immigrants who supplanted the Irish influx. The child of peasants who knew neither the language nor the law, who were suspicious of all authority, Costello respected only the code of silence, the code that had always insulated his Southern Italian forbears from oppressors. His was the New York where some sixty-six thousand dank tenements housed two million of the poor; where two-thirds of the factory workers earned wages far below subsistence; where gangs of hoodlums like the Gophers and the Car Barn boys ruled the railroad yards and the docks. Young Francesco turned first to petty thievery, then to assault and robbery. In early 1915, at the age of twenty-four, he was convicted—after numerous brushes with the law—of carrying a concealed weapon and given a year in prison.

"Will your Honor give me another chance?" Costello said, just before sentencing.

"You have had chances for the last six years," the judge replied. "These chances have to cease sometime."

"You could put me on probation," answered Costello.

"I have got it right from your neighbors that you have the reputation of being a gunman, and that you were armed, prepared to do the work of a gunman."

"But your Honor, the revolver wasn't found on me. It was found one hundred feet away."

"That is right. The officers followed you and saw you throw the gun away, and they first captured you and then took you back and got the gun. Your actions were those of a guilty man. I sentence you to the penitentiary for one year."

After Costello's release from prison, he was a far more mature individual—a criminal who realized that carrying a gun was no substitute for careful planning.

"I knew I had been stupid," he later told a friend. "Carrying a gun was like carrying a label that says, 'I'm dangerous, get me off the streets.' I made up my mind I'd never pack a gun again. And I never did."

Within a few years, Costello—much impressed with the methods used by the legendary gambler Arnold Rothstein—moved into bookmaking. With the coming of Prohibition in 1920, he went on to bootlegging, and by mid-decade he was a wealthy man, smuggling liquor across the border from Canada or landing it on New York and New Jersey beaches from offshore cargo ships.

"He was a man of his word," a Canadian liquor broker would say of Costello. "He had the money to spend and you could trust him. He'd ask you what you had, make notes, and place an order. You'd hand him the tab, and he'd take the money out of his pocket and pay you."

Toward the end of Prohibition, Costello expanded his gambling activities, going into slot machines, casinos, and layoff betting. Soon, acting in concert with Charles "Lucky" Luciano, Joe Adonis, Meyer Lansky, and Benjamin "Bugsy" Siegel, he became a criminal force, a man to be reckoned with in the underworld. During the 1930s, the farseeing Costello and his colleagues recognized the need for a National Crime Syndicate, helped found that organization, and then, bloodily, assumed its leadership. But all the while, the prime-minister-to-be remained as much as possible in the background. He was nothing more than a businessman, he maintained—an entrepreneur slightly ahead of his time, slightly ahead of the legalization of both liquor and gambling. Costello's friends in high places were many, and were bought by favors and by money. None of the sporadic investigations of his emerging empire, accordingly, caused him more than temporary inconvenience. His public posture was one of injured innocence. "I have been prejudged," he would say to the inquisitive, if he offered any comment at all.

By the time of O'Dwyer's December, 1942, meeting with Costello in the latter's apartment, only the naïve would have been surprised that the immigrant Irishman would have found the immigrant Italian a power worth courting. Costello was then on intimate terms with the Democratic leaders of at least ten of Manhattan's sixteen districts. A half-dozen of them regularly went to his home for dinner. Others met him at his favorite restaurants and watering spots—L'Aiglon, the Waldorf-Astoria Hotel, the Copacabana. Moreover, many politicians of Italian descent were related by blood or marriage to well-known mobsters. "I know the leaders, know them well, and maybe they got a little confidence in me," Costello would say. This confidence was well placed. In New York alone, within the next few years, some $3 billion annually would be bet through the prime minister's gambling network; millions of dollars would be paid annually for police protection; unknown sums would be passed under the table to understanding public servants.

Meanwhile, law and order ostensibly prevailed: New Yorkers could still stroll through Central Park after dark, unescorted women were not allowed in respectable nightclubs and bars, and the citizenry could feel secure—no matter what the hour—riding the Third Avenue El from the Bowery to the Bronx. Cobina Wright, Jr., having had her run as deb of the year, was being pressed for tabloid space by other madcap socialites; the big bands of Kay Kyser, Tommy Dorsey, and Benny Goodman were playing "Let's Remember Pearl Harbor," "Praise the Lord (and Pass the Ammunition)," and "Don't Sit Under the Apple Tree (with Anyone Else But Me)"; Greer Garson was keeping eyes wet and home fires burning in *Mrs. Miniver.* while Celeste Holm was doing her bit in the smash musical, *Oklahoma.* For most Americans on the home front, life was most pleasant.

Pudgy, moon-faced Irving Sherman, who during the 1930s had served as a front man for the racketeers who preyed on the garment industry, was still another witness to O'Dwyer's 1942 call on Costello.

"O'Dyer and I are going up to Costello's home," he would quote James Moran as saying. "Will you join us?"

Sherman, who testified he had been introduced to both O'Dwyer and Moran by a detective named Jack Gorman ("He is dead now"), could not recall that any politics were discussed at the meeting. But he did admit that his acceptance of Moran's invitation caused him considerable inconvenience, in 1945, when O'Dwyer made his second, and successful, run for the mayoralty.

"I was at a dinner given by the 3-G clothing manufacturers. I was there with Mrs. Sherman, Jack Gorman, several others. A man came in and motioned to Gorman to come over. Jack went and talked with him, got finished, and then took me aside. He said, 'O'Dwyer would like you to leave town immediately.' "

"What reason was assigned for the request you leave New York?"

"The only thing Gorman told me, this man gave him a message that there was going to be a terrible blast in the newspapers, and O'Dwyer didn't want them to get ahold of me and have a chance to talk with me."

Years after his visit to Costello's apartment, ex-mayor O'Dwyer, having resigned under fire, would say he did not know why Kennedy, Stand, and Sherman were present.

"I didn't expect to see any one of them. There was a conversation between Costello and me. And that conversation was not in the presence of the others. My best recollection would be that I talked to Costello about the contracts, and who was doing business at Wright Field, and did he personally have any interest in the contracts. There was an anonymous letter. . . ."

"Who got this anonymous letter?"

"The letter came to Moran in Brooklyn, and he mailed it to me."

"Just what did Costello say?"

"That in effect he knew the Joe Baker mentioned in the letter, knew him very well, had no interest in the contracts, and had no interest in any air force contracts. I told him the air force didn't want anyone in Wright Field unless they were legitimate people."

"Was there anything about Frank Costello that demanded your personal attention, as contrasted to Baker, who did not?" O'Dwyer was asked.

"I felt I could get information. I knew Costello had money. I knew he was the one who would finance the business . . . if anyone did."

"You knew Sherman was a good friend of Costello's?"

"That's right."

"Did you know Sherman's business?"

"He was working, when I knew him, for a shirt manufacturing company that was doing business with the navy."

"Don't you feel, with the knowledge you had of Costello, it was unfortunate of you to have visited his house?"

"It was very fortunate for the army, but it was unfortunate for me politically."

"Don't you think the same results for the army could have been obtained by having Costello come to you?"

"It was a question of my authority. I was not a district attorney with a fistful of subpoenas then. I was just a major in the air force."

"A funny thing, the magnetism that Costello had. How can you analyze it?"

"It doesn't matter whether a man is a banker, a businessman, or a gangster," Bill-O admitted. "His pocketbook is always attractive."

Costello would agree with O'Dwyer that future mayoral considerations were not discussed during their meeting and, going further, would insist that he was a nonpolitical creature.

"I have met these people, but I have absolutely divorced myself from any participating in politics," the prime minister solemnly declared.

"Yet you have continued to associate with a great many people in politics, have you not?"

"I don't know if you'd call it associate. If I meet them, I will talk to them, and they talk to me."

"What else do district leaders talk about but politics?"

"I don't know. Don't you know any of them?"

"As a matter of fact, I don't."

"Maybe you are better off," replied Costello.

But Costello's influence stretched well beyond New York City. Through Joe Adonis in Brooklyn, upstate New York, and New Jersey, Meyer Lansky in Miami, and Bugsy Siegel in California and Nevada, as well as lieutenants like Phil Kastel in New Orleans, he truly controlled a national gambling organization.

2

Cold-eyed, smooth-faced Joe Adonis was born near Naples in 1902. His real name was Joseph Doto and he had been a major Syndicate figure since 1931 when, at the behest of Lucky Luciano and Costello, he was one of four gunmen who shot to death Giuseppe "Joe the Boss" Masseria—the other assassins being Albert Anastasia, Bugsy Siegel, and Vito Genovese. In 1942, Adonis was a principal partner with the prime minister in the Piping Rock Casino in Saratoga, New York, a posh gambling establishment that had been operating illegally for almost a decade. Inside the casino, where Saratoga police were forbidden by their superiors to enter, Joey A— as he was known—would sit at a private table, watching the croupiers, dealers, and dicemen. With his low voice, gentlemanly manner, and conservative tailoring, he might have been a banker. "It's not what we win, it's what we earn," he would say.

During the gambling season, certain Saratoga police passed their duty hours by delivering supplies of cash to Piping Rock and ferrying customers back and forth—for a fee, of course.

"I had no reason to go into the casino," Detective Walter Ahearn explained. "We were just charging the passengers riding with us, and then we would go back to the police office."

"Do you remember that you said, as a reason you didn't go in, 'I still wanted to work'?" an investigator asked.

"That's right."

"Who did you think would fire you if you went in there?"

"It would be the chief or the commissioner."

Though his activities coincided with Costello's in many places, Adonis's power base lay in Brooklyn. Ruggedly handsome (hence the alias), he grew up in the Eighth Assembly District, around the waterfront and the Gowanus Canal, an area that produced such gangland notables as Frankie Yale, Albert Anastasia, and Al Capone. It was Yale, then the boss of Brooklyn, who made the young Adonis his protégé, initiating him during the 1920s into the mysteries of bootlegging, hi-jacking, and bribery. After his patron, Yale, was killed in an internecine dispute, Joey A, already a power in the mob, shifted his allegiance to Anthony "Little Augie" Carfano (also known as Anthony Pisano), becoming his chief aide. In 1933, Little Augie withdrew from the Brooklyn rackets to devote himself to gambling and horse racing in Florida and Adonis became the number one man.

With Prohibition coming to an end, Joey A, like Costello in Manhattan, decided to concentrate on gambling. Casinos, bookmaking, policy numbers, slot machines, floating crap games—all these undertakings offered the potential for immense profits. But first, of course, Adonis needed to insure police and political protection. Into his restaurant in South Brooklyn, the Italian Kitchen (originally located at the corner of Fourth Avenue and Carroll Street), flowed a steady stream of the borough's news-worthy names. Jerome Ambro, who was defeated as leader of the Nineteenth Assembly District to a large extent because of Adonis' enmity, and who attributed his loss to "floaters, thugs, and money," would be asked who had introduced him to the mobster.

"One of a number of men," he replied. "Bill O'Dwyer, Assemblyman Irwin Steingut, Sheriff and Fire Commissioner Frank Quayle, Democratic county leader Frank Kelly."

"And thereafter, did you go quite frequently to a restaurant owned and operated by Joe Adonis?"

"That's right."

"Was it a gathering place for politicians?"

"It was for the Who's Who of Brooklyn, the hoi polloi, the big names. . . ."

Ambro would maintain that, while he was still in Adonis' good graces in the early 1930s, he helped further O'Dwyer's career. After a chance meeting at the Italian Kitchen, Bill-O, then serving temporarily as a city magistrate and hoping to be confirmed in the post, asked Ambro to put in a word for him with Kenneth Sutherland, a top Democratic leader who was himself an Adonis friend. Ambro did, and, since both Sutherland and Joseph V. McKee, the acting mayor at the time, were caught up in a reform wave and looking for new faces, the magistrate's appointment was made permanent.

Besides supplying the cash that every politician needs for campaigning (discreet white envelopes were served with coffee at the Italian Kitchen), Adonis supplied the muscle. His goons roughed up and otherwise intimidated rival leaders and workers and, on election days, herded hundreds and even thousands of floaters—illegal voters—into key districts in order to tip the balance. Poll-watchers knew better than to complain: the police were mysteriously absent. The City Democratic Club, on Brooklyn's Clinton Street, became a favorite Adonis hangout, and there he and his cronies freely mingled with sheriffs, district attorneys, and judges. Most notable among the mobsters were Louis Capone, Adonis's liason with Murder Inc.; Albert Anastasia, whom Joey A personally selected as the leader of that lethal organization and who came to be called the lord high executioner; and

Anthony Romeo, a Murder Inc. killer who would himself be shot to death.

Through Albert Anastasia and his brother Anthony, Adonis ruled the Brooklyn docks, breaking up unionization efforts among the workers while on the payroll of the employers, and simultaneously gouging the same employers by taking a commission for safely unloading their goods. Moreover, he used his control of the waterfront to move into the already-burgeoning narcotics traffic. In similar industries where great numbers of low-income people were employed—trucking, the garment center, the fish markets—he shared in the extortion rackets of Louis "Lepke" Buchalter and his pleistocene sidekick, Jacob "Gurrah" Shapiro. Yet in 1940, when the spotlight of Bill O'Dwyer's Murder Inc. investigation would be turned on these arrangements, Joey A would remain in the shadows. He would be obliged, after conferring with Costello, to surrender Lepke to the law, and barely succeed in saving Anastasia, but his own connection with these lieutenants would never be proven.

On the surface, Adonis lived respectably, even philanthropically. Soon after his marriage (one of the witnesses signing the license was Lucky Luciano), he moved with his bride into a stucco mansion in Bay Ridge, then one of the borough's most exclusive residential areas. Remembering the needy, he gave thousands of dollars to his mother, Mary Doto, who still lived in his old tenement neighborhood, urging her to buy food and coal for the poor, or pay the rent for the indigent.

More and more, Joey A began to use mob muscle to go into legitimate businesses. Within weeks after he set up his Kings County Cigarette Service, his hoods managed, miraculously, to install ten thousand cigarette-vending machines in the borough's bars, hotels, and restaurants. Meanwhile, his rival cigarette distributors were plagued by hi-jackings and, over a four-year period, lost $6 million worth of stock. Amid the turmoil, Adonis prospered mightily. Observed one police officer of the obvious: "Hi-jacked cigarettes can be sold at one hundred percent profit." Other Adonis investments included three automobile agencies (White Auto Sales, a Ford agency located across the street from the Italian Kitchen, was the showpiece) and two liquor distributorships. Perhaps his most impressive acquisition, however, was the Automotive Conveying Company of Cliffside Park, New Jersey, which monopolized the delivery of Ford cars assembled in New Jersey to agencies throughout the Middle Atlantic States and New England. For most of the 1930s, Ford paid this Adonis-controlled company $1 million yearly. Much later, when Adonis would be asked why he had expanded his activities to New Jersey, he would say: "I like the climate there better."

"Was it cooler than Brooklyn?" his questioner inquired.

"About three hundred feet above sea level," replied the unperturbed Joey A.

The real reason why Adonis, starting in 1937, began to move his operations to New Jersey was the heat he was receiving in New York from Fusion Mayor Fiorello LaGuardia. Four years earlier, when the rotund, cigar-smoking La-Guardia had squeaked out a narrow victory over two Democratic rivals (and a divided Democratic party) for his first mayoral term, Joey A had supported the Little Flower with words ("The Democrats haven't recognized the Italians") and with cash (a twenty-five-thousand-dollar campaign contribution). During this period, coincidentally, even while La-Guardia was making Costello in Manhattan a whipping boy, and forcing him to move his slot machines down to Louisiana, he acted as if Adonis in Brooklyn did not exist.

But in 1937, Joey A made a mistake: he supported Democratic candidate Royal S. Copeland against the entrenched LaGuardia, who promptly trumpeted the city was being threatened by "a leader of the underworld" and "a tin-horn gambler." The police then took an unusual interest in the gangster's affairs, asking him, first, about a truck hi-jacking and, second, about the murders of three minor hoods who had optimistically stuck up a crap game under his protection. The charges were soon dropped, but the distractions served their purpose—keeping Adonis from getting out the Copeland vote. Laguardia easily won a second term.

So loud was the Little Flower's recurring invective against his onetime supporter, however, that Governor Herbert Lehman appointed a special prosecutor, John Harlan Amen, to look into the Brooklyn rackets. (This inquiry functioned apart from the Murder Inc. investigation.) In April of 1940, Amen filed kidnapping, extortion, and assault charges against Adonis and a bodyguard, Sam Gasberg, alleging that they had abducted two associates, Isidor Wapinski and Isidore Juffe, who Joey A felt owed him twenty-thousand-dollars, had taken them to the soundproof office in the rear of the Italian Kitchen, and there had beaten them until they returned part of the money. ("Joey A is supposed to be tight in money matters, which is why the boys don't like him too good," a disinterested party would comment.) So severe was the beating that Wapinski died. A nation-wide alarm went out for Adonis, who had been spending most of his time during the months of the Amen investigation in Florida, and he soon surrendered. In October, the case went to trial with Juffe the state's principal witness, only to collapse when the defense destroyed his credibility by showing he had been a professional swindler for two decades. Amen had no choice but to move, in February of 1941, for dismissal of the charges. Though this brush with the law was never a serious threat to

Joey A, it made him all the more appreciative of New Jersey's climate.

Throughout the Amen and Murder Inc. investigations, Adonis continued to shift his gambling and narcotics enterprises across the Hudson. In Cliffside, New Jersey, opposite Palisades Amusement Park, he established a restaurant headquarters, Duke's, that was a replica of the Italian Kitchen— replete with mobsters, politicians, and, of course, a soundproof office. The owner of record was Johnny "Duke" DeNoia and, though Joey A himself in the early 1940s kept a low profile, the restaurant's regulars included Willie Moretti and his brother Solly, veteran New Jersey Syndicate figures; Arthur Longano, an Adonis confidante; and Thomas "Three-Finger Brown" Lucchese, the Upper-Manhattan–based boss of one of New York's five Mafia families. Keeping in the background, too, was Abner "Longy" Zwillman, the onetime Newark bootlegging czar who had since infiltrated a dozen legitimate businesses. Meanwhile, Adonis took special care to insure the good will of the local authorities. Cliffside's chief of police would admit under subsequent questioning, for instance, that his annual income was five times his salary.

Willie Moretti, a close friend of Costello's since their boyhood days in East Harlem and one of the few loquacious Mafioso, would nonetheless debunk the whole idea that a criminal conspiracy existed.

"People of character don't need introductions," he said. "They know each other automatically. You go to the racetracks and you go to Florida and you meet people. A man that is well-known meets everybody."

"Are these people the mob?" Moretti's interrogator asked.

"The newspapers calls them the mob. I don't know, if they would be right everybody would be in jail."

"Is that what *you* mean when you say the mob? These

people you meet at racetracks and gambling places?"

"People are mobs that make six percent more on the dollar than anybody else."

"You mean these people are called a mob because they make more money?"

"That is right."

Moretti would claim that Duke's was no different than any popular restaurant.

"I would class Duke's like Lindy's on Broadway," he said.

"What do you mean by that?" his questioner persisted.

"You get good meals there, and you hang around there like everybody else does."

"Have you ever seen Longy Zwillman and Joe Adonis there?"

"Yes, sir."

"And there would be a lot of those people who make six percent more on their money?"

"How can I answer that? I don't ask people their business."

Some idea of the magnitude of the New Jersey gambling operation in the early 1940s can be gleaned from the bank deposits of Frank Erickson, the suave middleman the newspapers called king of the bookmakers, who for years had served Costello, Adonis, and Meyer Lansky as a national clearing house for all wagers. During 1941 and 1942, in just one Jersey bank, Erickson's deposits totalled more than $2 million. Obviously, Joey A was becoming as untouchable in his new Republican stronghold as he had been in Democratic Brooklyn. And riding high with him were his fellow Syndicate overlords—Costello, Lansky, and Bugsy Siegel—all interlocked in the business of crime.

3

In New Orleans in 1942, Broadway expatriate Phillip "Dandy Phil" Kastel, who had once run a string of bucket shops selling fraudulent securities and had served a three-year prison term for his initiative, administered Costello's multi-million-dollar slot-machine empire. The two men had begun their placement of the machines in New York in 1928, evading the intent of the law by having the slots dispense packages of mints to players and slugs to winners—the slugs being convertible to cash. All went well for a half-dozen years. The Tru-Mint Novelty Corporation put some five thousand machines into bars, restaurants, and candy stores, the Syndicate saw to it that competition was discouraged, and the annual gross reached at least $3 million. In the candy stores, stepladders were provided to help schoolchildren reach the counters on which the machines rested. But early in 1935, reform-minded Mayor LaGuardia, overcoming a restraining order from a judge favorably inclined to the subterfuge, went to the U.S. Supreme Court and had the slots declared illegal, thereby driving them from New York.

"The Supreme Court held that the slot-machine business was illegal?" Costello would be asked.

"Well, it had been mint machines. I believe that was the question," he answered.

"If you had a little package of mints in the machine, and they dropped out when somebody put a coin in, that made it a legal machine?"

"That's right."

"And finally the Supreme Court refused to accept that?"

"Right."

"It was an attempt to get around the law?"

"We were told we were in the right."

"The lawyers told you you were within your rights?"

"Yes."

"And as long as the injunction stayed in effect, you made a lot of money?"

"You would make money, naturally."

Within weeks, however, Costello and Kastel found a haven for their machines in Louisiana, where they already had established several gambling clubs. Their protector was Huey P. Long, the raspy-voiced populist politician who ruled that state, largely on the strength of his promise to re-distribute the wealth. A former traveling salesman among the "rednecks" of back-country Louisiana, Long had earned a law degree, attracted public attention by representing the people of the state in public-utility litigation and, in 1928, had overwhelmingly been elected governor. In that post, he pushed through the building of badly-needed roads, hospitals, and schools, raised taxes drastically among the well-to-do, and—through his bullying of the legislature and control of the police—virtually suspended the state's democratic processes. Though he resigned the governorship in 1931 to enter the U.S. Senate, the "Kingfish," as he was known, continued to rule Louisiana from Washington. During his periodic drinking bouts, Long frequently ran afoul through an inability to distinguish a prostitute from somebody's wife. It was because of this failing that he made Costello's acquaintance.

"One time Huey went up to New York," New Orleans politician Peter Hand volunteered, "and he went into the powder room of one of the clubs, I think it was Long Island somewhere, and somebody punched him in the mouth, and one of Costello's friends saved him from getting a beating, and he became very friendly with Costello." The demagogic Long would explain his involvement with the prime minister another way. "The people seem to want gambling, so let them gamble," he said.

"Huey Long came to New York in 1935 and asked you if you would come to New Orleans and go into the slot-machine business?" Costello would be asked.

"That is correct."

"How did he broach the subject?"

"He said that he wanted me to go to Louisiana and make a survey, because he wanted to put these slot machines there, and to pass legislation in order to get revenue for an old-age pension."

"And did you go down there?"

"I went down and left Mr. Kastel there to survey it."

"Was the use of slot machines in Louisiana illegal?"

"I presume they were," said Costello, "otherwise Governor Long would not look to pass legislation."

"So you had Costello in New York, who dealt in these things, and then you had the Governor of Louisiana, putting their heads together to break the state law?"

"If a governor tells me he wants to find locations, and that he wants legislation, he is not breaking any law."

"You put the machines in, didn't you?"

"Then I broke the law," Costello said. "He never broke it."

"The governor knew you were putting them in, didn't he?"

"I don't know if he did or not. Six months later, he passed out, and I hadn't seen him."

Long had of course "passed out" by means of his assassination, in September of 1935, in the corridors of the State capital at Baton Rouge. (The assassin, Dr. Carl A. Weiss, was killed in turn by the Kingfish's bodyguards.)

Long's death in no way curbed the Costello-Kastel operations in Louisiana. In fact, it soon became evident that the Kingfish, whose share of the profits was to have been a mere $250,000 annually, had badly underestimated the appeal of the slots. "It knocked a hole in all the other kinds of gambling," said Peter Hand. "Put a nickel in, and the nickels come out. Put a quarter in, and the quarters come out. We hadn't seen that in forty years around here." Dandy Phil Kastel, who in a few short months had already developed both a southern accent and a sizeable reputation among the madams of the French Quarter, went from dealing with Long to bargaining with Hand and his associates. "I told him we wanted fifty percent," remembered Hand. "I thought I was talking to a baby, but I found out that I was talking to a very smart fellow. He told me, 'That's your deal and that's that. I got to take care of the police, city hall, and everybody. . . .' "

The extent of the Costello-Kastel profits, in 1936 and 1937 alone, can be estimated from their indictment, in 1937, on charges of evading five-hundred-thousand-dollars in federal taxes on $3 million income from the slots. An acquittal soon followed, and day-by-day operations were never affected.

Debonair in dress, quiet in manner, polished in appearance, the ever-efficient Kastel was well-liked in New Orleans. Even his marriage to a local prostitute named Margie Dennis did not keep him from mingling in polite society. "Phil Kastel was a refined man, a highly intelligent man," reminisced a New Orleans criminal court judge. "He wasn't pushy or anything like that. Let's face it, he came down here to make friends and he made them." But there was no mistaking that Costello was in charge, even seeing to it that Kastel found work in the slot-machine racket for his four brothers-in-law —Dudley, William, Harold, and Jerome Geigerman.

"Tell me, Mr. Costello," the prime minister would be asked, "did Phil Kastel ever say anything but okay to you?"

"Naturally, he had said other than okay."

"Do you deny that Kastel took orders from you about the slot-machine business in New Orleans?"

"He might have taken some suggestions."

4

Russian-born Meyer Lansky, who emigrated with his family to America in 1911 at the age of nine, had come to hold, by 1942, a unique place in the underworld. As a young Jewish gangster on the Lower East Side, he had early cast his lot with emerging Mafia leaders like Lucky Luciano and Costello against the older Italian bosses—the so-called "Mustache Petes." After Luciano and Costello triumphed in the struggle, Lansky became the liason between them and non-Italian hoodlums, including those in cities other than New York. In 1934, with the backing of Luciano and Costello, as well as Adonis, Bugsy Siegel, and Louis "Lepke" Buchalter, Lansky played a major role in organizing the National Crime Syndicate during the legendary meeting at Manhattan's Waldorf-Astoria. The guest list featured such luminaries as Hymie Abrams of Boston, Harry Stromberg—also known as Nig Rosen—of Philadelphia, Abner "Longy" Zwillman of New Jersey, Moe Dalitz of Cleveland, Isadore "Kid Cann" Blumenfield of Minneapolis-St. Paul, and Phil Kastel (boss-designate of New

Orleans). Johnny Torrio, a gangland elder statesman who during his years in Chicago had been the mentor of Al Capone (now finally in jail for tax evasion), and who disapproved of the bloody disputes there among Jewish, Irish, and Italian mobsters, prevailed upon Paul "the Waiter" Ricca to represent the Windy City. Meanwhile, Anthony "Little Augie" Carfano, Adonis's former chief, was summoned from Miami. This meeting created a hierarchy of crime, capable of making joint decisions for the common good and, after Luciano was sent to prison by Special Prosecutor Thomas E. Dewey in June of 1936, Costello—as Luciano's heir—emerged as its chief beneficiary.

Ironically, Lansky's first brush with the law, and his first meeting with Luciano, came in 1918, when he was arrested for brawling with the Italian over a prostitute. A perhaps apocryphal part of the story is that the diminutive but feisty Meyer was defending Bugsy Siegel, then a precocious lad of twelve, who had not paid Lucky for the girl's services. Whatever the truth, the fact remains that soon afterward Luciano, Lansky, and Siegel—together with Costello, whom Luciano introduced to the group—began to work as a team: running floating crap games, shaking down push-cart operators, burglarizing warehouses.

In 1920, Lansky organized a group of young Jewish gunsels and went into the stolen car business, with Siegel as his lieutenant—and so the Bugs & Meyer mob was born. He would change the appearance of a car for resale, rent out getaway vehicles to other gangsters, haul Prohibition booze, even contract to use the cars for paid killings. In this way, the Bugs & Meyer mob would evolve (after Lansky and Siegel went on to less overtly homicidal endeavors) into Murder Inc.—the enforcement arm of the Syndicate-to-be, largely staffed by Jewish hitmen. "I was about a head taller than this midget,"

Luciano would say, referring to one of his early meetings with Lansky, "but he looked up at me without blinkin' an eye, and he said, 'Fuck you.' . . . Next to Benny Siegel, Meyer Lansky was the toughest guy, pound for pound, I ever knew in my whole life." But, more importantly, Luciano saw in Lansky the same reflective quality that he and Costello possessed: "We was like analyzers."

Now Meyer, in the manner of a successful businessman, began to think about taking a bride. In May of 1929, he married Anna Citron, a respectable Jewish girl who knew little of his gangland background, and honeymooned with her in Atlantic City, New Jersey. When Anna did learn of his activities, the couple became emotionally estranged, though they continued though the 1930s to live as man and wife—whenever Lansky's trips on behalf of the Syndicate did not take him away from New York. Her growing depression would eventually lead, years later, to a divorce.

In 1931, Lansky solidified his relationship with Luciano and Costello, helping them eliminate two underworld archrivals. First, he loaned them the services of Siegel for the assassination team that shot to death "Joe the Boss" Masseria, then he provided Sam "Red" Levine and three other Jewish gunmen to kill Salvatore Maranzano. So the stage was set, a few years later, for the organization of the National Crime Syndicate. "Meyer Lansky understood the Italian brain almost better than I did," Luciano would say. "That's why I picked him to be my *consigliere.* Someplace he must've been wetnursed by a Sicilian."

As the 1930s progressed, Lansky turned his attention southward. Louisiana became a way station, and he and his brother Jake worked with Costello in setting up gambling clubs there under the aegis of Carlos Marcello, the Tunisian-born Mafia boss of the state. But Lansky soon moved on, leaving others to run the day-by-day details, contenting himself with a piece of the take. "There was just too frigging much to do elsewhere," he explained. 'Elsewhere' was the Gold Coast of Florida, to the north of Miami, where he obtained a monopoly on the national wire service that transmitted track information, and so was essential to bookmaking. South of Miami he operated through Frank Erickson, Costello's gambling coordinator, in converting Tropical Park from dog to horse racing. Even though Prohibition was repealed in December of 1933, the Syndicate continued to market liquor without paying taxes, and Lansky turned to Cuba for the supplies of molasses that were used in manufacturing alcohol. (His Molaska Corporation supplied more than a dozen illegal distillers throughout the eastern half of the United States.) While in Havana, he also arranged with Fulgencio Batista, the Cuban dictator, for he and his colleagues to control the island's gambling. "We hadda put up three million in cash, up front, for Batista, and Lansky did it by opening an account in Zurich for him," Luciano would say. While Cuba was then still a playground for the rich, Meyer's initiative presaged the Syndicate's domination of gambling, during the post-World War II period, throughout the Caribbean.

"When were you in business in Cuba?" Lansky would be asked.

"In the later years of 1937," he would reply.

"What business did you have there?"

"I had the race track and a casino at the Hotel Nacional."

"Who were your partners?"

"I don't know."

"Was Frank Costello a trustee?"

"No, no."

"Did Frank Erickson have any interest in the track?"

"I don't remember."

"Was the race track and the casino at the Hotel Nacional a million-dollar operation?"

"We tried to develop it. Unfortunately the war broke out."

In 1942, the peripetetic Lansky ended a short stay in Los Angeles, where at age thirty-nine he had registered for the selective service draft, and returned to New York—where he would spend the war years developing the jukebox market, pushing the machines into bars and restaurants with the help of Syndicate muscle. So important had he become in the underworld that he and Costello would soon negotiate with the United States government for the release from prison of Luciano, claiming the Italian could make a major contribution to the war effort. Lansky was now, through adoption, a full-fledged member of the Honored Society—unobtrusive, feared, respected.

5

By the mid-1930s, Benjamin "Bugsy" Siegel had graduated from merely being Lansky's lieutenant and had become the undisputed leader of the Lower East Side Jewish mobsters. Not only did Philip "Little Farvel" Kovalick, Hyman "Curley" Holtz, and Harry "Big Greenie" Greenberg obey his orders, but even Louis "Lepke" Buchalter and Jake "Gurrah" Shapiro heeded his advice. Besides the usual run of illegal and homicidal endeavors, his interests included an insurance business. ("Insurance against getting knocked off," cracked one insider.) Like Luciano and Costello, Siegel enjoyed the prestige of accomodations at the Waldorf-Astoria; meanwhile, he established his wife and two young daughters in a luxurious suburban home in Scarsdale. The money was rolling in: his tax returns from 1929 to 1935, which were not overly scrupulous, showed a net income of some $380,000. In his snap-brim hat and velvet-collared Chesterfield, the smiling, boyish-looking Siegel epitomized gangster glamour. "These fellows were like gods to me," reminisced actor George Raft of underworld chieftains in general and Siegel, his longtime friend, in particular. "They all had Dusenbergs and sixteen-cylinder Cadillacs and wherever they went there were police captains and politicians bowing to them, and I thought, 'These fellows can't be doing anything wrong.' "

Sometime in 1937, Siegel—with the full approval of Costello and Lansky—moved with his family to Los Angeles. There he joined the Hillcrest Country Club, sent his daughters to daily lessons at the Du Brock Riding Academy, and eventually settled into a thirty-five-room Holmby Hills mansion, where his neighbors included Claudette Colbert, Bing Crosby, Judy Garland, Humphrey Bogart, and Alan Ladd. He settled into the local rackets as well: gambling concessions in Redondo Beach, a dog-racing track in Culver City, and a glittering gambling ship twelve miles off Santa Monica whose customers wore evening dress. With the same tenacity that his colleagues in the East had gained control of the garment, market, and dock workers, Siegel began the organizing of the movie extras. Soon producers and stars were thrusting unsecured "loans" upon him to prevent possible delays in filming; in one year alone the extortion brought him four-hundred-thousand-dollars.

Siegel's primary interest on the West Coast, however, was in gaining control of the national wire service that supplied bookmakers—for graduated fees ranging from $150 to $1500 weekly—with the racetrack information they needed. This was where the money lay, for without a wire service to give them entries, odds, scratches, and payoffs, off-track bookmakers could not operate. For two decades, the number one racing news service had been Continental Press of Chicago. Now, in the 1940s, the lieutenants of the jailed Al Capone set about supplementing it with a rival wire called Trans-America, and Siegel became its Western director. In collaboration with Jack I. Dragna, the Mafia representative in Los Angeles, and aided by gambling wizard Moe Sedway, Bugsy soon saw to it that local bookmakers in California, Nevada, and Arizona switched their allegience from Continental to Trans-America—or else. His share of the racket was estimated at three-hundred-thousand-dollars yearly.

Years later, an investigator, questioning Moe Sedway about his and Siegel's livelihood, would say:

"You are growing rich. Yet you don't contribute a thing in the way of production that makes real wealth. What you do is peel off in these games of chance. If you had your life to live over again, would you play the same kind of game?"

"I would not," replied Sedway. "I would not want my children to."

"You are in cahoots with a lot of people like Bugsy Siegel, and I wonder whether it all pays, and what it amounts to, and why men do these things."

"You see what it got for me," said Sedway. "I have had three major coronaries, and I have had diarrhea for six weeks, and I have an ulcer, hemorrhoids, and an abcess in my upper intestines."

"What I am asking is this: What does it all amount to?" continued the pious investigator.

"You go into this type of business and you stay in it."

"You say you knew Luciano? He is the scum of the earth. When decent men want to make a living, these men peel it off. They may have money but that is all they have."

"We don't get as rich as you think we do," said Sedway defensively. "I work pretty hard."

While he was establishing himself financially (his checking account deposits at the Union Bank & Trust Company often exceeded eighty-thousand-dollars monthly), Siegel simultaneously pursued the Hollywood social scene. His entrée was the Countess Dorothy DiFrasso, the plump and fortyish American-born heiress to a leather-goods fortune who had acquired her title through marriage to an Italian nobleman. The Countess, who entertained Hollywood notables at parties featuring boxing matches, found in the much younger Siegel the man of her delusions. In short order, she saw to it he was hob-nobbing with such stars as Gary Cooper, Clark Gable, and Cary Grant. Meanwhile, the trysting couple (Bugsy must have had a sense of humor, no matter how homicidal) embarked on a series of misadventures that must have greatly puzzled the circumspect Costello and Lansky.

The first of these enterprises was an attempt to find the millions in gems and gold supposedly buried a century before on Cocos Island—off the coast of Costa Rica—by the infamous crew of the English vessel, *Mary Deere.* Mesmerized by a mysterious map, the Countess and Siegel assembled a bizarre group of treasure hunters, including Marino Bello, whose strongest credential was that he had been the stepfather of the late Jean Harlow; Richard Gully, an English interpreter of the good life who later became Jack Warner's (of Warner Brothers) social secretary; Dr. Benjamin Blank, official physician for the Los Angeles County Jail; and Harry "Champ" Segal, a mob hanger-on who whiled away the time as Bugsy's sparring partner. The rag-tag outfit set sail from Mexico in

September of 1938 aboard a three-masted, diesel-powered schooner, armed with dynamite, rock drills, spades, caviar, and fine wines. They found nothing of value on Cocos Island, but not for lack of trying. "We drilled through rocks and shale," declared a searcher. "We dynamited whole cliffs." After ten days they returned to Hollywood—blistered, bitten, and beaten.

Just before World War II began, the Countess and Bugsy sought to corner the market for what they thought to be a super-explosive. With Mussolini preparing for war, Dorothy imagined she had the perfect buyer. Through her husband in Rome, she arranged for a demonstration to take place before members of the Italian government, and she and Siegel traveled to Europe for the festivities. Unfortunately, the test was a failure: there was no explosion. Mussolini was so miffed he expropriated the Countess's Italian property. So it went with the madcap couple. A stomach-turning venture into soybeans, a precocious committment to zippers when the country still accepted only buttons, an abortive attempt to extract Vitamin A from sharks' livers . . . all failures.

Occasionally, Siegel had more serious problems. In November of 1939, when the Murder Inc. investigation involving Louis "Lepke" Buchalter was accelerating in Brooklyn, Bugsy decided to do a favor for his Eastern colleague, who had just surrendered to the authorities. Harry Greenberg, a former Lepke henchman, was in Los Angeles, threatening to testify against his former boss unless he was provided with hush money. Not only did Siegel arrange a "hit" on Big Greenie but, inexplicably, he himself took part in the ambush. Several months later, when the still-developing Murder Inc. probe got around to Greenberg's death, one of the participants, a gunsel named Allie Tannenbaum who was now in police custody in New York, proceeded to implicate Bugsy.

Corroborating Tannenbaum's testimony was Abe "Kid Twist" Reles, the principal state's witness. During the summer of 1940, Tannenbaum and Reles were flown to Los Angeles to repeat their statements, and Siegel and four others were indicted for the homicide. "Early in August, Allie and Reles were loaded aboard a plane in utmost secrecy in New York and flown across the continent," said Burton Turkus, the Brooklyn assistant district attorney who, working under O'Dwyer, was chief prosecutor of Murder Inc.

By December, however, the indictment was dismissed, since the testimony Tannenbaum and Reles had given before the Los Angeles grand jury would have had to be repeated— for technical reasons—and District Attorney O'Dwyer adamantly refused to expose the two men to "the natural hazards" of a second trip. The kindest thing one can say about O'Dwyer's decision was that he was being short-sighted: in his desire to nail down a conviction against Lepke in New York, and so insure for himself the mayoral nomination, he would not risk his witnesses to press the case against Siegel in the West.

It was not until September of 1941 that O'Dwyer relented, agreeing to send Tannenbaum to the West Coast once more, and Siegel promptly was re-indicted. But before he could be brought to trial, Reles, stashed in a Brooklyn hotel room under the protection of six policemen, took a still-unexplained fall to his death. Without his corroboration, Tannenbaum's testimony was worthless and, in February of 1942, the murder indictment against Bugsy was again dismissed. "If all the sighs of relief were laid end to end," said Turkus, referring to the loss of Reles's testimony, not only against Siegel, but against Adonis, Anastasia, and other Syndicate chieftains, "the breath expended would have come close to filling one of the navy's larger lighter-than-air ships."

Subsequently, O'Dwyer would be asked in considerable detail about the circumstances of Reles' death.

"Apparently there were six men in the room of Reles, and he was fully dressed at five o'clock in the morning, and he got out the window. It seems, on the face of it, that the police officers weren't paying attention? . . ."

"They were careless," replied O'Dwyer, "and there is no question about it."

"What did you do about it?"

"The men, as I remember it, were punished."

"Weren't you reported as having appeared at the police trial to defend them?"

"Not to defend the particular act of carelessness, but to tell what I knew about them."

"And did you not, four years thereafter, take the head of the squad and make him seventh deputy police commissioner?"

"Yes," Bill-O admitted.

Fortunately for Siegel, the only penalty he suffered for Big Greenie's killing was his forced resignation from the Hillcrest Country Club. Even during the period of his indictment, he spent as much time out of jail as in it, largely due to the efforts of Dr. Benjamin Blank, the physician for the Los Angeles County Jail who had accompanied the Countess and Bugsy on their buried-treasure search. During one monthly period, Siegel left the jail—with doctor's permission—no less than eighteen times. And while he sometimes did have dental work done, he spent far more time partying at fashionable Beverly Hills bistros. (When the story of his permissiveness came to light, Dr. Blank, claiming he was not getting "a square deal," was fired.)

By 1942, Costello and his allies, the young "turks" who had brought down Masseria and Maranzano, had solidified their control of the Syndicate, and had branched out far beyond New York. None knew it better than Bill O'Dwyer.

"Bugsy Siegel, was he one of the top men?" O'Dwyer would be asked.

"I know how much trust they put in Siegel. He was big," Bill-O would reply.

"Albert Anastasia was the boss of the New York waterfront? And he was also the boss of Murder Inc?"

"He was the director."

"And Anastasia had a boss named Joe Adonis?"

"Here is one place where I wouldn't quibble."

"And whereas Anastasia had the waterfront, Adonis had the gambling?"

"That is the impression I got from my informants."

"And Siegel had a partner named Lansky? Was he big?"

"He would be on the same level as Siegel, except that it is quite possible Lansky went in for a lot of things other than gambling. Narcotics is one of them."

"Then there was Luciano?"

"He was very big."

"What is your present view about Costello in this over-all gang picture?"

"I never did find his name mentioned in connection with any murder in Brooklyn. . . ."

PART TWO

1890-1941:
Beginnings

1

WILLIAM O'DWYER was born July 11, 1890, in the village of
Brohola, County Mayo, in the windswept northwest of Ireland. Actually, he came into the world four days earlier, but
a registry mishap made the July 11 date the official one, and
nobody, Bill would later say, was ever the poorer for it. His
father, Patrick O'Dwyer, was a country schoolteacher, having
come to Brohola a few years before, in answer to an advertise-
ment placed by the parish priest. Formal education was then
fairly new in Ireland. Previously, the people had been forced
to rely on itinerant teachers, relics of the era when English
law made it a crime to teach them to read and write. After
settling into his job, Patrick married a local schoolmistress,
Bridget McNicholas, and began raising a family: William was

the couple's first child; ten more would follow. He was a bright lad, and his mother had one ambition for him—throughout his adolescence, she was convinced he had an avocation for the priesthood. Eventually, she persuaded him to enroll at the University of Salamanca, the great Jesuit seminary in Spain.

But the young O'Dwyer was not that sure what he wanted to do with his life. "My God, the past takes me back to when I was a boy in Ireland," he would reminisce. His father had painstakingly led him through the mysteries of quadratic equations, logarithms, and inclined planes. The boy read Locke and Bellamy, was taught about Drake, Magellan, Cortes, and Columbus. His father, too, had spoken to him about his future. "Nothing we can do for you here can compare with the United States of America," was the elder O'Dwyer's advice. "All the girls will stay here, the boys will go to the USA."

A year at Salamanca made William realize the priesthood was not for him, and whetted his appetite for America. A trifle shamefacedly, he wrote his mother of his decision and took steerage passage for New York, where he landed, in the summer of 1910 at age twenty, with $25.35 in his pockets. Of sturdy build, with the broad forehead, bushy brows, and clear blue eyes characteristic of the O'Dwyers, he briefly worked as a coal-passer on the docks, a stoker on an Argentina-bound freighter (an experience that brought the weight on his five-foot-eight-inch frame down from 155 pounds to 135), a fireman on the boats that traveled the Hudson between New York and Albany. By 1911, he was a hod carrier and a plasterer's apprentice, equally incongruous occupations for a youth familiar with *The Oxford Book of English Verse*, but jobs that enabled him to make his way in America. He helped build the Hotel McAlpin, the Woolworth Building, and other New York landmarks and, years later, still carried his union card.

"When we took time off for lunch, I would read westerns to the other hod-carriers," Bill-O would say. "Little did the boys realize I was practicing pronunciation."

Soon afterward, O'Dwyer switched to bartending, first at the Ritz-Carlton, then at the Vanderbilt and Plaza hotels. While working behind the bar, he met many of New York's noveaux riches, and for them he reserved a special contempt. "I wish you could have seen them swarming into this town," he once told some friends. "The cattlemen, the copper kings, the sports, all with buckets of money, and they didn't know how to behave in a great city, especially toward the help." There was the night Diamond Jim Brady came into the Vanderbilt with the Dolly Sisters, one of whom had taken to wearing a live monkey as a fur piece.

"Boy, check this," she told the hat-check man, a pal of O'Dwyer's named Barney.

"Madame, it would please me to oblige," replied Barney, "but there is no guarantee the monkey is housebroken. It will have to be put in the basement, where the dogs are kept."

While the Dolly Sister screamed in rage, Diamond Jim shouted for the manager. "Fire that man!" he yelled, indicating the offending Barney. "Yes, sir," answered the manager, just before advising his subordinate to disappear himself for a while in the basement, until Brady left the hotel.

Years later, when O'Dwyer was a magistrate in Brooklyn, Barney came before him to answer for a parking ticket. It was God's providential way of rewarding the man for telling off the Dolly Sister, Bill-O would think. "I dismissed the case, and I always felt that justice was done."

It was at the Vanderbilt that O'Dwyer met a lively, outspoken Irish girl named Catharine Lenihan, a telephone operator, and in 1916, the same year he became a naturalized citizen, they were married. "Only by the intercession of the supernatural," a friend of Mrs. O'Dwyer once remarked, "would it have been possible for a husband of hers to become a stuffed shirt." (Three decades later, when President Harry S. Truman, then at the low point of his popularity, visited New York and was greeted by an equally beleaguered Mayor O'Dwyer, she neatly summed up the uncertainties of politics. "Amos and Andy," she commented.) The couple settled in Brooklyn's Bay Ridge section and in 1917, seeking security, O'Dwyer won an appointment to the police department. "I became a member of the police department and remained there about seven years," he would say. "At that time crime was more or less localized. Every city had their criminals. They had their thugs. But they were individual operators. Also, they were not regarded as respectable." Prohibition, of course, would change all that. "The customer, the speakeasy owner, and the bootlegger became partners in a gay lark and —worse than that—the criminal was made respectable. . . . Then hi-jacking caused the bootleggers to take defensive steps, and the violence that accompanied it resulted in alliances among the underworld."

Invariably, O'Dwyer's stories of his police years dealt with the eccentrics he had met. One such character was Big Nell Flaherty who, like O'Dwyer's friend Matty Culhane, was six-feet-two, which "was not so good for a woman, and as a result Big Nell took to drink." After a few pops, she was likely to stretch out in a doorway where she "dreamed, I should imagine, of love and affection." But if a cop tried to rouse her, the raw-boned Nell was a tiger to handle. "Police records reveal," O'Dwyer remarked, "that Big Nell was never taken into custody by less than six officers until her 74th year." At that time, only two cops were required to book her, and one of them was Matty Culhane.

"Do you desire justice, Nell, or do you wish to go to Special Sessions?" the magistrate asked.

"Last time you told me that," Nell replied, "it resulted in 30 days."

"Your Honor, I will take care of the lady," volunteered Matty.

"Nell, you're not getting any younger," Culhane told her. "I'm taking you over to the hospital and getting you a good cleaning-out".

"I want no sympathy from no cop," said Nell.

But Matty checked Nell into the hospital anyway, and soon afterward she passed away. "I killed her," a remorseful Culhane told O'Dwyer. "It wasn't the humiliation of having two cops bring her in, it was the cleaning-out."

April 20, 1918, was the turning point of O'Dwyer's police career. Dispatched from the station house to break up a family fight in a Bay Ridge flat, he was met on the street by a hysterical fourteen-year-old boy, who said his father, crazed by drink, was threatening to shoot his mother. Bursting into the apartment, O'Dwyer found himself facing a man with a loaded pistol and, to save his own life, fired first. Though the shooting was clearly justifiable homicide, the incident left its scars on the young policeman. In later years, he would help the man's son through school and eventually secure him an appointment to the police force. But, more immediately, the shooting ended O'Dwyer's enthusiasm for police work. In his off-duty hours, he began to study law. Five years later, in 1923, he would graduate from Fordham Law School.

"I remember one Saturday when I was on the force," he would say of those days. "I was married to Kitty and I had 470 books and I was studying law at Fordham at night." That particular Saturday evening, O'Dwyer dropped into a tailor shop, run by two acquaintances named Nat and Herb, to have his suit jacket pressed. "Nat was in the rear, where I thought he was pressing my jacket, and Herb—out front—kept saying to me 'How come you study so much? What ambition you got!' " The young patrolman soon realized why the tailor was chattering away so nervously. He had interrupted some improvised arson, so Nat and Herb could collect on their fire insurance.

O'Dwyer resigned from the police force shortly before passing the New York bar examinations in 1925 and, for the next seven years, practiced law in Brooklyn. A good Democrat, he knew the benefits that could accrue to his practice by establishing friendships in the political clubhouses—his early law partner, for instance, was George Joyce, a power in Joe Adonis's district and a longtime acquaintance of the mobster. But, despite his growing popularity in the Irish-American community, O'Dwyer never succeeded in gaining the favor of the snowy-haired, cherubic John H. McCooey, the Democratic ruler of Brooklyn throughout the twenties and thirties. Undaunted, Bill-O founded the County Mayo Men's Association, becoming its first president, and began importing Gaelic football teams into the metropolitan area. He made sure, of course, that the teams were available to play benefit games for Mrs. William Randolph Hearst's Free Milk Fund for Babies, and thus became friendly, not only with the Hearst sportswriters and columnists, but with reporters on non-Hearst newspapers. It was understandable then, in 1932, when Joseph V. McKee became New York's acting mayor after James J. Walker resigned in disgrace, that, prompted by the press, he should notice O'Dwyer. The independent McKee, feuding with Tammany Hall in Manhattan and McCooey in Brooklyn, was looking for men who, ostensibly at least, had little or no connection with the Democratic party regulars. He appointed O'Dwyer a city magistrate at a salary of twelve-thousand-dollars yearly.

"Did you know Joe Adonis?" Bill-O would be asked years later.

"I met him casually someplace. I don't know when, I don't know where."

"Were you familar with the restaurant he ran?"

"I remember it very well."

"Did you ever go there?"

"Never. I never crossed the door."

"You and Adonis did, however, have certain friends in common? Was George Joyce one of them?"

"Yes," O'Dwyer replied.

"Was George Joyce a law partner of yours?"

"About six months, yes, but he was and is one of my dearest friends."

"Did you know whether, after Joyce became a judge, he continued to know Adonis?"

"Well, he knew him. I think they knew one another as boys. But how often he met him I don't know."

As a magistrate, O'Dwyer was called humane by his admirers and soft-hearted by his critics. He realized he was presiding in a poor man's court where, for the most part, the infractions were minor and the defendants uneducated. Early in his tenure, he faced a Brownsville courtroom filled with forty unlicensed street peddlers who had been given summonses by a single policeman—and not one of them rose to answer the charge. They were victims of a periodic drive against street merchants, an offense that was usually ignored. "Judge, I don't think you're going to do any business today," a court attendant whispered. "With an Irish cop giving the summonses and an Irish judge on the bench, these Jewish peddlers don't think they'll get a decent break." O'Dwyer understood: the street merchants were gambling that if the cases were postponed the system of rotating judges might mean that the next time a Jewish—and presumably sympathetic magistrate—would be on the bench. Nothing nonplussed, O'Dwyer told the courtroom that he would be sitting in Brownsville for the entire month. Then he recalled the defendants.

The first peddler hesitantly stepped forward.

"Guilty or not guilty?" O'Dwyer asked him.

"Guilty," the man said.

"Sentence suspended," O'Dwyer ruled.

In similar fashion, all forty cases were disposed of, and Bill-O's reputation as an understanding judge began to grow.

During these decades, the male members of O'Dwyer's family one by one followed him to America. True to his father's prediction, Bill-O's five sisters stayed in Ireland, while four of his five brothers emigrated (the fifth, Tommy, died in Ireland while still in his teens). Jim served in the U.S. Army during World War I, then joined the New York Fire Department. He was killed in 1926, when his fire truck collided with a motorcycle while answering a false alarm. Frank came over next, got a job in the produce market on Fourteenth Street, eventually became a melon buyer. He soon developed his own produce business in California, and Bill would often visit him, during the mayoral years, on brief vacations. Brother Jack tried managing prizefighters, then opened a restaurant in Brooklyn. In 1934, he was with a detective friend in a tavern when four men attempted a robbery. Jack's friend pulled his gun and, during the ensuing fusillade, Jack was fatally wounded. Paul, the youngest O'Dwyer and Bill's junior by seventeen years, came to New York in 1925, took jobs as an elevator operator, silk-packer, and longshoreman while working his way through law school, and received his degree four years later. He would practice in Brooklyn until 1940, and would then move out of the borough—to avoid any conflict-of-interest charges about Bill, who was serving as district attorney.

After six years on the magistrate's bench, O'Dwyer was appointed by Governor Herbert H. Lehman, in 1938, to fill a vacancy in Kings County Court, at a salary of twenty-five-thousand-dollars, and within months was elected to a full fourteen-year term. Now his future seemed laid out—from immigrant to policeman to law school graduate to jurist. But in 1939, with stormy charges of official corruption hanging over gangster-ridden Brooklyn, he decided to escalate his ambitions, running for, and winning, the Brooklyn district attorney's post, taking a five-thousand-dollar cut in pay in the process. The spotlight was beginning to focus on Murder Inc., and the criminal Syndicate that used that organization to keep its minions in line. And the politician who prosecuted Murder Inc., O'Dwyer realized, would have the same spotlight trained on him, to use in running for higher office.

But publicity can transform its heroes into villians, and O'Dwyer's at first much-heralded work against Murder Inc. would eventually be questioned and re-questioned—as his tenuous connections with mobsters were examined and reexamined. For facts can have many interpretations, and no one knew that better than he. "Say, do you remember old O'Sheehan who played the violin and had the big ears?" he would say of the tricks memory can play. "And everyone said, 'Do we remember O'Sheehan!' And it was like yesterday and you couldn't figure out how the years had passed. But none of us *really* remembered old O'Sheehan. And yet we knew he must have played the violin and had big ears, and what *more* do you need to know?"

2

Frank Costello, who was christened Francesco Castiglia, was born some six months after William O'Dwyer, on January 20, 1891, in the tiny town of Lauropoli, in Italy's southern-most province of Calabria. He was the youngest of six children—four girls and two boys. Directly across the Strait of Messina, just a few miles from Calabria, lies Sicily, and through the centuries both Calabrese and Sicilians have shared a common burden of oppression, poverty, and violence. So poor was the Castiglia family that Luigi, the father, could take only three of his children with him when he emigrated to America in 1893, leaving behind his wife, two daughters, and Francesco. For the next two years, while she waited for her husband to send the money for their passage, Maria Castiglia eked out a bare existence for her brood—working as a mid-wife, begging food on the promise to pay. In the late 1920s, when the success-ful Costello would return to Lauropoli on a visit, he redeemed from a local merchant one of the bills his mother still owed. "She always swore she never done anything wrong in her life," Costello would say. "I wanted that piece of paper to show her she beat the poor old guy out of two sacks of flour."

In 1895, Maria Castiglia set sail for New York with the four-year-old Frank and one daughter, forced to leave the last child with relatives in Italy because there was no money for her ticket. "All we took with us from the old country," Frank would say, "was this big iron pot my mother cooked in. She fixed up the pot by putting in a blanket, and that's where I slept for the crossing."

The Castiglia family was re-united in the East Harlem area of Upper Manhattan, where Francesco's father had a tenement flat on 108th Street and nearby ran a small grocery. Because he found it difficult, in the Italian ghetto there, to learn English, young Frank did not enter public school until he was nine; he stayed there only until the fifth grade and then, a headstrong thirteen-year-old his parents could not control, he went onto the streets, where he joined with other teenage rowdies in loose-knit gangs that mugged, pilfered, and stole. East Harlem in those pre-Prohibition days was run by Ignazio "Lupo the Wolf" Saietta, the head of the Sicilians-only criminal organization that Americans were already beginning to know as the Mafia. (One of Lupo's chief aides, Ciro Terranova, had his headquarters just around the corner from the Castiglia flat; when the building was finally torn down, the remains of some twenty unidentified men were found in its walls and beneath its floors.) While Frank did hold a succession of temporary and menial jobs, his avocation clearly was crime. His first arrest came in 1908, when he and two other youths were accused of beating a coal dealer and robbing him of $17.50. His second arrest, in his twenty-first year, came in 1912, when he was arraigned for assaulting a neighborhood woman on the street and stealing $1600 from her handbag. In both cases, the charges, miraculously, were dismissed.

Soon afterward, Costello formed a friendship with a young man from Sicily who was undergoing a criminal apprenticeship much like his, but on the Lower East Side of Manhattan. (The West Side was then the exclusive preserve of the Irish gangs, while the Italians and the Jews shared the East Side.) The Sicilian's name was Salvatore Lucania, and he came to be known as Charles "Lucky" Luciano. Costello and he first met at a silent-movie house in Times Square, an area that served as a buffer between the uptown and downtown gangs.

"We liked to go to the movies because the silent pictures had titles and they helped us learn English," Luciano would remember. The young toughs usually sat in the balcony, where they hooted, whistled and made general nuisances of themselves. One night, the manager decided to restore order, and the various gang factions were thrown out of the theater. "One of the guys was a little older than us and he had an outfit called the One hundred and Fourth Street gang," Luciano would say. "We got together and it turned out he was a Calabrese. His name was Francesco Castiglia. . . ."

Luciano was struck by the huskiness of his new friend's voice. "I had to lean over to hear him." In those days, Luciano would explain, Italian mothers were likely to have their children's tonsils and adenoids removed on the slightest pretext. Quite often, the doctors they went to did slipshod work, and a child would later talk "like he had a permanent sore throat. That's what happened to Frank."

With his criminal career still developing, the twenty-three-year-old Costello decided to marry. Through an acquaintanceship with her brothers, he had met a dark-haired, vivacious Jewish girl named Loretta Geigerman, who her friends called Bobbie. Friendly and outgoing, she was everything the watchful and suspicious Costello could not allow himself to be, and he was immediately attracted to her. Costello was not a handsome man—his brow was too narrow and his nose too fleshy—but Bobbie was fascinated by his brooding eyes and quiet manner. "When I met Bobbie, it was like meeting one of my own people," he once explained. "She didn't talk Italian, but the German dialect of her parents was foreign, like mine. Bobbie and me got along great from the first, although neither of our mothers was too happy." In

September of 1914, Frank and Bobbie, who was then fifteen years old, were married—not by a rabbi or a Catholic priest, but by a Protestant minister.

Six months later, Costello was arrested again, for carrying a concealed weapon, and this time the charge stuck. Not that Frank did not play the helpless immigrant: he pretended he needed an interpreter, gave his name as both Saverio (his mother's maiden name) and Stello, insisted he was the sole support of aged parents. After spending several weeks in the Tombs because he could not raise bail, he agreed to engage in plea-bargaining. Accordingly, the charge against Costello was reduced to a misdemeanor, with a maximum one-year penalty that he imagined would be suspended, and he filed a plea of guilty. When he went before General Sessions Judge Edward Swann for sentencing, however, he encountered an unsympathetic jurist.

"This young man in his younger days has not led the life he should have," Costello's lawyer told the judge. "But now, since he is married and starting to earn a living, I ask your Honor to be as light with him as you can."

Judge Swann was unimpressed.

"I find that appeals were also made for him in those assault and robbery cases," he replied. "One case he robbed a woman going to the bank with sixteen-hundred-dollars. I commit him to the penitentiary for one year, and this is the last time appeals will do him any good."

About 1918, Costello joined forces in earnest with Luciano—and with Luciano's Jewish colleagues Lansky and Siegel. (Adonis would fit into the combination in 1920 with the coming of Prohibition.) All were tough, shrewd, and intelligent, all would within a decade develop the concept of organized crime and sit on the Syndicate's board of directors. "We was the best team that ever got put together," Luciano would say.

Whether or not it was true, Luciano always claimed it was he who gave Costello his new name. The group was planning the robbery of a dockside warehouse, with Siegel designated to strongarm the night watchman, when Lanksy demurred. "Why should the Jews, Benny, and me, always go first?" he said. "We've got two Italians, why don't you take the same chances?"

"Whadda you mean, two Italians?" Luciano replied. "We're one wop, one mick, and two Jews."

"Where's the mick?" demanded Lansky.

Luciano, starting to laugh, pointed at Franceso Castiglia. "I said, 'Him. He's Irish. You know, Frank Costello.' Of course, when we got up to our ears in New York politics, it didn't hurt that we had an Italian guy with an Irish name."

With the profits from their thievery, Costello and his friends began to move, around 1919, into gambling—buying into established bookmaking operations. To protect their investment, they created a slush fund for bribery; initially, it was only a few thousand dollars, but within twenty years it would grow into the millions. "We always knew that people could be bought," Luciano would say. "It was only a question of who did the buyin' and for how much."

During this period, Costello learned most of what he knew about bribery and bookmaking from Arnold Rothstein —the man who supposedly had fixed the 1919 World Series, the most famous gambler of his era. "All I know I stole," Frank once said, meaning he aped the ideas and mannerisms of those he considered his betters. "If I saw you hold a cigarette a certain way, and I liked it, I would hold it that way." Rothstein, on his own way to success, had early struck up an accomodation with the politicians of Tammany Hall—and the police and judges they controlled. He was the buffer between Tammany and the mobsters, passing on the bribes and alloting the protection, and meanwhile taking his cut. Rothstein then used the money to become a discount man for bookmakers—giving them insurance, for an added fee, when bettors wagered too heavily on various favorites. When he died, in 1928, the victim of a cardsharp's gunshot, he left an estate of some $3 million. Costello "stole" from Rothstein, first by simply observing his methods of doing business, later by becoming a minor associate. After Rothstein's murder, it was only natural that Frank should inherit his contacts with Tammany Hall.

Soon after Prohibition went into effect, on January 16, 1920, Costello—together with Luciano, Lansky, Siegel, and Adonis—moved into bootlegging. They were still, of course, only middle-echelon hoodlums. Giuseppe "Joe the Boss" Masseria was running the Manhattan Mafia, having succeeded Lupo the Wolf, and Luciano had not yet established himself as Masseria's lieutenant. In Brooklyn, Adonis was still only the protégé of Frankie Yale. Other big names in the booze trade included the Bronx's Arthur "Dutch Schultz" Flegenheimer, New Jersey's Abner "Longy" Zwillman, the East Side's Irving "Waxey Gordon" Wexler and Owen "Owney" Madden. But Prohibition was offering enough bootlegging revenue for everyone. Luciano, with Costello as his key advisor, was taking special care to forge new underworld alliances, preparing the way for the Syndicate-to-be. Meanwhile, if muscle was needed, Lansky and Siegel were adding to the Jewish gunsels in the Bugs and Meyer mob, Murder Inc.'s forerunner.

Initially, Costello and his friends imported liquor from Canada—borrowing the money for their purchases from Arnold Rothstein and cutting the gambler in for a share of the profits. Then, sometime around 1923, Costello went into partnership with William "Big Bill" Dwyer—the most flamboyant bootlegger of the twenties. Just why Dwyer invited Frank into his operation is uncertain: perhaps it was the promise of relief that the Bugs & Meyer mob could offer him from the worsening hi-jacking. "Costello was one of the 'legitimate' bootleggers," George Wolf, his onetime attorney, would recall. "By that I mean he imported the liquor which the 'illegitimate people attempted to hi-jack. An unofficial partnership sprang up between Frank and Bill Dwyer. Frank put armed guards on his trucks. He had to play rough to survive."

Dwyer, a former longshoreman out of Manhattan's Hell's Kitchen (and no relation to William O'Dwyer) was already several times a millionaire by the time he met Costello. An entrepreneur rather than a gunman, he was the first bootlegger to take full advantage of Rum Row—the name given the line of ships, laden with cases of legal liquor picked up in St. Pierre or Nassau, that peddled their wares off the New York–New Jersey coast, outside the three-mile teritorial limit. Dwyer not only employed a fleet of ocean-going speedboats that could outrun the U.S. Coast Guard vessels, he also bribed dozens of Coast Guardsmen to look the other way. On one occasion, he even arranged for a Coast Guard cutter to make a pick-up. Once the booze was ashore (two favorite droppoints were the Brooklyn waterfront and the East River near 132nd Street), he was generous with the police as well. A Coast Guardsman or policeman who let a load of Dwyer's liquor go through untouched needed only to show up the next morning at his offices in the Loew's State Theater building in Times Square, mention his service and collect his reward. To Dwyer and Costello, the bribes were simply business expenses.

The profits that could be made from bootlegging were staggering. A case of Scotch, for instance, could be brought for $8 in Great Britain, then sold for $65 off the ships in Rum Row. By the time the case of Scotch got to dry land it was worth $120. Then the bootlegger would cut each bottle to one part Scotch, three parts grain alcohol and water. The original $8 case was now worth some $400.

Obviously, the greatest risk involved in bootlegging was transporting liquor by truck from coastal drop-points to inland delivery sites. Since this had to be done at night, and along lonely roads, blockades were common. Costello set up a system where one member of the Bugs & Meyer mob rode in the truck, to fight a delaying action, thereby giving the other gunsels, following in a roadster, a chance to catch up. During one of the first attempted hi-jackings, according to Wolf, nineteen-year-old Bugsy Siegel himself sat in the truck. It was most unfortunate for the hi-jackers. By the time his confreres reached the blockade, Siegel was in complete control: Three of his adversaries lay dead, and four more stood with their hands in the air. The word quickly spread—stopping the Dwyer-Costello trucks was a high-risk enterprise.

By 1925, Costello had become wealthy, but not, like Dwyer, ostentatious. He and Bobbie did move out of Harlem, but only to a middle-class home in Bayside, Queens. And while they were often seen in expensive restaurants and nightclubs, so were hundreds of other conservatively-dressed businessmen, relaxing with their wives. To justify his income, Costello, who was in the process of becoming a naturalized citizen, went into trucking with his none-too-bright brother Edward (who played only a hireling's role in the bootlegging), bought and sold real estate, even bought a company that made ice cream pops. In a New York filled with notorious hoodlums like Dutch Schultz, Jack "Legs" Diamond, and Larry Fay, as well as boisterous speakeasy personalities like Toots Shor, Texas Guinan and comedians Clayton, Jackson, and Durante, Costello remained virtually unnoticed. (Just how much money he made from bootlegging in the twenties is difficult to estimate, but his partner, Dwyer, eventually was sued by the federal government, for unpaid taxes during that period, for almost $4 million.)

In December of 1925, Dwyer's life-style all but forced the federal government to take action against him. U.S. District Attorney Emory Buckner, using the testimony of Coast Guardsmen who had been on the Dwyer-Costello payroll and who had turned state's evidence, exposed what the *New York Times* called a $40-million international liquor ring, and eventually brought indictments against several dozen men. So numerous were the indictments, in fact, that the defendants were split into two groups. Dwyer and one group were brought to trial first, Frank and Edward Costello and the rest later. At the conclusion of Dwyer's trial, in July of 1926, only he and one henchman were convicted; Dwyer himself was given a two-year sentence. Very much the sportsman (he already owned two racetracks and would soon launch a third in Miami, to be called Tropical Park), he answered prosecutor Buckner's question as to whether he had received "a square deal" with a smiling reply: "Positively."

Predictably, Costello's trial received little attention in the press—his reward for staying in the background. In January of 1927, the case against him collapsed when the jury could not agree on a verdict, while his brother and most of the other defendants were acquitted.

"What happened with your trial?" he would be asked sixteen years later by George Wolf, the prime minister's attorney. "It was a hung jury, wasn't it?"

"Yeah," replied Costello. "I hung it."

The jury, he explained, voted eleven to one for conviction, but "I owned the one."

"What took the government so long to re-try the case?"

"The witnesses ain't in the phone books these days, and the file kind of got lost."

What neither man mentioned, but what Wolf knew, was that two years after the trial, the federal judge in the case, Francis A. Winslow, was forced to resign after a House Judiciary Committee accused him of "corruption, collusion, favoritism, oppression, and judicial misconduct." Winslow's handling of the Costello case was brought up as evidence of his misfeasance.

3

In 1928, realizing it was only a matter of time before Prohibition would be repealed, Costello began broadening his gambling operations. First he formed the Tru-Mint Novelty Corporation, as we have seen, and with the help of Dandy Phil Kastel placed some five thousand nickel slot machines in New York City's bars, restaurants, and candy stores. "If a guy named Hershey can make all that dough on a five-cent candy bar," he told Kastel, "maybe there's an angle." The resulting cascade of nickels created a gross of $3 million annually, the law being circumvented—initially at least—by having the machines pay off with mints to losers and slugs to winners. Of course, the slugs were convertible to cash. Then, within weeks after Arnold Rothstein's slaying in November of 1928, Costello, aided by the suave Frank Erickson, moved swiftly into a second area of big-time gambling, taking over Rothstein's lucrative clearing-house monopoly—accepting layoff bets from lesser bookmakers. Erickson was the front man, Costello the enforcer, with the business being conducted from offices at 1960 Broadway.

"You used the office for gambling?" he would be asked.

"Well, not for gambling," Costello hedged, "but to meet certain people I had to pay off or collect from. . . ."

"Did you take bets there?"

"No, I never took bets."

"But you met people with whom you were gambling?"

"No," Costello insisted, making a fine distinction, "I gambled myself."

By now Costello and his associates, who clearly saw the need for the creation of the Syndicate, were ready to set about its organization. A rash of gangland shootings had aroused the public, and even the most neanderthal mobster could see that the uproar was bad for business. In New York, Frankie Yale had been slain, and Legs Diamond and Dutch Schultz were warring incessantly. In Chicago, Al Capone had punctuated his long-standing emnity with the late Dion O'Bannion's gang by machine-gunning to death seven of its members in the St. Valentine's Day Massacre, and George "Bugs" Moran, the O'Bannion's leader, was vowing to respond in kind. And so, when Costello initiated the first of several crime conventions, in the spring of 1929, at Atlantic City, New Jersey, gangland's rulers saw fit to attend. From Chicago came Capone himself, together with Frank "the Enforcer" Nitti and Jacob "Greasy Thumb" Guzik; from Boston, Charles "King" Solomon; from Philadelphia, Max "Boo-Boo" Hoff, Waxey Gordon and Nig Rosen; from Cleveland, Moe Dalitz; from Detroit, representatives of the Purple Gang; from northern New Jersey, Longy Zwillman. But the New York delegation was the largest. Besides Costello, it included the glowering, bushy-browed Luciano, now Joe Masseria's lieutenant in Manhattan; Lansky, who was honeymooning with his bride Anna; and Adonis, now the number two man in Brooklyn. Though Enoch "Nucky" Johnson, Atlantic City's crime boss, was the gathering's ostensible host, Costello—the chief spokesman for New York's young turks—delivered the keynote talk, stressing the need for a national Syndicate. According to George Wolf, his longtime attorney, his words went straight to the point:

"We got to put ourselves on a business basis," Costello declared. "We got to stop the kind of thing," he said, taking special care not to look at Capone, "that's going on in Chicago.

"You guys are shooting at each other in the streets and people are starting to squawk. If they squawk loud enough, the Feds start cracking down. And you know what that means.

"We're going to have a national commission with every family represented. The old way, killing a guy who's in your way, is no good any more."

So receptive were the delegates to Costello's plan that they straightaway voted to end violence—at least in the liquor trade. Moreover, they even accepted Frank's next suggestion: that they take the heat off themselves by sending Capone to jail. "Tell me when I'm supposed to laugh," Al is reported as saying. But Costello and the New York contingent had its way, and for the good of the Syndicate-to-be (and perhaps to escape Moran's wrath), Capone dutifully stopped off in Philadelphia after leaving Atlantic City, was picked up on charges of carrying a concealed weapon by two detectives who had once been his house guests, and thereafter served a brief prison sentence. Though this was the first of the "deals" that Costello would arrange for the embryo crime organization, it would not be the last. The Syndicate was being formed.

If there was a stumbling block to criminal co-operation, it existed, ironically, in New York. Joe Masseria's leadership of the Mafia there was being challenged by Salvatore Maranzano, and the two hard-line dons, each an autocratic Mustache

Pete with his own army of gunmen, were not farseeing individuals. As the squat, earthy Masseria's deputy, Luciano was walking the proverbial thin line—working for Joe the Boss until he, Costello and the others were strong enough to take over from him. Meanwhile, the Castellammarese War, so-called because Maranzano came from Castellammare del Golfo in Sicily, and Masseria had declared anyone from that region fair game, continued to be fought. "They came from opposite sides of Sicily," Luciano would say of the two adversaries, "and both of them brought the whole idea of vendetta with them when they came to America. All us younger guys hated the old mustaches. We knew the old guys and their ideas had to go."

Several months after the Atlantic City meeting, Masseria began to force Luciano's hand. Long resentful that Lucky and his colleagues had grown rich out of Prohibition by working part-time for themselves, Joe the Boss demanded they give up this profitable sideline. What triggered his rage was that, while Luciano had been picking up a shipment of bootleg booze in New Jersey, two mob gunmen—Abraham "Bo" Weinberg and Charley "the Bug" Workman, had been picked up by the New York police. "It's your district," he ranted over the telephone in the early dawn. "When I need your muscle, you ain't around no more. That's gotta stop."

Hoping to placate Masseria, Luciano asked him to drop in at his Barbizon Plaza Hotel suite as soon possible. Then he called Costello, asking him to join them.

When Joe the Boss arrived, his rage was unabated.

"Who the hell do you think you are?" he shouted, striding into the apartment. "When I need you you're off runnin' your own fuckin' stuff."

Then Massetia saw Costello.

"What the hell is he doin' here?"

Luciano, all too aware that Masseria's private army outnumbered his five to one, tried to calm him down. The reason for Costello's presence, he explained, was that Frank was the man whose connections with the police could release Weinberg and Workman from jail.

"Stop the horsehit," snapped Masseria. "From now on you work for me twenty-four hours a day."

"Joe, we got a deal. We shook hands. You're not in the whisky."

"The whisky belongs to me," bellowed Masseria. "I break the handshake."

Later that day, Luciano met with his partners: Costello, Lansky, Adonis, Siegel. They knew they could play for time before bowing to Masseria, but they also knew he had five hundred soldiers in his army.

"What'ya thinkin', Little Man?" Luciano asked Lansky.

"This thing between Masseria and Maranzano's gonna bust open. Charlie, we have to pick the winner now, and then go with him."

Eliminating either Masseria or Maranzano, of course, would take careful planning. In October of 1929, Luciano, trying to play one Mafia leader off against the other, came close to losing his life. He went alone to meet Maranzano in Staten Island—to discuss switching his allegiance from Masseria. But when he balked at Maranzano's suggestion that he himself kill Joe the Boss, instead of using intermediaries— Sicilian tradition decreed that a leader's actual killer could not succeed him—he was beaten and tortured. At one point Maranzano viciously slashed Luciano's right cheek, severing the muscles and giving his captive the squint-eyed look that thereafter characterized his appearance. Yet Maranzano allowed Luciano to live. He had little choice: he knew that only one of Masseria's lieutenants could get close enough to his rival to slay him, and he gambled on Luciano changing his mind. Consoling their recuperating friend later, Costello and Lansky called him "Lucky," and the nickname stuck.

What gave Luciano and Costello a manuvering interval during the Castellammarese War was the October 29 stock market crash. So hard-hit were most Americans by the disaster that bootlegging, gambling, and protection profits likewise plummeted. Masseria and Maranzano were forced to delay their showdown while each concentrated on his own affairs. But an increase in loan-sharking, the establishment of a national wire service for off-track betting, and the stability of the nickel-and-dime numbers game soon brought the rackets back to normal, and the two dons were once again at each other's throats. To further fuel passions, Luciano and Costello, in the latter part of 1930, covertly arranged the assassinations of key aides to Masseria and Maranzano, staying in the background themselves and making sure that each don held the other responsible. Two prominent members of the Luciano-Costello group, Vito Genovese and Albert Anastasia, performed the killings. Maranzano was enraged, but stymied. Again, he came to Luciano and this time they struck a pact. Luciano and Costello would arrange for Masseria's murder, in return for guarantees of personal safety and noninterference in their own rackets. "Masseria's luck was holding and Maranzano couldn't get within a mile of him," Luciano would remember. "He had to have me to settle this thing."

Maranzano professed delight. "Whether you like it or not, Salvatore Lucania, you are my bambino," he declared.

Masseria's assassination was staged in classic gangland style. On the morning of April 15, 1931, Luciano met with his chief on the Lower East Side. After putting Masseria in a relaxed mood by describing a fictitious plan, supposedly long in development, for the elimination of top Maranzano men like Joe Bonnanno and Joe Profaci, Luciano suggested a drive to Coney Island for lunch—to the Nuova Villa Tommaro, a favorite mob hangout. Masseria agreed. The restaurant was jammed when they arrived, but nearly empty three hours later when they finished their meal. Always a prodigious eater, Joe the Boss had worked his way through great quantities of antipasto, shellfish, and pasta, digesting his food with glass after glass of Chianti. It was three-thirty in the afternoon when the restaurant's owner dropped over to their table, left Luciano and Masseria with a deck of cards, and mentioned he was going for a stroll on the boardwalk. The two men had barely begun to play when Lucky excused himself to go to the men's room. Whereupon the assassination team—Joe Adonis, Bugsy Siegel, Vito Genovese, and Albert Anastasia—entered the Villa Tommaro, fired a score of bullets at Joe the Boss, and left him dead and bleeding, still seated at the table. The same limousine that had brought the killers from Manhattan then sped them away. The blood-letting was over within minutes, witnesses were conspicuously absent. As for Luciano, he did what any concerned citizen would have done: he phoned for the police. "The cops asked me where I was when it happened," Luciano would say. "I said to them, 'I was in the can takin' a leak. I always take a long leak.'"

Now a flamboyant Maranzano sought to establish himself as undisputed Capo di Tutti Capi—Boss of All Bosses. At a ceremonial banquet in the Bronx that was attended by hundreds of mobsters from all over the country, he divided spheres of influence, named capos—heads of "families," demanded discipline worthy of Caesar's legions. Simultaneously, he declared he was Caesar, and that tribute was due him: he would receive a piece of all the rackets, and he alone would decide how large a piece. Ostensibly cowed, one guest after another approached Maranzano, after his speech, with cash-filled envelopes. The initial tribute totalled some $1 million. But Maranzano's imperial style was no more suited to the emerging Syndicate than Masseria's naked threats, and no one knew this better than Costello. "As Frank once said, 'A greaseball is a greaseball,' " George Wolf would remember. "What he meant was that Maranzano, despite his polished appearance, was of the same ilk as Masseria."

In the weeks that followed, Luciano and Costello began sounding out their peers, in New York and other cities, about Maranzano's heavy-handedness. Everywhere there was dissatisfaction. Then, in August of 1931, Costello was informed, by Nig Rosen of Philadelphia, that Maranzano was planning his murder—and that of Luciano, Adonis, Genovese, and others. Vincent "Mad Dog" Coll, a particularly vicious killer, had been given the assignment. (For some reason, possibly because Maranzano did not believe that Jews could be real threats to him, Lansky and Siegel were not on his hit list.) "I can't get along with these guys," Maranzano is reported to have said. "We got to get rid of them before we can control anything." Forewarned, the Luciano-Costello group accelerated its own assassination plans. What better way to get to their enemy, they reasoned, then to impersonate Internal Revenue agents? In his offices at 230 Park Avenue, where he conducted both his legitimate businesses (real estate and import-export) and his racket activities, Maranzano had grown used to seeing IRS representatives, who called periodically to inspect his books. Lansky and Siegel straightaway chose four Jewish gunmen, men whose faces the Italian and his bodyguards would not know, and held them in readiness. On September 10, only hours before Luciano and Genovese were due to report to a Maranzano summons (and be murdered themselves by Coll), the bogus IRS men entered the offices, easily disarmed the confused bodyguards, and then stabbed and shot Maranzano to death. The guards, an informer later would say, "were all sitting around in the outer office when these four Jews walk in and flash badges. Charlie Lucky could use them, because his family had sided with Lansky. The old man stuck his head out of the inner office to see what was going on, and one of the fake bulls says, 'Who can we talk to?' and the old man says, 'You can talk to me.' So two of them go in with him, and the other two keep an eye on the crowd. A long time after this I meet one of the boys who went in with the old man. His name was Red Levine. I said, 'I hear you were up there.' Levine said, 'Yes, I was there. He was tough.' He told me the idea was to use a knife, so there wasn't any noise, but the old man starting fighting back, and they had to use a gun."

Even as the assailants fled down the building's staircase, Vincent Coll reportedly was on his way up, primed to gun down the supposedly waiting Luciano. But the young turks had struck first. That night, in a half-dozen cities, a score or more of lesser Mustache Petes, older Italians too wed to the old ways, were similarly eliminated, in the so-called "Night of the Sicilian Vespers," and the leadership of organized crime underwent a convulsive change.

In short order, Luciano, Costello, and their friends set up another banquet meeting—this one in Chicago—to tell their colleagues how the Syndicate they envisioned would be run. "I explained to them that all the war horse-shit was out," Lucky would say of his recruiting work, "that every outfit in every city would be independent, but there would be a national organization to hold things together." Crime was big business. It required a board of directors, and while Luciano would be willing to serve as board chairman, he was insisting his appointment be by general consent. When some of the banquet-goers attempted to present him with the traditional cash-filled envelopes, he refused to accept them. "Why should you be paying anything to me when we're all equals?" he asked.

Time was needed for the Luciano-Costello group's ideas to sink into the collective mob consciousness. It would not be until the spring of 1934, at the climatic meeting in New York's Waldorf-Astoria a few months after the repeal of Prohibition, that the National Crime Syndicate would fully come into existence. By then, Luciano was living in the Waldorf-Towers, having been impressed by the way Costello (who now lived on Central Park West) conducted business in the hotel's barbershop and bar. Almost every Italian underworld leader attended the meeting (except Capone, who was in jail for tax evasion), and Lansky saw to it that the non-Italian leaders were present: Louis "Lepke" Buchalter, Hyman Abrams of Boston, Nig Rosen, Longy Zwillman, Moe Dalitz of Cleveland, Kid Cann of Minneapolis-St. Paul, The speeches were laudatory and the back-slapping exuberant, and before the night was over the Syndicate was firmly rooted in American society.

During this transitional period, Costello solidified his contacts with Tammany Hall—the political organization that controlled the city. So influential was he becoming that, while attending the 1932 Democratic National Convention in Chicago—a gathering torn between Franklin Delano Roosevelt and Alfred E. Smith—he could share a suite with James J. Hines, a Roosevelt man and the city's most powerful district leader. Meanwhile, he could arrange for Albert Marinelli, a Smith backer and Tammany's only Italian district leader, to room with Luciano. The Syndicate spread its bets.

Nothing in Jimmy Hines's appearance or background spoke of weakness. Square-jawed and still muscular in his late fifties, he was a personable man with a ready smile and icy, pale-blue eyes. Growing up in the neighborhood around Eighth Avenue and 116th Street in the 1890s, the son of a blacksmith, he worked long hours at the forge himself— though he was always willing to doff his apron to help a friend. Politically ambitious, he lived by a simple code: if you help your neighbor, he will vote for you. "When Jimmy Hines was shoeing horses and somebody came to tell him that Aloysius Boyle, or maybe Hymie Klotz, was in trouble," explained a backer, "Jimmy would go to the front for Aloysius or Hymie. He's like that now. That's why we love him." Hines put his philosophy more pragmatically: "In politics the thing to do is build yourself an army. I see hundreds of people every day. It's a lot of hard work, but I keep it up." In 1911, after mounting a series of challenges to the entrenched leader of the Eleventh Assembly District that culminated in his punching the man in the jaw at a heated political rally, Hines became the leader himself. "You stuffed in as many ballots as you could and let the counters do the rest," he would admit. And in 1921, though he was only one of some three dozen district leaders, his influence was so great he could defy even Tammany Boss Charles F. Murphy, who wanted to oust him. "You are a millstone around the neck of the Democratic party," he would tell Murphy to his face at a Tammany executive meeting.

Hines's Eleventh Assembly District lay between Eighth Avenue and the Hudson River on the Upper West Side. Originally Irish and Jewish, by the 1930s it had come to include Blacks and Puerto Ricans. In a typical day Hines would see hundreds of petitioners, starting in the early morning at his 111th Street apartment while still in his dressing gown and pajamas, continuing through the afternoon at his Forty-first Street business office (centrally located because of his city-wide influence), ending in the evening below Morningside Heights at his Monongahela Club. Hines took special pains never to turn a constituent away empty-handed; if he could not fill a request, he would provide a reasonable substitute. A woman might want a job for her truck-driver son: Hines would call a city contractor. A highways department laborer who lived in Manhattan would complain he had been transferred to Staten Island and could not afford the commuting fare: another phone call rectified the injustice. A woman with a babe in her arms wanted bail money for her husband: Hines provided it.

A great deal of cash passed through Jimmy's hands (he kept neither a savings nor a checking account), but he maintained that the money came from well-wishers (not mobsters or people making kick-backs for city contracts), and that it was spent, as fast as it came in, on the innumerable charitable acts a district leader had to perform. Indeed, Hines and his wife lived relatively simply, if one allowed for Jimmy's expansive racetrack betting. Yet his critics would counter that his rise to real power, during Prohibition, coincided with the rise of the rackets. Hines did nothing to dispel the gossip by unabashedly frequenting the prizefights at Madison Square Garden in the company of Dutch Schultz, one of the city's biggest bootleggers. Nor could it be denied that Attorney Joseph Shalleck, the longtime Hines supporter with whom he shared his midtown offices, at various times represented both "Big Bill" Dwyer and Owney Madden. In 1929, too, Jimmy was tied to Racketeer Larry Fay, who was then being investigated for his protection efforts in the milk industry. "I have met Fay in connection with my political duties," he explained smoothly. Subsequently, Hines's name was likewise connected, in the newspapers, with narcotics and gambling investigations. But no wrong-doing, and no financial connection with the mobsters, had thus far been proven.

For some half-dozen years after Franklin Roosevelt's 1932 election victory, James J. Hines, FDR's early supporter, controlled federal patronage in Manhattan. By dispensing these plums wisely, he strengthened his authority over the police and the courts. Frank Costello and the Syndicate naturally took pleasure in their man's success. "I *know* Jimmy all right," a friend would say of the shrewd, enigmatic Hines, "but honestly, I don't know a thing about him. He always worked too smoothly for me."

Albert Marinelli, the only Italian in the almost solid phalanx of Irish Tammany leaders, did not suffer from his 1932 allegiance to Al Smith. Syndicate support saw to that. His Assembly District, the Second, was on the Lower East Side —specifically the Bowery, the area south of Fourteenth Street. If Costello moved easily among the Irish, the other Italian mobsters did not, and Marinelli's rise was traceable to their insistence they be represented by a man bound to them by blood-ties as well as money. Marinelli got into politics before World War I, when he became a ward heeler for the Second Assembly District's crusty Timothy "Big Tim" Sullivan, a saloon keeper who ruled the Bowery like a feudal fief. After Big Tim's death in 1916, the leadership eventually passed on to two men: Christopher Sullivan (Tim's cousin) and Harry C. Perry. But Marinelli throughout the 1920s came to exercise more and more power in the district and, helped by the 1931 publicity attending Judge Samuel Seabury's investigation of gambling in Perry's clubhouse, that year he officially displaced him. There was no formal election; the story goes that a couple of the Luciano-Costello group's hoods walked into Perry's office, showed their guns, and suggested he retire. For years thereafter, though Christy Sullivan remained the Second Assembly District's nominal co-leader, Marinelli controlled its political clout—for the good of the Syndicate.

Nor did Costello neglect expanding into legitimate businesses. In late 1933, just as Prohibition was coming to an end, he and Phil Kastel worked through Irving Haim, a former bootlegger, to form Alliance Distributors, a liquor wholesaler. In turn, Haim arranged with the William Whitely Company of London for the exclusive right to distribute in the United States such brands of scotch whisky as House of Lords and King's Ransom. A few years later, Costello and Kastel tried to buy the Whitely firm, prevailing upon Haim and millionaire sportsman William Helis ostensibly to put up the $325,000-down payment and staying in the background themselves. Only at the last moment did the Whitely firm discover who the Haim-Helis backers, and the endorsers of the note, really were. To this day, it is uncertain whether the revelation actually cancelled the deal.

"It was a Helis note for three hundred, twenty-five thousand dollars, which you and Phil Kastel endorsed?" Costello was subsequently asked.

"Yes, I endorsed that note," he admitted.

"This was in connection with the William Whitely Company of London, whereby Phil Kastel received an interest in that company?"

"I believe so."

"What did you get out of this deal?"

"Nothing."

"You mean you would sign a three-hundred-twenty-five-thousand-dollar note for nothing, Mr. Costello?"

"Absolutely nothing. Pure friendship."

"Weren't you actually negotiating a contract whereby you

would succeed Phil Kastel as the man who got five shillings on every case of whisky exported to the United States by Alliance Distributors?"

"Yes, I had a talk with Mr. Haim."

"Well, you were going to get a large number of shillings on certain types of whisky sent over here from London, a deal that would net you hundreds of thousands of dollars. So that is really the consideration for your generosity in signing the note?"

"I don't know what the consideration was. There was never any talk on that subject."

"Is it not a fact that Phil Kastel and Irving Haim were to buy that distillery, and you were to succeed Kastel as the man who got the big commission?"

"All I know is, I was offered the overriding."

"What happened so that the deal fell through, Mr. Costello?"

"I don't know the details."

"Haim and Helis's family did buy the distillery. What happened to you in the deal? Somebody objected to your being in it?"

"I heard there was an objection."

"And the contract with you never was signed?"

"Never signed, no."

"Is it not a fact that after you stepped out of the Whitely Distilleries deal, you continued to have an interest in Whitely? You continued to receive money from Irving Haim?"

"No."

"I would like to read you a telephone conversation, an incoming call to your home, and it was you calling Mrs. Costello. You said, 'What time will you definitely be home this afternoon? I'm expecting a package. Irving Haim will bring it.' Mrs. Costello said, 'I will be home by five o'clock.' And you said, 'Irving will bring it and it will be in an envelope. You know where to put it.' What did you mean, Mr. Costello?"

"I don't remember that at all."

4

During the early 1930s, while Costello was helping set up the National Crime Syndicate, young federal prosecutor Thomas E. Dewey was laying the groundwork for investigations that would bring to grief many of Frank's colleagues—thereby creating a leadership vacuum that would, ironically, result in Costello becoming prime minister of the underworld.

Dewey, a native of Michigan who migrated to New York to study both voice and law (a case of laryngitis ultimately persuaded him to concentrate on the latter), had graduated from Columbia Law School, spent a couple of years with a Wall Street firm, and worked in local Republican politics. Then, in 1931, his friend George Medalie, the U.S. Attorney General for the Southern District of New York, named him, at age twenty-eight, as his chief assistant. For the next two and one-half years, Dewey and his aides painstakingly collected evidence of income-tax evasion, through records and checks, against two of the East's biggest bootleggers, Irving "Waxey Gordon" Wexler and Arthur "Dutch Schultz" Flegenheimer. As it happened, this initiative did not displease Costello and his friends. Both Gordon and Schultz, despite their high status in the rackets, were freelancers by temperament, and would not fit into the embryo Syndicate. "Who sold the beer barrels to the Gordon organization?" Dewey later wrote of his modus operandi. "Who sold the malt? Who sold the fleet of trucks the Gordon organization used for distribution? How were all the goods and services paid for, and in whose names had delivery been taken? What did the sellers' books show?" Frequently, when Dewey's agents did ask for a bank's records, the bank would tip off the Gordon people and, even while the agents waited in a vestibule, the mobsters would make off with the evidence. But Dewey persevered. Hard-nosed digging produced an incriminating trail of cancelled checks, fictitious accounts, and fraudulent signatures.

In November of 1933, Dewey brought Gordon, a former pick-pocket with a genius for organization, to trial for tax evasion, asserting that Waxey's net income—from beer alone —was $1.3 million in 1930 and $1 million in 1931. In cross-examination, the prosecutor conclusively proved that such income was reflected in Gordon's style of living: four automobiles, a ten-room apartment on West End Avenue, antique furniture, servants, jewelry for his wife, periodic vacations to Miami and Hot Springs, Arkansas.

"In 1928, you filed a return for six thousand, eight hundred and fifty-two dollars and paid a tax of fifteen dollars, isn't that right?" Dewey asked the bootlegger.

"That is possible," Gordon replied.

"For 1929, seven thousand, three hundred and ninety-four dollars, right?"

"I guess that is right."

"For 1930, eight thousand, one hundred and twenty-five dollars, right?"

"That is right."

"Then, for 1931, after your conference with the agents of

Internal Revenue, for the first time in your life you filed a tax
return of more than eight thousand, one hundred and twenty-
five dollars?"

"That is right."

"Did you have insurance on your household furniture for
one hundred thousand dollars in 1931?"

"I did."

"How did you acquire one hundred thousand dollars
worth of property?"

"I won it on the racetrack."

"That is your testimony?"

"Yes, sir."

"Did your wife have a new Cadillac in 1930?"

"She didn't."

"Was one registered in her name?"

"It was."

"Whose car was it?"

"A fellow by the name of Louis Parkowitz. He owned the
car, and I bought it from him. I paid five hundred dollars for
it."

"You paid five hundred dollars for a new Cadillac sedan?
Is that your testimony?"

"That is right."

"You were paying twenty-four hundred dollars a year for
life insurance?"

"Yes."

"Where did you get the money to pay twenty-four hundred dollars in the years when you reported a six- or-seven-
thousand-dollar income to the government?"

"I was borrowing it."

"That is your testimony?"

"That is my testimony."

So obvious did Dewey make Gordon's tax evasion that the

jury debated less than an hour. He was found guilty, and sentenced to ten years in the penitentiary.

Shortly after Gordon's conviction, the presence of a Democratic president in the White House forced a re-shuffling of U.S. Attorneys, and Dewey lost his federal job, temporarily halting his investigation of Schultz. Back in private practice, he nonetheless continued his interest in criminal law, suggesting, through his membership in the Bar Association, a far-reaching reform program. Then, in mid-1935, a runaway grand jury in New York County defied the Tammany district attorney, claiming that the political machine was protecting Schultz and other mobsters, and demanding that Governor Herbert Lehman appoint a special prosecutor. After much procrastination and repeated urging from prominent attorneys and the Bar Association, the Governor named Dewey to the post.

In August of that year, Schultz was acquitted, in the improbable jurisdiction of Malone, New York, on charges of evading $92,000 in taxes on $480,000 income during the 1929–1931 period. "Before I discharge you," said the chagrined judge to the jury, leaving no doubt he felt it had been tampered with, "I will have to say your verdict is such that it shakes the confidence of law-abiding people in integrity and truth." Despite Mayor Fiorello LaGuardia's warning that "there is no place for him here," Schultz arrogantly returned to the New York area, and to Dewey's subpoena powers.

The Dutchman, who had not gotten into bootlegging until 1928, had parlayed a fleet of rickety trucks, innate administrative ability, and a savage, violent nature into perhaps the biggest beer business in the country. Into his Bronx warehouses, equipped with huge elevators, night after night rolled empty trucks; they were swiftly brought below-ground to his breweries, loaded with vile, adulterated beer, and sent off to speakeasy owners too cowed to argue about quality or price. Along the way, Schultz eliminated a score of gangland rivals, including Vincent "Mad Dog" Coll. Now in 1935, with Prohibition at an end, he was firmly entrenched in the numbers racket. This was a lucrative business in which countless nickels and dimes were wagered on the chance of guessing the last three numbers of the daily parimutuel total at the racetrack —and it was truly a racket since the odds against the bettor were one thousand to one, while the payoff was only half that. "It was worth anything from $20 to $50 million, depending on whom you listened to," Dewey would say of the numbers operation, "and Schultz was using the proceeds to infiltrate legitimate industries and pay off law-enforcement people."

Though still another federal charge hung over the Dutchman's head (an indictment for failure to file tax returns—a mere misdemeanor), he realized the threat Dewey represented. According to Burton Turkus, who later brought Louis "Lepke" Buchalter to justice as O'Dwyer's chief aide in the smashing of Murder Inc., Schultz actually worked out the details of an assassination plan. He had learned that Dewey stopped off each morning, on his way to the office, at a nearby drugstore where he made his confidential phone calls—a precaution lest his office phone was tapped. Meanwhile, the prosecutor's bodyguards waited on the street. Schultz's idea was for a hitman, whose revolver would be fitted with a silencer, to go into the drugstore a few minutes before Dewey. The assassin would then gun down his target, shoot the drugist as well—relatively without noise—and then quickly leave the premises, calmly walking past the guards. The Dutchman pushed his plan before the Syndicate, but found no support. "Dewey was bound to Manhattan by jurisdictional limits," Turkus would explain. "Assassinating a prosecutor could stir up such righteous indignation that it could dam up the financial flood from the rackets in all other places."

Despite the disapproval of Luciano, Costello, and the other Syndicate leaders, Schultz decided to go ahead with Dewey's killing. "I say he ought to be hit," he insisted. "And if nobody else is going to do it, I'm gonna hit him myself. . . ." His target date was October 25.

The Syndicate was not pleased with such initiative. "They could not risk the crazy man any longer," Dewey would say laconically. On the evening of October 23, the crime organization dispatched Charlie "the Bug" Workman to the Palace Chop House in Newark, New Jersey, whose backroom the Dutchman was using as an informal office. Workman entered the Palace unnoticed and walked past the few patrons at the long bar, stopping before going to the rear to check out the men's room for any Schultz bodyguards. There he found a man who looked familiar, and he shot him without hesitation. As the customers rushed out the front, and the bartender flattened himself to the floor, Workman ran to the back, where he found Bernard "Lulu" Rosenkrantz and Abe Landau, two of Dutch's aides, and Otto "Abadaba" Berman, the mathematical wizzard responsible for rigging the numbers racket's odds. In the exchange of gunfire that followed, Workman fatally wounded all three. Only as he was fleeing the restaurant did he realize it was Schultz who has been his first victim. But the Dutchman was not yet dead. For the next three days, as the tabloids zealously reported the event (including the financial news that the adding machine Abadaba was using carried totals of $313,000 and $236,000), the delirious Schultz lingered on.

"Was it the boss who shot you?" he was asked.

"Who shot me? No one," was the Dutchman's reply, and soon afterward he died.

Ironically, Luciano within a few months would come to

regret the part he played in saving Dewey's life. In July of 1936, the special prosecutor scooped up some one hundred people in a series of vice raids, and encouraged them to testify against the Syndicate leader in an effort to prove he controlled the city's vice trade. "The arrested women were told," Dewey would admit, " 'We are not in the business of prosecuting prostitutes and madams and pimps. We are here to get the big-shots.' " Though there is doubt to this day that a mobster of Luciano's pre-eminence, despite certain other social dis-qualifications, would have any real connection with prostitu-tion, Dewey assembled a credible case. ("Frank Costello told me it was a bum rap," attorney George Wolf would say. "Witnesses were being 'persuaded' to link Luciano with so-called 'organized prostitution.' Frank said, 'It was as orga-nized as a flea circus.' ") Among Dewey's witnesses:

- *Nancy Presser*, a prostitute and drug addict, who—in the prosecutor's own words—"told us that Luciano, on several occasions, had sent for her to visit him at the Barbizon Plaza and the Waldorf Towers. She said he had told her how the prices in the houses were going to be raised."

- *Florence "Cokey Flo" Brown*, the mistress of vice figure Jimmy Frederico and also a drug addict, who testified that "With Frederico, she met Luciano and dined one evening with them. In a car on the way home, Frederico began to talk about prostitution. There was some discus-sion, which Luciano ended by saying, 'Have them all come down and we will straighten the matter out.' "

- *Mildred Balitzer*, another addict, who swore that she had asked Luciano to let her husband out of the racket— "I said to him, 'You know I am married to Pete now. I want Pete to get out of the business.' Luciano said, 'He can't get out because of the money he owes. As long as he owes it he can't get out.' "

On April 1, Luciano was arrested in Hot Springs, Arkansas, a favorite gangster health spa, and later extradited to New York. Charged with sixty-two counts of compulsory prostitution, he came to trial in mid-May. After giving the court the testimony of prostitutes (who, some said, had perjured themselves for freedom from prosecution), Dewey called upon Marjorie Brown, a surprise witness who worked as a chambermaid at the Waldorf Towers. ("A decent, hard-working girl who traveled to Manhattan every day from Union City, New Jersey. . . . completely fearless and completely believeable," was the way the prosecutor described her.) It was she who was able to tie Luciano to a number of vice organizers who were his co-defendants—Abe Wahrman, Little Davie Betillo, Jimmy Frederico.

"What are your duties in the Waldorf Towers?" Marjorie was asked by Dewey.

"To clean the bathrooms and pantries," she answered.

"Do you see anyone in the courtroom who was a guest at the Waldorf during the past year?"

"Yes," the young chambermaid said, and pointed out Luciano.

"Under what name did you know him there?"

"Charles Ross."

"During the time he was there, did you see a number of people going in and out of his apartment?"

"Yes."

"Will you stand up now and point out anybody in the courtroom whom you saw?"

"Yes—the fellow in the gray suit with the polka dot tie."

"Indicating the defendant Wahrman," Dewey said for the record. . . ."Have you seen him there on several occasions?"

"Oh, I can say about twenty."

"In the apartment of the man you knew as Charles Ross?"

"Yes."

In short order, Marjorie similarly identified Betillo and Frederico as having been frequent visitors to Luciano's apartment. Her testimony was extremely damaging.

When George Morton Levy, Luciano's attorney, brought his client to the stand, he asked the witness if he had ever met any of the prostitutes who had testified.

"There has not been a witness that has got on this stand of Mr. Dewey's that I ever saw in my life," Luciano insisted, exempting the Waldorf chambermaid from his denial.

"Did you ever receive the earnings of a prostitute?" Levy asked.

"I gave to 'em. I never took," the Syndicate leader replied.

The jury did not believe Luciano. Found guilty on all sixty-two counts, he was sentenced in 1936 to thirty to fifty years imprisonment—an amazing penalty considering the nature of the case against him. ("How can I convince the jury," Luciano's attorney had asked Dewey, referring to the fact that the testimony of fifty prostitutes was no more meaningful than the testimony of one, "that a mountain of manure is no better than a cupful?") Naturally, Dewey was exhultant. "The top Mafia leader in New York has been convicted," he would say, "and I felt that the majesty of the law had been vindicated." As for Luciano, he must have wished he had taken the advice of Albert Anastasia, the head of Murder Inc.

"The Dutchman was right, we gotta knock off Dewey," Anastasia had told Lucky just before the prostitution indictment.

"We don't want the kind of trouble everybody would get

if we knocked off Dewey," Luciano had said.

Decades later, Lucky would explain his forbearance. "I was sure no jury was gonna sit there and listen to a bunch of broken-down broads claimin' I was their boss. I was sure that as soon as George Morton Levy got'em in cross-examination, the jury'd laugh the whole thing out of court."

Now Luciano, incarcerated in a Dannemora, New York, penitentiary, was effectively removed from day-to-day control of the Syndicate. More and more, Costello assumed his role. Meanwhile, Dewey continued his crusade, turning his attention to Louis "Lepke" Buchalter and Jacob "Gurrah" Shapiro. "Lepke was the brains of the team," the prosecutor would say. "He was slim, handsome, and acted like a respectable businessman. He lived in a luxurious apartment. He traveled about town in a high-powered limousine driven by a chauffeur. Gurrah was a short, bettle-browed, bull-necked thug . . . coarse, hoarse-voiced, and violent." Lepke and Gurrah formed their partnership during the 1920's. At first, they were free-lancers, hiring out their muscle in industrial arguments. Then they joined with Jacob "Little Augie" Orgen's mob and, after his death in a gangland dispute, became preeminent in the New York rackets. Lepke and Gurrah bulled their way into the garment industry in 1927, taking over the cutters' union—and without the cutters no suits could be made. Next they brought their strong-arm tactics to bear on the truckers—and without trucks no goods could be moved. Their control gradually extended to machinists' unions, furmakers' unions, even movie projectionists' unions. "They built up and dominated great industrial rackets," Dewey observed. "Whenever a gorilla called on a businessman and said, 'I'm from L & G,' the victim paid whatever he was asked to pay."

To achieve this kind of respect, Lepke needed muscle.

With Siegel's and Lansky's approval, he first assimilated the old Bugs & Meyer gang, and then expanded the army of Jewish hitmen. As the Syndicate evolved, these killers, known as Murder Inc., became its enforcement arm. And Lepke, Luciano, Costello, Lansky, and Adonis, to keep a buffer between Murder Inc. and themselves, appointed Anastasia its titular head.

Assembling his case against Lepke and Gurrah, Dewey decided to focus on their takeover, in the early 1930s, of the flour-trucking and baking industry. Typically, they had gained control of the industry by arranging the murder of an honest union official. Now, in 1937, Dewey and his staff gathered evidence to show the two men had been behind the assassination. Simultaneously, they subpoenaed the books of the baking industry—and other industries as well —poring over the ledgers to trace the trail of protection money. "The machine-controlled district attorneys were sleeping peacefully," Dewey would say of the corrupt political system in New York. "Lepke and Gurrah invaded a flour-trucking union and gave out new orders. From then on strikes would be called when they said so. Strikes would be called off only after the businessmen had paid a large extortion. The gangsters intended to set up a trade association with lawyers and front men protecting them. And they did."

Once again, the pressure exerted by Dewey and his task force proved overwhelming. By mid-summer of 1937, even as the indictments were being prepared against them, Lepke and Gurrah went into hiding, setting the stage for Bill O'Dwyer's investigation of Murder Inc. that was to follow. About this time, the politically-ambitious special prosecutor gained the Republican Party's nomination for Manhattan district attorney, and subsequently was swept into office. "There is an alliance of long standing between crime and certain elements of Tammany Hall," he charged during the course of his campaign. "This alliance must be broken."

Still another Syndicate leader who fled from Dewey's subpoena powers in 1937 was Vito Genovese, who had been Luciano's lieutenant and, because of his ruthlessness, might have been a real threat to Costello. That Genovese was not adverse to violence is indicated by his marriage of several years earlier, to Anna Vernotico, just twelve days after her husband was found strangled to death on a rooftop, a tightly-drawn sash cord around his neck. At least one mob informer claimed that Vito unblinkingly ordered the killing, so that Anna would be free to re-marry. Dewey's developing case against Genovese centered on his alleged involvement with the murder, in 1934, of Ferdinand "the Shadow" Boccia, who had demanded too large a share in the $160,000-proceeds of a crooked card game. But Vito was not without a strong sense of self-preservation. Carrying $750,000 in cash in a suitcase, he departed Dewey's jurisdiction for Italy, where he developed strong contacts with Mussolini and the Fascists. After World War II, he neatly switched back to Democracy—uncovering black-market operators for the American Military Government, and then replacing them with men of his own choosing. He would return to New York, beat the Boccia murder indictment, and begin a long, bloody campaign to unseat Costello from his prime ministership.

Gordon, Schultz, Luciano, Lepke, Genovese—why did Costello not come under Dewey's scrutiny? Attorney George Wolf would say it was because Frank was "legitimate"—at least in underworld parlance. "He wasn't in narcotics. He wasn't in numbers. His source of income, so far as the authorities knew at the time, was the slot machines in Louisiana, outside of Dewey's jurisdiction." For business advice, Costello relied on Adonis, whose Brooklyn base was also outside of Dewey's subpena powers, and Lansky, who likewise preferred "legitimate" deals. For general head-cracking, from which he kept himself several levels removed, Frank could count on Albert Anastasia, the Brooklyn dock-boss. So the prime minister slipped uncaught through Dewey's crime net—"By saying nothing, and lying low."

In 1938, Dewey capped his investigations by indicting James J. Hines on numbers racket charges. The case came to trial in mid-August and, though most of the evidence against Hines, the district leader who dealt only in cash, was provided by witnesses trying to save their own skins, its sheer weight was impressive. In Dewey's words:

- *George Weinberg*, a former Dutch Schultz aide, said he had heard Schultz telling Hines "he had to have protection. Weinberg testified that Hines replied he could take care of the Sixth Division in Harlem . . . Schultz then paid Hines one thousand dollars and instructed him, Weinberg, to pay Hines five hundred dollars a week."

- *Dixie Davis*, Schultz's onetime lawyer, "testified that thousands of dollars had been paid to Hines for top-level protection in the distict attorney's office."

- *Big Harry Schoenhaus*, a Schultz aide, "testified that Hines had been on the payroll for three years."

- *Internal Revenue Service* wire-taps "picked up Hines when he called Dixie Davis with reference to his weekly payments."

- *A Democratic county leader* in Troy, New York, "testified that Hines had telephoned him repeatedly and asked him to stop the local police from 'pushing Dutch Schultz around.' "

The case against Hines was temporarily interrupted by the granting of a mistrial on a technicality, and the precocious, thirty-five-year-old Dewey—now the Republican gubernatorial candidate—used the time, in the fall of the year, to attempt to oust Herbert Lehman from the Governor's mansion. He failed, but only by the narrowest of margins, thereby serving notice he would be a potent political force for years to come.

In the early part of 1939, Dewey brought the sixty-three-year-old Hines to trial again, and on this second occasion made the charges stick. New York's most powerful district leader was found guilty on February 25, and sentenced to four to eight years in the penitentiary. "How would you feel," he said in answer to a reporter's question, "if you were kicked in the belly?" Not until late 1940, however, when the appeals process was exhausted, did Hines begin serving his time at Sing Sing.

5

In the fall of 1939, helped by widespread charges of corruption among the borough's law-enforcement officials, William O'Dwyer was elected Brooklyn's district attorney, resigning from his Kings County judgeship to take a job that, at twenty thousand dollars yearly, involved a five-thousand-dollar cut in pay. As O'Dwyer assumed his new duties, he would say, "I had no notion there was organized crime all over the country. But I did look at the murder records, and the number of homicides in Brooklyn that were not solved by the police was astonishing. In a certain part of Brooklyn, there were gangs, small but frightfully active, extorting from shopkeepers, throwing stink bombs, committing assaults and murders. The

hoodlums would be arrested with great fanfare, brought before Magistrates' Court, and charged with disorderly conduct
—nothing more. If you made the bail at one thousand dollars,
they put their hands in their pockets, peeled off one thousand
dollars, and walked out. This had been going on for years."

The part of Brooklyn O'Dwyer referred to was its north-
east triangle—the districts known as Brownsville, East New
York, and Ocean Hill. Brownsville's and East New York's
rackets had been ruled, since 1931, by Abe "Kid Twist" Reles,
whose principal aides were Bugsy Goldstein and Harry
"Pittsburgh Phil" Strauss. On their way to the top, Reles and
his men efficiently disposed of the notorious Shapiro brothers, the district's previous overlords: Irv Shapiro was shot
eighteen times, Meyer received a single bullet through his left
ear, Willie was buried alive. Allied with Reles was Ocean
Hill's leader, Happy Maione, whose lieutenant was Frank
"Dasher" Abbandando. The Brownsville-Ocean Hill mobsters even had a front man, Louis Capone, who ran a pastic-
ceria—a coffee shop—where they gathered to discuss business. As the National Crime Syndicate evolved, Reles and
Maione came under the supervision of both Lepke and Albert
Anastasia, and they and their men—together with the rem-
nants of the Bugs & Meyer mob—thus became a part of Murder Inc. "In a ten-year period, upward of one thousand murders were committed," Burton Turkus, O'Dwyer's chief
assistant in the district attorney's office, would say. "They
were done for the Syndicate. But murder was not the big
business. The rackets were. The assassinations were ordered
solely to sustain the rackets."

It was not until late January of 1940, in fact, that O'Dwyer
and Turkus began to realize there was a Murder Inc. "We
knew there were mobs working," Turkus would remember.
"We knew that Kid Twist Reles, fat and vicious, had an outfit

in Brownville with his pal, Bugsy Goldstein. We knew Happy Maione in Ocean Hill had a gang of hoodlums." But initially, Turkus emphasized, the law did not realize that these men were carrying out mob assassinations on a national scale.

That January, even as the O'Dwyer office was exerting pressure on the Brownsville-Ocean Hill gangs, a jailed hoodlum insisted to Turkus he had seen Reles and Goldstein— together with an underling named Dukey Maffetore—several years earlier kill a man. Maffetore, a twenty-five-year-old with a fondness for comic books, was brought in for questioning —under the theory he would be most likely to crack. He proved to be innocent of the original charge but, under intensive interrogation, admitted participation in two entirely different slayings. And so the unraveling of Murder Inc.'s multiple homicides began.

"When I was twenty," Maffetore began, "I got in with the mob. I went into the shylock business. Pittsburgh Phil gave me the territory. Pretty Levine was my partner. In 1937, Pittsburgh Phil tells us to steal a car." They did and, following orders, delivered the auto to Maione and Dasher Abbandando.

"A couple of days later," Maffetore said, "I see in the papers a guy was found dead in the car."

Almost as an afterthought, Dukey described a second killing—one that took place just a few months before. At Goldstein's direction, he had driven "a little guy" he didn't know to Reles' house. "They choke him there. Then Bugsy sets fire to him on a vacant lot."

These homicides turned out to be the slayings of George "Whitey" Rudnick and Irv "Puggy" Finestein, and the solving of the crimes eventually brought down Murder Inc. But first corroboration was needed.

"You should go get Pretty," Maffetore suggested. "He is smart. He knows more than me."

Pretty Levine was more intelligent than Dukey and he took much longer to crack. Trying to go straight after the Rudnick killing, he moved from Brownsville and took a truck-driver's job. But he still feared his former bosses. Only after the police put his wife in protective custody did Levine talk. "Why should I keep my wife in jail for these rats?" he said.

And then Abe "Kid Twist" Reles, who with Happy Maione was being held in the Tombs on minor charges, announced he wanted to make a deal. "You were in on the Puggy Finestein job," Turkus told Reles. "On that," the Kid replied smilingly, "you ain't got no corroboration."

Reles was right. "A Kid Twist could say, 'Me and Bugsy and Happy did such-and-such a job,'" Turkus would admit. "Yet, unless an outside witness—one neither accomplice nor principal—substantiated him, Bugsy and Happy would walk out of court free." That was New York criminal law.

But Reles knew who in the underworld could provide that substantiation. "I can make you the biggest man in the country," Kid Twist told O'Dwyer. "But I got to make a deal."

After considerable haggling, O'Dwyer agreed that Reles could keep his immunity from prosecution—based on the information he provided. In other words, he could not incriminate himself in those murders he described to the grand jury. "I can tell you about fifty guys that got hit," Kid Twist bragged. "I was on the inside." He kept his promise. After twelve days, his testimony—filled with minutest detail—took up twenty-five stenographer's notebooks. A cold-eyed killer, he was as skillful at his work as any craftsman.

One can only conjecture why Reles decided to talk. The most plausible answer is that he sensed the halcyon years of Murder Inc. were drawing to a close, that the Syndicate—

becoming more respectable on the eve of World War II—was finding its enforcement arm an embarassment. At any rate, Reles not only exposed the Brooklyn operation of the mob, but gave O'Dwyer and Turkus a view of the national set-up. "Me and my partners are in shylocking, the restaurant business, the garment industry—through Lepke, crap games, slot machines, bookmaking . . ." he would say. "We got connections. New Orleans, Florida. We are like this with the Purple Mob in Detroit. We work with Bugsy Siegel in California."

Now the prosecutors moved swiftly to jail additional witnesses, before the Syndicate could silence them. Among those caught in the net:

- *Julie Catalano,* whom the newspapers would call the "Kings County Canary." Perhaps his most notable assignment was driving the getaway car the memorable night Happy Maione, dressed as a woman, shot to death two members of a plasters' union who were resisting his extortion attempts.

- *Sholem Bernstein,* who went out of his way to give friends automobile rides. Unfortunately, the friends invariably met with accidents. "I will become a rat and tell everything," Sholem said.

- *Blue Jaw Magoon,* who when he was not driving murder cars was fond of partying. "I went out social with all the guys," he would reflect. "When Pittsburgh Phil is with the big-shots he wines and dines them, but with the little guys he argues about a nickel. Reles is ungenerous, too, but he puts on no airs."

On May 13, 1940, O'Dwyer and Turkus brought Ocean Hill's Happy Maione and Dasher Abbandando to trial for the murder of suspected stoolpigeon Whitey Rudnick, whose death three years before has been caused by sixty-three stab wounds in the chest, a smashed skull, and strangulation. Dukey Maffetore's part in the homicide, as we have seen, was stealing a car for Happy and Dasher—on orders from Pittsburgh Phil.

"Me and Pretty Levine took the car," Dukey testified, "and brought it to Atlantic Avenue and Eastern Parkway—to the garage there. Happy and Dasher was there."

The most important testimony, of course, came from Reles, who with Julie Catalano was present in the Sunset Garage—where Dukey and Pretty delivered the auto—the morning Rudnick was murdered. "I walk in," said Reles, who was admitted to the garage by Maione. "Over there on the floor, Rudnick is laying. Abbandando is holding him around the shoulders and Pittsburgh Phil is putting a rope around his neck."

Later, Reles said, "Abby grabed Rudnick by the feet and drags him over to the car. Phil and Happy grab it by the head, They put it in the car. Somebody says, 'The bum don't fit.' So, Abby pushes. He bent the feet up."

"You mean the legs?" interrupted the judge.

"Yeah, he bent up the legs," continued Reles. "Then, just as they push the body in, it gives a little cough or something. With that, Phil starts with the ice pick and begins punching away at Whitey. And Maione, he says, 'Let me hit this bastard one for luck,' and he hits him with the cleaver, someplace on the head."

The trial lasted just ten days. Found guilty of murder in the first degree, the defendants were later sentenced to die in the electric chair. Though the conviction was reversed, eight months later, on a technicality, a second trial brought a new conviction and a similar sentence. On February 19, 1942, Happy and Dasher died in Sing Sing.

On September 9, 1940, O'Dwyer began trial proceedings

against Brownsville's Bugsy Goldstein and Harry "Pittsburgh Phil" Strauss—Reles' two best friends—for the murder, the year before, of gambler Puggy Finestein.

"Albert gave me a contract to take some guy," Pittsburgh Phil told Reles at the time.

"Who is the guy?" the Kid asked.

"I don't know. Some small fellow. His name is Puggy . . . with a pug nose. You can't miss him."

"Who is Albert?" the prosecutor asked Reles during the trial.

"That is our boss," Kid Twist replied.

"What is Albert's full name?"

"Albert Anastasia." And thus Anastasia's name was introduced to the investigation. Through him the trail could have led to Adonis, even to Costello. Yet, as we shall see, O"Dwyer's pursuit did not extend that far.

For the next couple of weeks, Phil and Bugsy Goldstein unsuccessfully sought Puggy Finestein. Then, one evening out of the blue, their quarry approached the defendants and Reles while they were standing on the street—to ask their help in finding a shylock named Tiny, to whom he owed some money.

"What happened next?" the prosecutor asked Reles.

"Me and Phil and Bugsy got into a consultation."

"What was said?"

"I says to Phil, 'What are you going to do with him?' He says, 'Take him to your house.' 'Why my house?' I says. And Phil says, 'You're moving anyway.' Then Bugsy says to me, 'My wife is going over to your wife to go to the movies, so I don't think your wife is home.' That settles it. Phil says to Bugsy, 'Ride him around about an hour. Make believe you're looking for Tiny. Then bring him there.'"

Bugsy needed a car.

"Phil spots Dukey Maffetore over at a newstand," Reles continued. "He says, 'Dukey will take you. Don't tell him nothing.' "

While Bugsy kept Puggy occupied, Reles went home to set the stage for murder.

"When I got inside, I see my wife there, and Bugsy's wife, Betty, and the old lady—that's my wife's mother. I tell my wife, 'Go to the movies with Betty.' So her and Betty leave, and the old lady goes to bed."

Phil joined Reles a half-hour later. "Albert says it's okay —but do it clean," he reported.

"What happened then?" the prosecutor asked.

"Phil asks me have I got a rope and an ice pick," Reles said. "So I go into the bedroom where the old lady is sleeping. I ask her, 'Where's the rope we used up at the lake last summer for the washline?' She says, 'Down in the cellar in the valise.' Then I ask the old lady, 'Where's the ice pick?' She says, 'In the pantry.' Phil says to the old lady, friendly-like, 'Why don't you go back to sleep?' "

"When Bugsy and Puggy walked in, what happened?"

"As soon as Puggy passes the chair, Phil jumps up and puts his arm around him . . . mugs him. Puggy wiggles around. So Phil throws him on the couch. I put the radio on louder, because Puggy is making noise. Phil is like laying over Puggy so he should not move. Bugsy is hitting him to make him quit. I give Phil one end of the rope. He ties him up like a little ball. If he moves, the rope will tighten around his neck more."

"After the job was finished, was anything said?"

"Pittsburgh Phil says, 'We better burn this bum up so nobody will know him.' He says to Bugsy, 'Go get some gas.' "

"What was done?"

"Me and Phil pick up Puggy and we take it out the side door and put it in Dukey's car," Reles testified.

After the cremation, which took place in a nearby vacant lot, Bugsy encountered Blue Jaw Magoon. He jumped from Dukey's car, the gasoline can still in his hand, and ran over to Magoon's auto.

"What did Bugsy Goldstein say?" the prosecutor asked Magoon.

"I says, 'What's the excitement?' Bugsy says, 'Me and Dukey just burn a guy.' I says, 'Who?' 'A guy named Puggy,' he says. It didn't mean anything to me."

Further corroboration, unwittingly, came from Reles' mother-in-law, who was questioned about what took place the next morning.

"Phil was saying to my son-in-law that his finger is bitten, and he wanted Mercurochrome," she testified.

"Did you do any housework?"

"Yes, I cleaned up the living room," she said. "Things were very disturbed."

Pittsburgh Phil and Bugsy were convicted of murder and, like Happy and Dasher, condemned to die in the electric chair. The sentence was carried out in June of 1941.

Lepke, as we have seen, had been in hiding from prosecutor Thomas E. Dewey since mid-1937. Two years later, the law still did not know his whereabouts—although he had remained in Brooklyn, concealed by Anastasia in a succession of comfortable apartments. But then a worried Frank Costello and Joe Adonis, concerned about the growing public outrage that Lepke could not be found, and the damage it might do the Syndicate, convinced Lepke to give himself up —telling him that a "deal" had been arranged. Intermediaries were easily found in Broadway columnist Walter Winchell and FBI director J. Edgar Hoover, two men who never shied away from personal publicity. Only Anastasia did not concur with the Syndicate decision. "What's the hurry?" he told Buchalter. "While they ain't got you, they can't hurt you." But Anastasia's advice went for naught and, on the night of August 24, 1939, an auto pulled away from lower Third Street in Brooklyn, rolled across the Brooklyn Bridge, and made its way to Fifth Avenue and Twenty-eighth Street in Manhattan. In the back seat of the car, which was driven by Anastasia, were Lepke and Louis Capone's sister-in-law, the woman carrying a baby to make the trek look like a family outing. On Fifth Avenue, Lepke walked over to a waiting limousine. "Mr. Hoover, this is Lepke," said Winchell, making the introductions.

"Glad to meet you, I'm sure," said Lepke, while the stony-faced FBI director stared at him in silence. When Hoover did speak, the mobster learned the truth: there was no deal. "I wanted to get out of the car," the mobster later remembered. But it was too late. FBI agents had already surrounded the limousine.

Within a few months, not only was Lepke convicted by the federal government on narcotics charges, and sentenced to fourteen years imprisionment, but he was nailed by Dewey, who would soon successfully run for governor, on bakery-racket charges, and given an additional thirty years. A third conviction—this one for homicide—was to come.

In September of 1936, Lepke had ordered the killing of Joseph Rosen, a garment-center trucker he had put out of business and was threatening to go to the law. Suave Louis Capone had arranged the hit and muscular Mendy Weiss, another Lepke confidante, had—together with the ubiquitous Pittsburgh Phil—early one Sunday morning pumped ten bullets into Rosen, who had been reduced to running a candy store.

Now, in September of 1941, O'Dwyer and Turkus brought Lepke, along with Capone and Weiss, to trial for the murder. Providing the initial evidence against the defendants was Max Rubin, a onetime labor-racket henchman of Lepke's. Rubin testified that, on several occasions in 1936, Buchalter had threatened to "take care of" Rosen. Finally, a few days before the killing, the usually calm Lepke exploded in anger.

"I stood enough of this crap," he was quoted by Rubin as saying. "That son-of-a-bitch Rosen—he's around again, and shooting off his mouth about seeing Dewey. He and nobody else is going anyplace and doing any talking."

Corroborating Rubin's testimony was Allie Tannenbaum, a Murder Inc. hireling whom O'Dwyer and Turkus had persuaded to talk.

"On the Friday before Rosen's death, where were you?" he was asked.

"That was the day I went up to the office to report to Lepke," Allie replied.

"Who was there?"

"Lepke was there. He was with Max Rubin. His face was flushed. Lepke was hollering. He says, 'There is one son-of-a-bitch that will never go down to talk to Dewey about me.' Max was trying to calm him down. He was saying, 'I'll handle Joe Rosen—he's all right.' "

"What did Lepke say to that?"

"He says, 'You told me that before.' He says, 'I'm fed up with that son-of-a-bitch, and I'll take care of him.' "

The final prosecution witness, Blue Jaw Magoon, strengthened the case against the defendants. After the Rosen killing, he swore, he had been ordered by Louis Capone to commit another murder—near Sutter Avenue, where Rosen had been slain, and where Magoon was known.

"I asked Capone if it was advisable for me to work there,

because I hung out only a block away, right off Sutter Avenue, and I might be recognized," Blue Jaw testified.

"Did Capone answer?"

"He says, 'What are you worried about? I worked on the Rosen thing, and it was right on Sutter Avenue, and I wasn't recognized.' "

On November 30, 1941, Lepke—along with Capone and Weiss—were found guilty as charged. Though sentenced to die in the electric chair, various appeals and delays would stay their execution until March of 1944.

Yet the investigation of Murder Inc. would never go beyond Lepke—to Anastasia and Adonis, to Siegel in California, even to Costello. For in the early morning of November 11, 1941, Abe Reles, the only man whose testimony could have insured this prosecution, although guarded by six policemen, plunged to his death from the sixth floor of the Half Moon Hotel in Coney Island, where he was being held in protective custody. Terming the death accidental, the Brooklyn district attorney's office promptly issued a report, which said in part:

- There are detectives working in eigh-hour shifts keeping a strict supervision over the material witnesses—who include Allie Tannenbaum and Sholem Bernstein.

- After the witnesses go to bed, the doors to the rooms are opened. Reles was sleeping alone in room 623. His door was open.

- The rooms in which the witnesses are kept are visited at fifteen-minute intervals.

- Sometime between 7 A.M. and 7:10 A.M., a detective went to Reles' room. He discovered Reles was missing, although the slacks usually worn by him hung across a chair. He looked out and saw the body of a man on the extension below.

• It was discovered that two bedsheets were knotted together, one end of which was attached to about four feet of wire, the end of the wire being wound around the radiator.

• At the time, the radio was playing, and Reles probably left it on all night.

• It is the belief of the district attorney's office that Reles probably tried to swing into the room below, room 523, recently vacated, in order to effect his escape. The sheets were only long enough for him to reach the floor below.

. . .

To at least one member of the district attorney's office, Burton Turkus, the escape theory was ridiculous. "Here was a veteran murder specialist," Turkus would say. "Yet the opinion created by the death scene would have you believe that, risking his own neck, Reles tied a knot that came undone almost as soon as his weight pulled against it."

For similar reasons, Turkus disregarded a second theory —that Reles was trying to play a practical joke on his guards.

Police captain Frank Bals, an O'Dwyer friend who was in charge of the guard detail, would testify about Reles's death.

"When I saw him, he was lying on an extension roof, and there was an indication that he had tied a bedsheet and tried to slide down to the floor below to a vacant apartment. But the bedsheet he used, he used along with a piece of wire, and little did he know you cannot tie a knot in that thing."

"Were Reles, and the detectives guarding him at the Half Moon Hotel, under your command?"

"Yes," Bals replied. "There were six men always guarding him. Not him alone, there were other witnesses there."

"Were certain of these detectives in Reles's room an hour prior to his death?"

"Well, the room was practically all in one. It was a suite of rooms, and there were no doors."

"And there was a man watching Reles at all times?"

"There were men in the suite. But they evidently fell asleep."

"This is your explanation?"

"Well, how could Reles do it if they did not?"

"What did the detectives say in extenuation of their being asleep?"

"I do not recall," Bals said.

"Reles was the most influential witness you had. You were the ringmaster, and your six dummies let the man go out the window. I think the thing is shady."

"My thought is he just tried to play smart and sneak down to the next floor."

"How many prisoners, other than the Murder Inc. group, have you ever had in a hotel room?"

"They are the first."

"Who gave the order? District Attorney O'Dwyer?"

"That is right," Bals replied.

It remained for Burton Turkus to put Reles's "accidental" death in proper perspective. "Reles would have had to be unconscious," he would say of the fall. "Otherwise the Kid would have had plenty of time in a drop of forty-two feet to have let out at least one substantial scream. The fact that Reles's body was found more than twenty feet from the wall of the building definitely leads to the conclusion he exited with some force. Murder by one or two men is the likeliest of all the theories advanced for Reles's startling end."

6

Reles's death effectively destroyed the developing case against Albert Anastasia, the lord high executioner, for the 1939-murder of Morris Diamond, a trucking-union leader who had been defying extortion demands. Allie Tannenbaum had testified that he had, on Anastasia's orders, "fingered" Diamond for Dandy Jack Parisi, the actual gunman, and Julie Catalano, the getaway-car driver, had sworn that Anastasia himself had plotted the crime. But they were accomplices. Only Reles, the nonparticipant, could have provided courtroom corroboration. From Anastasia, of course, the trail could have led to the highest levels of the Syndicate.

"I come over to talk to Albert about our bookmaking business," Reles had said during his interrogation, describing a visit to Anastasia's house, "and these two guys are sitting there. They are discussing a Morris Diamond matter. 'Everything is ready and you still don't tell us where the bum lives,' Albert says. 'I'm working on it, Albert,' he is told. 'When I get it, we will take care of him,' Anastasia promises."

Knowing that Reles was telling the law everything he knew, Anastasia remained in hiding throughout 1940 and 1941. He need not have bothered: during the eighteen months that O'Dwyer had Reles in custody, he made no effort toward getting a murder indictment against Anastasia. Finally, in May of 1942—six months after the Kid's death and while Albert was still in hiding—the "wanted" cards on Anastasia, and on Dandy Jack Parisi, were removed from the police investigation bureau files. This ammounted to formal notice, to all concerned, that the Morris Diamond case was closed and the mobsters were no longer being sought for questioning.

"Referring to the Anastasia case," O'Dwyer later would be asked, "is it not a fact that you commented at the time that the police had a perfect case of murder in the first degree against him?"

"For indictment?" O'Dwyer asked.

"For indictment."

"Yes, sir."

"Was Reles an important witness?"

"Reles was the one witness who was not involved in the crime. I depended on him as the independent proof."

"And that's why he was locked up at the Half Moon Hotel?"

"Not for that one case alone, but that's why he was in the hotel."

"And what is your version of the facts about his death?"

"That he tried to escape."

"Then your testimony conflicts with Captain Bals, whose thesis is that Reles didn't try to escape, that he let himself out the window with the intention of climbing in the floor below and coming up and tapping on the door and saying, 'Peek-a-boo, I'm back again.' "

"How could anyone tell what was in Reles's mind?" said O'Dwyer. "What he was trying to do will never be known."

"Is there an explanation for the fact that proceedings against Anastasia were not pursued, in view of the evidence you had against him?"

"Yes, sir, there is a very good explanation," O'Dwyer replied. "One of the first things that happened was that Anastasia and Jack Parisi went into hiding, and we were never able to find them. There was another witness besides Reles. He was a small boy, who was reported to me as delicate, and I think had some trouble with one eye. He was apparently sitting on a stoop, very early in the morning, when Mr. Diamond was going to work and Parisi killed him. Now the story I was told by Reles was that Anastasia not only arranged the details of the crime but had a conversation regarding it in the presence of Reles. I have said that was a perfect case. But a perfect case to me means a perfect indictment case. This little boy—first of all, he was delicate, secondly, there was the danger of these gangsters threatening his father and mother. In my opinion, it was not a good thing to put this case to the grand jury until I knew that I had Anastasia in custody and, if possible, Parisi."

The "little boy" in question, it should be noted, was a sturdy sixteen-year-old at the time of the Diamond killing, and it was he, as he was opening his father's grocery store for business, who had seen Parisi pump a clip of cartridges into Diamond.

O'Dwyer then was asked about the "wanted" cards on Anastasia and Parisi.

"Now, in May of 1942, a month before you left the district attorney's office to go into the army, weren't the cards removed from the files of the police department?"

"I didn't know about that until later," O'Dwyer replied. "Should I be held responsible for what was done or not done in that office when I was in army uniform?"

"Did you visit Brooklyn between 1942 and 1945?"

"I lived in it."

"And you frequently saw Jim Moran, the chief clerk in the office?"

"That's right."

"Did you ever check up on what had been done about this

case—the most important in your entire career?"

"I had my army work and my army responsibilities," O'Dwyer maintained.

James J. Moran, the man who ordered the removal of the "wanted" cards on Anastasia and Parisi, would vehemently defend his actions.

"There never was a case against Albert Anastasia for the Morris Diamond murder," he would say. "There was no sense cluttering up the files with cards."

"Would you give us your opinion why you thought there was not a good case?"

"I didn't think they had sufficient corroboration. The witness was no good. The witness couldn't see three feet ahead of him."

"Who was that witness?"

"It was a boy, at the time about nine or ten years old. They had him around the office for months."

"Was Abe Reles another witness?"

"As to the actual killing, I don't know for sure."

In the fall of 1941, nominated as the Democratic candidate for mayor on the strength of his new-found fame as a crusading district attorney O'Dwyer waged a vigorous campaign—the issues of which can best be described as trivial—against the entrenched LaGuardia. On election morning, after a barber had given him a shave in the second-floor bedroom of his house on Brooklyn's Seventy-ninth Street, he went downstairs, as usual, to breakfast with his wife.

"Hello, cabbage-head," he was greeted by Edna Davis, the Negro maid, who was measuring several drops of iodine into his orange juice.

"When you get to be fifty-one and start campaigning," the unruffled O'Dwyer observed, "you need your iodine."

Late that evening, it became apparent that Bill-O's efforts

—this time at least—had been in vain. By a narrow margin, LaGuardia won his third straight mayoral race. Within a few months the Murder Inc. investigation would come to a close, and O'Dwyer would spend the war years in the army air force. Uppermost in his mind, however, was another bid for the mayoralty.

PART THREE

1943-1945: Interregnum

1

DURING THE WAR YEARS, New York was a place of gas rationing, blackouts, and food coupons, of young Frank Sinatra presiding over teenage riots at the Paramount, of snooty headwaiters and free-spending patrons at the Copacabana, the Latin Quarter, and the Diamond Horseshoe. It was also a place, increasingly, that Frank Costello was coming to dominate. At no time was this clearer than in August of 1943, when a police wiretap on the phone in Costello's Central Park West home picked up the following call from Magistrate Thomas Aurelio, who had just received the Democratic nomination for State Supreme Court justice.

"Good morning, Francesco," Aurelio began. "How are you, and thanks for everything."

"Congratulations," Costello said. "It went over perfect. When I tell you something is in the bag, you can rest assured. . . . We'll have to have dinner soon."

"That's fine," Aurelio replied. "But right now I want to assure you of my loyalty for all you have done. It's undying."

In short order, disbarment proceedings were begun against Aurelio—on the logical grounds that no jurist should be so friendly with a member of the Syndicate. Called to testify, Costello, knowing he had committed no crime in recommending Aurelio's candidacy, simply told the truth.

"What business do you now have?" he was asked by Manhattan District Attorney Frank Hogan.

"Candy machines. When you put in a nickel and pull the handle, a pack of mints drops out."

"Isn't it true that once in a while some slugs drop out with the package?"

"Yes."

"Isn't the machine commonly called a slot machine?" Hogan asked.

"I guess that's right."

Before testifying about Aurelio, Costello revealed that he had been instrumental, the year before, in putting in office Tammany Boss Michael Kennedy—a man he often saw "at racetracks, bars, restaurants, and Madison Square Garden."

In view of that help, Costello went on to explain, he fully expected Kennedy's support when, later, the gambler and the district leaders he controlled met with Kennedy to discuss Aurelio's candidacy.

"The meeting was for the specific purpose of talking to Mike Kennedy about putting Judge Aurelio on the bench," Costello said. "I said that would be a very fine thing. Kennedy said he was going to give it a lot of consideration."

Within a few weeks, however, Frank learned from Bert Stand, the Tammany secretary, that Kennedy was under pressure, from President Roosevelt among others, to see that an Irish-Catholic congressman received the Supreme Court nomination. "You ought to talk to that fellow," Stand advised the mobster. "He's cooling off on the Italian."

The news made Costello furious. "I told Kennedy," he testified, " 'Now you've got to be either a man or a mouse. Declare yourself. You're the leader of Tammany Hall. Are you going to be the boss or not?' "

Then and there, Costello said, "Kennedy told me he was definitely going to have Judge Aurelio on the ticket."

In rebuttal, Aurelio's attorney tried to bring out the supposition that his client did not know the details of Costello's past.

"Have you in the last nine or ten years tried to conduct your life in a decent way?"

"I have," replied Costello.

"You are reluctant to give us the names of some of the decent people you associate with?"

"I know some of the finest, biggest businessmen in the country. I wouldn't want to embarass them. I gamble, but I never stole a nickel in my life. My word is my bond."

When the graying, meek-looking Aurelio took the stand, the jurist did not deny that he had asked Costello's help, but insisted that he had not known his background. This was a startling claim from a man whose two decades of experience as an assistant district attorney and a magistrate must have made him knowledgeable about the underworld.

Aurelio remembered Costello telling him, "Everyone believes you are going to get the nomination. As a matter of fact, it's in the bag."

As for his offer of "undying loyalty," the jurist had a ready explanation. "That's just the way some Italians express things," he said.

Charles B. Sears, the referee in the disbarment proceedings, agreed with Aurelio. On October 30, 1943, he found there was insufficient evidence to assume that the jurist knew the character of the "Francesco" to whom he had been so profuse in his thanks. "Not proven" was the verdict.

A few days later, his bi-partisan place on the ballot secure, Aurelio was elected to the New York Supreme Court.

Ironically, Costello did not benefit, in the years that followed, for his sponsorship of the judge. "Early in Aurelio's career as supreme court justice, Frank sent an intermediary to 'feel the judge out' concerning the forthcoming trial of a friend," Attorney George Wolf would say. "He was icily rebuffed. 'A lousy ingrate' was one of the lesser terms Costello used about Aurelio. To newspapers he coined a phrase which became famous, 'I can't even get a parking ticket fixed with him.' Aurelio's phone call had sprung Frank into the spotlight of publicity. Overnight he became the number one criminal in New York, and he blamed the little judge."

One of the "decent people" with whom Costello was associating about this time was George Morton Levy, the wealthy trial lawyer (he had defended Lucky Luciano) and racetrack operator. For years, he and Levy had been golfing companions at the posh Lakeville Country Club in Great Neck, Long Island, where they were often joined by Frank Kelly, the Brooklyn Democratic leader, and gambler Frank Erickson. Then, in 1943, a second wiretap on Costello's phone revealed that he had been asked by Levy, whose Roosevelt Raceway was then operating at the Empire State Racetrack in Yonkers, to rid the track of bookmakers—so as to keep the

State Harness Racing Commission from revoking its license.

"Have you got a minute, Frank?" Levy began the conversation.

"Sure," replied Costello.

"Pinkerton sent us a contract" [to police the track] "and it is the most blankety-blank thing I ever saw. They can refuse to let in anybody they choose. I called Empire State for a conference and asked them if we could get our own agency. They turned the idea down. We did not think we could open today. We saved this thing by putting in a twenty-four-hour cancellation clause. If we could only get Empire to budge. We can't jeopardize the bookmakers. Pinkerton can put out anyone. What a blankety-blank bunch of morons. They're just as liable to arrest President Roosevelt's wife as not."

"I see."

"It's like holding a gun up against you. Pinkerton may have enough pride to step out. I don't want them."

"If they make any arrests" [and cannot prove the men are bookmakers] "you are subject to a suit."

"As boss, you should be able to tell them the way things stand now," Levy said.

"Okay." Costello agreed.

"I can't play golf Sunday," Levy continued, now more relaxed. "I ran a pencil into my hand—can't hold a club."

"I'll probably see you Sunday anyway," replied Costello. "We can sit on your front lawn and cut up your business."

Later, Costello would be asked what he meant when he said he and Levy would "cut up" the latter's business.

"That is just a saying," the gambler answered. "Maybe we would cut up some touches. You know, just slang. What business can I cut up on a lawn?"

"You were hired in 1943, apparently to chase bookies off

a track. You were paid fifteen thousand dollars a year. Do you remember Mr. Levy saying to you, 'We can't jeopardize the bookmakers'. . . ."

"I don't remember him saying that to me."

But Costello did recall being approached by Levy.

"He told me he was having difficulty at the track, at Roosevelt Raceway. He told me he might lose his franchise. Bookmakers were there, and the Racing Commission had told him that if he didn't clean it up he might lose his license. I says, 'What way can I help you?' He says, 'Can you suggest something?' I says, 'Haven't you got a detective agency there?' He says, 'There have been a lot of complaints. I personally don't think there's any more bookmakers there than any other track, but there have been a lot of complaints.' I says, 'Nothing I can do for you, George.' So he says, 'Maybe you can think of something.' I says, 'What I can do, George, I can spread the propaganda around that they're hurting you and you're a nice fellow, and I can tell them that if there's an arrest made, it's going to be very severe. I don't know how much good it's going to do, but I'll talk about it.' He says, 'I wish you would,' and I did."

"Did you think that your passing the word around would have some influence on bookmakers?"

"I didn't think so, and I still don't think so."

Subsequently, Levy—under attack for allegedly having Costello as a silent partner—would give his version of his dealings with the gambler.

"I said, 'I will want to pay you.' He said, 'There is no necessity to pay. I will do what I can.' I said, 'I insist on paying.' "

"How much did you pay?"

"Sixty thousand dollars. Fifteen thousand dollars a year."

"What did Costello do? He has told us that he wandered

around to a few bars and talked to some people, none of whom he can remember, and he says that all he said was that if there were any bookies caught at the track they were going to get heavy sentences, and they had better be careful. Does that sound like sixty-thousand-dollars worth?"

"I don't know whether he did sixty-thousand-dollars or sixty cents worth of work. He did the job, in my opinion, when there was no revocation proceeding. The mere hiring of the fellow was invaluable."

2

Throughout the 1940s, Costello's authority in the underworld —despite sporadic investigations—continued to grow. Moreover, his money and his success were bringing him semi-respectibility. Tammany leaders, judges and favor-seekers openly called at his homes on Central Park West and in Sands Point, Long Island, and dropped in at the Waldorf during his business mornings, at the Madison Hotel where he often lunched, at L'Aiglon where he dined. At one point, Costello bought into Wall Street—taking title to three buildings in that hallowed area, re-naming them the 79 Wall Street Corporation, and installing himself as the company's president.

"Where did you get the money to invest in 79 Wall Street?" he would be asked.

"Well, it was a surplus," Costello replied.

"Where did you get the surplus?"

"From slot machines and so forth," Costello answered, giving the usual answer to explain his income.

"And the sales price was four-hundred-thousand-dollars?"

"That's right."

In interviews with reporters and columnists, Costello would insist that he was no Syndicate leader, he was simply a gambler. "I'm cleaner than ninety-nine percent of New Yorkers," he told *Newsweek*. "I'm like Coca-Cola. There are a lot of drinks as good. Pepsi is a good drink. But Pepsi never got the advertising Coca-Cola got. I'm Coca-Cola because I got too much advertising."

With the New York *Journal-American*'s Bob Considine, he took a similar line. "If you say I was or am a racketeer, I guess you're right. I have decided that a racketeer is a fellow who tries to get power, prestige, and money at the expense of entrenched power, prestige, and money. I figure that if I'm a racketeer, so are—let's say—editors. They'll print your articles in the hope of stealing circulation from rival newspapers."

To Walter Winchell, to whom each year he would give one-hundred-thousand-dollars in cash for the Damon Runyon Cancer Fund, Frank would say, "I can honestly say that, since I'm old enough to know right from wrong, I've tried to lead a good life. I've been married to the same girl for thirty years. How many of my critics can match that?"

Costello, like most *Mafioso*, expected his wife to be seen and not heard. Bobbie had her charge cards, her dinners and evenings out on those social occasions when she was needed, her periodic vacations. In return, she was expected to be cheerful, keep sumptious and quiet homes where Frank could relax, and—above all—be discreet. But the Costellos were childless and, with no career of her own, Bobbie must often have wondered how to busy herself. Each year, the Christmas holidays provided a poignant outlet for her energies: she would write out and address more than a thousand Christmas cards. She kept two dogs, worried about her weight, and always remembered the birthdays of friends.

For years, Costello kept a mistress, a former showgirl, in a Fifth Avenue apartment. They were never seen together in public, but Frank would regularly visit her in the late afternoon, stay several hours, and then go about his evening's work. In everything he did, he kept a low profile. "He never let you know he was Frank Costello," saloon-keeper Toots Shor would recall. "He acted like just another guy. He loved to bet and talk sports. I never saw him with anybody but his wife. He had too much respect for her to be seen with someone else." Everything about Costello was keyed to the unobtrusive. His tailoring, for instance, was expensive but conservative. Even when provoked, he took care not to raise his voice: he let his silence indicate his displeasure. He was a soft touch for those short of cash, endorsed the *macho* pleasures and prejudices of his day, and never talked about Syndicate business.

Costello could also be protective. When, about 1943, his longtime friend Willie Moretti began violating the code of silence—some say because of a syphilitic condition that affected his mental faculties—Frank saw to it Willie was spirited from the New York Area. To some extent, Costello was jeopardizing mob interests in New Jersey by this decision: Joe Adonis, Frank Erickson, and Longy Zwillman were uneasy about the free-talking Moretti. But Frank, who had been best man at Moretti's wedding, prevailed. Accompanied by male nurses, Willie was hustled out to the West Coast for several months—until his condition improved.

"Of course, there's a Mafia," Moretti would momentarily babble to a law-enforcement official. "I'm just what you claim I am, I'm the head man in my territory. But what's so bad about that? We don't harm anybody outside our own people.

We don't run to the cops when someone gets out of line. We settle things among ourselves."

"But what about the mob locking up the olive-oil business, the artichokes, the fish?" Moretti's questioner insisted. "If I, or my brother-in-law, tried to break into something that you've got controlled, we'd get a new hole in the head."

"Well, maybe that might happen once in a while," Willie conceded.

Just as embarassing to Costello as the Moretti and Aurelio matter was the time, in 1944, when he left $27,200 in cash, stuffed into two envelopes, in a taxi—and the newspapers learned of his forgetfulness. Frank had been given the money, part of the regular profits from the New Orleans operation, by Phil Kastel at the Hotel New Yorker near Pennsylvania Station, and had then taken a cab to the Sherry-Netherland at Fifty-ninth Street and Fifth Avenue. When he discovered the loss, he quickly checked with the doormen at the respective hotels, but they could not identify the driver. Meanwhile, the cabbie—in an exemplary display of honestly—had turned the money in to the police. "I thought it was counterfeit," he would explain. It is also possible, of course, that he knew who the cash belonged to—Costello's picture was often in the tabloids and his initials were on the envelopes—and only wanted protection.

The Syndicate leader's initial reaction was not to claim the money.

"You can't just forget it, Frank," Attorney George Wolf told him.

"Why not?"

"Because you'll look like you're hiding something. You've got to be forthright. Come with me down to the police property clerk's office."

"Can't we just forget the whole damn thing?"

"You left your handwriting all over the envelopes. The police will trace it."

"Damn that cabbie!" Costello swore. "Why didn't he *keep* the money?"

By now, Mayor LaGuardia was in the act—specifically forbidding the property clerk's office from releasing the money to Costello.

"What I'm interested in," the mayor told reporters, "is where did the bum get the cash and where was he taking it?"

Frank then was forced to sue the city for the $27,200, while a succession of front-page newspaper stories eagerly covered daily developments. Supporting his suit as an interested party, incongruously enough, was the federal government, which had a judgment pending against him for unpaid taxes. The State Supreme Court ruled for Costello, but the victory, financially speaking, was a hollow one. Of the disputed money, $24,287 went to the United States Government. The prime minister could afford the loss. It was the publicity that bothered him.

3

With the outbreak of the war, O'Dwyer—as we have seen— went into the army air force with the rank of major, and soon was assigned to its procurement arm, charged with investigating fraud by air force suppliers. It was in this connection, he always claimed, that he and James Moran had visited Costello's apartment in 1942, to tell the Syndicate leader that "the air force didn't want anyone in Wright Field unless they were legitimate people," and not to seek Costello's political support. Be that as it may, then Colonel O'Dwyer's efforts for the military in early 1944 drew praise from Under Secretary of War Robert L. Patterson, who wrote: "Bill O'Dwyer has done more than anyone else to prevent fraud and scandal in the army air force. His work is of the utmost importance, and I deem him the best-qualified man for it." A few months later, with the war coming to an end, O'Dwyer was named by President Roosevelt to head the economic section of the Allied Control Commission and sent to Italy. From his Rome headquarters, he supervised both financial aid and food shipments to the newly-emerging Italian government, and performed his duties so diligently he was credited with saving thousands of civilian lives. A promotion to brigadier-general soon followed.

Back in New York as a civilian in 1945, O'Dwyer experienced little difficulty in again securing the Democratic party's mayoral nomination. His Murder Inc. prosecution was still fresh in the public's mind, his war record was impressive, his friends were the city's power brokers. With the scrappy LaGuardia declining to run after three straight terms as a Fusion candidate, the election of a Democrat seemed certain.

O'Dwyer was fifty-five years old. His thatch of hair was fast graying, the lines of care radiating from the corners of his blue eyes were deepening. Ever fond of story-telling and reminiscing, his soft voice retaining just the hint of a brogue, he was an unpretentious man, easily liked. Almost deliberately careless about clothes, he often wore suit jackets and trousers that did not match. His shoes were the thick, black oxfords favored by former policemen who remember the weariness of pounding a beat. His relaxation was a long, black cigar. "I shall never forget how hectic New York seemed to me, coming as I did from a small Irish town," he would say to a reporter. "It's no calmer now, but I am used to it—the same bustle, the same business, the same crowds. Yet there is no more law-abiding place in the world. I ought to know, I was a cop here. It's a place that demands the best. I have this from personal experience, too—I was a bartender in a swell hotel. But when I think about New York, I forget its colleges, its libraries, its skyscrapers. I don't give either Wall Street or Broadway a thought. To me, New York means thirteen thousand homes, each renting for fifty-dollars or less a month, in which 5 million of our people live. It is these folks who make the city what it is. They or their forebears came from the four quarters of the earth, and they live here in peace and harmony."

Yet Bill-O was not simply a gregarious politician: he was erudite, sensitive, and skillful at keeping his private feelings to himself. He could quote extensively from Dante, Byron, and Yeats, among dozens of poets. And he was fascinated by American history—his preoccupation extending from scholarly works to the novels of Kenneth Roberts to popular biographies of men like Sam Houston. He and his wife Kitty, to whom he was deeply attached, were childless. He spoke only to close friends of her declining health: Kitty O'Dwyer now rarely appeared with him in public and seldom ventured far from their Bay Ridge home.

O'Dwyer's Republican-Liberal-Fusion opponent in the mayoral campaign that fall, Judge Jonah T. Goldstein, culminated a series of attacks against him in late October that contained some shocking charges—even by the standards of anti-Tammany candidates. "I am a judge of the Court of General Sessions—the court of the highest criminal jurisdiction in this state," he told a radio audience just before the election. "In the course of my duties as a judge, I signed the wiretapping order against Frank Costello that revealed a sordid judgeship nomination. It is understandable why Costello and his pals—criminal and political—are campaigning against me. Moreover, it is apparent that O'Dwyer is not going to answer my charges that his nomination was engineered by Frank Costello, Joe Adonis, and Irving Sherman.

"A sly report fed out of O'Dwyer's headquarters suggests that O'Dwyer met Costello in connection with army operations. The war is over. There is no danger of military secrets falling into the hands of our enemies. Let O'Dwyer tell the public what military matters he took up with Costello.

"Frank Costello is not only the slot machine king, but also the Democratic machine king. He and O'Dwyer met and dined together. Costello has kept in touch with O'Dwyer directly and through intermediaries, and particularly through Irving Sherman, his front-man.

"Sherman visited O'Dwyer frequently in the Brooklyn district attorney's office, though his name was not entered in the visitors' register, pursuant to O'Dwyer's personal instructions. Sherman is an intimate of Benny Siegel, alias Bugsy Siegel. He and Siegel both started their careers with the Lepke and Gurrah gang. Today Bugsy is the underworld king of California. And Sherman is the representative of Frank Costello—the underworld king of New York.

"O'Dwyer first developed his friendship for Sherman when the Brooklyn district attorney's office was investigating Murder Inc. That was the time when Bugsy Siegel and many others were under investigation. There were matters in the district attorney's office that were, obviously, of interest to Sherman. He was not a lawyer. He was not a judge. He was not a detective. He was not even a stool pigeon. Yet he visited O'Dwyer frequently.

"Let me tell you more about Sherman. He lives at 299

West Twelfth Street, Manhattan. He has an unlisted tele-
phone number, which has been temporarily disconnected.
On April 12, 1945, he made a person-to-person call to O'Dwyer, who was then at the Hay-Adams House in Washington,
D.C. On May 6, 1945, Sherman made another person-to-person call to O'Dwyer, who was then in El Centro, California.
On May 25, 1945, Sherman again made a call to O'Dwyer in
El Centro. On June 5, 1945, Sherman made a fourth call to
O'Dwyer, when he was in New York. Sherman certainly kept
track of O'Dwyer—in Brooklyn, New York, Washington,
and California.

"Sherman had O'Dwyer's 'S-N-P' number in Brooklyn—
'special-non-published' number. Few, if any, of O'Dwyer's
close friends had that number. But Sherman had it—because
he called O'Dwyer at that number from outside the city in
February and April of this year. Sherman was also acquainted
with O'Dwyer's chief clerk, Jim Moran, and he would also
telephone Moran at the later's home.

"I have told you that Adonis supports O'Dwyer's candidacy. He is Brooklyn's Public Enemy number one. His
power is so strong he was able to tell the Brooklyn Democratic leadership that they had to nominate O'Dwyer. He
served notice that he would set up primary fights unless
O'Dwyer was nominated.

"Adonis now rules Brooklyn by remote control from Bergen County, New Jersey, where he lives, and where he runs
one of the biggest gambling operations in the country.

"These mobsters are playing for big game," Judge Goldstein summed up. "Rackets and big-time gambling in New
York will repay them many times over for all they have spent
in promoting O'Dwyer's candidacy, in building up their candidate, and in trying to get him elected."

A few days later, a Kings County grand jury handed up

a presentment accusing former District Attorney O'Dwyer and members of his staff with gross laxity, inefficiency, and maladministration in the course of the Murder Inc. investigation. The evidence had been laid before the grand jury by Brooklyn District Attorney George J. Beldock, a Republican appointed to the post by Governor Dewey when O'Dwyer resigned to run for the mayoralty. Accused with O'Dwyer were former Chief Assistant Joseph Hanley, former Assistant District Attorney Edward Heffernan, and Chief Clerk James Moran.

The grand jury had centered its investigation into the circumstances surrounding the murder of Peter Panto, a leader of the rank-and-file movement in a Brooklyn longshoremen's union. He disappeared on July 14, 1939, after being threatened by Emil Camarda, a high-ranking union official. Through the efforts of detectives working under O'Dwyer, Panto's body was discovered, on January 29, 1941, in the swamps outside Lyndhurst, New Jersey. No one was ever convicted of the crime. At the time of the disappearance, Panto had been leading some twelve hundred insurgent longshoremen in a movement against gangster domination of the Brooklyn waterfront—and was fighting the kick-back and extortion rackets.

Within twenty-four hours, District Attorney Beldock expanded upon the grand jury's charges against O'Dwyer, and explained who, in his view, Bill-O was trying to protect.

"Let us talk about a man who was strangled and buried in quicklime, and a criminal investigation which was kidnapped and strangled in its infancy," Beldock declared. "The strangling of Peter Panto suppressed a revolt of Brooklyn's longshoremen against a murderous mob which held a death grip on six of their union locals. The killing of the waterfront investigation gave a free hand to organized murderers to prey upon the workers.

Panto's murder — according to
Beldock
grand jury law of 1945

"The gangsters and the Camarda family dominated these locals. The Camardas were a clan of union officials headed by Emil Camarda, founder and general factotum of the City Democratic Club. In this hideout, union officials played pinochle with Albert Anastasia, boss of the Red Hook underworld. In this club, Anastasia met his henchmen, his board of directors in the waterfront branch of Murder Inc., the subsidiary of the underworld organization in which Frank Costello and Joe Adonis are the upper crust.

"Peter Panto's revolt was getting somewhere. One night he had twelve hundred followers at a meeting. Soon thereafter, Emil Camarda called him in for a fatherly talk.

" 'Peter,' he said, 'I wish you'd stop what you're doing. The boys don't like it.'

"Two weeks later, on the night of July 14, 1939, Panto told his sweetheart and his kid brother that he was going to meet some men he didn't trust, and asked them to notify the police if he did not appear next morning. Panto left in an automobile with Gus Scannavino, Emil Camarda, and Tony Romeo, a trigger man for Anastasia. He was never seen alive again.

[Years later, Burton Turkus would maintain that the oxlike Mendy Weiss, whom he had sent to the electric chair for the murder of Joseph Rosen, had done the actual Panto strangling. "I hated to take that kid," Turkus would quote Weiss as saying. "But I had to do it for Albert, because Albert has been good to me."]

"Panto's death raised a commotion," Beldock continued. "New York City's Commissioner of Investigation went to work on his disappearance. He obtained startling confirmation of the racketeering charges. Now Special Prosecutor John Harlan Amen picked up his ears. Appointed by Governor Lehman to probe official corruption in Brooklyn, Amen took over. Soon he had a blueprint of the rackets. He sent out grand jury subpoenas for the books of the looted union locals.

"The union locals got busy, too. They hired a lawyer to hold Amen in check. They set up phony substitutes for their books, which they had burned. But the locals lost their case. The Supreme Court ordered the books produced before the Amen grand jury.

"Then, with lightning action, District Attorney O'Dwyer interjected himself. He pulled a big raid. The police descended on the waterfront, seized more than a hundred witnesses and herded them to O'Dwyer's office. The phony books went along, too. O'Dwyer had kidnapped the case. He had the witnesses. He had the evidence. Before the night was out, his assistants had even obtained confessions. By midnight, Anthony Guistra, a union secretary, was held in fifty-thousand-dollar-bail. They said it was to protect his life. He had confessed writing up the phony books because, for years, he had been turning over the union's money to the triggerman, Tony Romeo.

"O'Dwyer's chief assistant, Joseph Hanley, announced that night that the racketeers had milked the hard-working longshoremen of more than six hundred thousand dollars in dues alone. O'Dwyer himself said the extortion was 'terrific.' It had been a big night's work. The case had been broken wide open.

"For three days, the district attorney's investigation went on at high pressure. Then suddenly the man in command, Chief Assistant Hanley, was ordered off the case by O'Dwyer himself. Assistant District Attorney Heffernan was placed in command. Heffernan made a show of activity. He actually opened the case before a grand jury. Evidence piled up. Witnesses were thrown into jail in default of heavy bail. O'Dwyer convinced Prosecutor Amen that all this activity was on the level.

"Prosecutor Amen gave O'Dwyer all his files, his testimony, his exhibits, and, on top of that, everything that had been dug up by the City Commissioner of Investigation. O'Dwyer now had the entire case in his own hands.

"Now what happened?"

"O'Dwyer promptly ordered the investigation dropped. This is the sworn testimony of his colleague, Assistant District Attorney Heffernan. Amen's records were buried in the files where they were never read. The jailed witnesses were never again questioned. The whole business was salted away.

"The grand jury before whom the case had been opened was allowed to hear the pre-trial testimony of a single witness. They never heard of the case again. All references to the case were carefully omitted form the grand jury docket book in the keeping of O'Dwyer's chief clerk, James Moran. The permanent trial sheet authorizing the commencement of the case mysteriously disappeared from the keeping of this same Moran.

"At the very time that O'Dwyer was personally convincing Amen that everything was on the level, he was conferring with Emil Camarda, the union boss. Oh no, Camarda wasn't questioned about his threat to Panto, or Panto's last ride. But Camarda's visit [in May, 1940] had an amazing sequel—the end of the racket investigation. In June, Camarda again visited the district attorney's office—this time to see Moran. After this, Heffernan wrote a whitewash report. Heffernan said the locals had been reorganized with new officials. In truth, the only officers missing from the list were known gangsters, at that very moment fugitives from justice. Back on the list went Guistra, the man who had forged the books.

"Even Heffernan was forced to admit in this 'whitewash' that one of the locals had not yet been able to reorganize because its leader was in jail. He was Gus Scannavino. Along with Camarda, he had been one of the men last seen with

Panto. Scannavino is the man who was never questioned about his presence in Camarda's City Democratic Club the night the murder was planned. Scannavino today, since the murder of Emil Camarda, has become his successor, the organizer of the six waterfront locals.

"These were the gentry to whom O'Dwyer returned control of the racket-ridden workers.

"But what about Anastasia? Who was protecting him?"

To both Judge Goldstein's and District Attorney Beldock's specific charges, O'Dwyer chose to respond with generalities.

"When I took over the office of district attorney," he said, "I began training a small group of men in the necessary work of careful criminal investigation. While these men were being broken in, I was working night and day to get enough information to present to a grand jury. On the second of February, 1940, about thirty days after I took office, I obtained my first indictment against three men for gangster murders. It took some time to work on these men. We finally broke one of them. It took several weeks to get him to give us the information which we knew he had about the workings of the underworld. From what we got from this one man we moved quickly onto others. It took us months and months before we finally put together the actual picture.

"When Abe Reles finally opened up in March or April of 1940, we then began to know where we were moving. We then knew what was going on not only in Brooklyn, but also in New York, in Newark, in Sullivan County, New York, and even in Los Angeles.

"Here is a clear picture of what we did in that first year in office:

"Not a single racket killing.

"Exposure and complete destruction of a nation-wide ring

of murderers with all the attendant crime prevention.

"The solution of fifty murders committed in Brooklyn, and the solution of eleven other murders committed in various parts of the United States.

"Talk about laxity?

"Now while all this was going on," O'Dwyer continued, "it is true that there were some people from the waterfront who were brought in and turned over to Mr. Hanley and Mr. Heffernan on the question of kick-backs. I was concentrating on murder and not kick-backs. There was a possibility that we might obtain from some of these people leads to Albert Anastasia who, we had found out, was the chief director of the killings in Brooklyn. Out of these witnesses came the information which led to the discovery of the body of Peter Panto. We did not want to lose any possible evidence against the leader of the gang—Anastasia.

"I made the decision that the important thing was to get the murder gang down to the last one. That is what I concentrated on. When we ended up, we had sent seven of them to the electric chair. As long as Abe Reles was alive, we had a perfectly good case against Albert Anastasia," said O'Dwyer, not mentioning the fact that he had not once moved to indict Anastasia—either for the Peter Panto killing or the previously-mentioned Morris Diamond murder—during the eighteen months he had Reles alive and in custody. "But the day Abe Reles went through the window and was killed [November 11, 1941], that particular case, for want of corroboration, was no longer a clear case. I asked Mr. Turkus and Captain Bals of the police department to make a careful study of the Anastasia case. They said this would require considerable further investigation. This was still a month or two before I went into the army.

"I joined the army on June 1, 1942. At that time, there was

no case that was barred by the statute of limitations, including the Anastasia case. It may interest District Attorney Beldock to know there is no statute of limitations against murder.

"My record is that, when I left for the army, Murder Inc. in Brooklyn was completely destroyed. Many had been executed and others were in jail for life. That is the picture.

"Talk about laxity?"

In the midst of the charges and counter-charges, O'Dwyer's popularity continued to grow. The fact he may have been supported by the Syndicate made little impression on the voters.

A more acceptable, and highly effective, political backer of O'Dwyer's in the weeks before the election was his old friend Al Rosen, a Hollywood movie and theatrical entrepreneur who had made a bundle with his production of "Ladies Night in a Turkish Bath." It was Rosen who had persuaded a reluctant Bill-O to submit to the pencils and paints of a make-up man for some well-received newsreel speeches. Nor was this Rosen's only campaign inspiration. He organized the drive to enlist grocers and butchers under the O'Dwyer banner. "Their opinion amounted to something in that post-war day of shortages," a reporter would write. "They talked to innumerable housewives. Al argued that the chatter would sound like the united voice of myriads. He flooded the town with emissaries who told grocers and butchers that O'Dwyer's blood boiled everytime anyone alluded to them as 'blacketeers.' " Rosen next lined up elevator operators for O'Dwyer. "His reasoning was that one big O'Dwyer button on the lapel of an elevator operator would be seen by thousands of people," the reporter continued, "and that a few hundred O'Dwyer buttons on elevator operators would create the effect of an irresistable trend working itself up into a tidal wave. The election odds were not far from even when Rosen started and were ten to one for O'Dwyer before Election Day."

On November 6, 1945, Bill-O the boy from Bohola was elected mayor of New York by a then record plurality of some 685,000 votes. O'Dwyer, running on both the Democratic and American Labor Party tickets, polled 1,119,000 votes to Judge Goldstein's 434,000, while Newbold Morris, the No-Deal candidate backed by LaGuardia, registered 399,000.

It was not until six weeks after the election—not that it would have materially affected the outcome—that the Kings County grand jury that had accused O'Dwyer and his aides of laxity in the Peter Panto matter revealed that O'Dwyer himself had admitted to mishandling the developing case against Anastasia. "The undisputed proof is," the grand jury declared, "that William O'Dwyer and Edward Heffernan were in possession of competent legal evidence that Anastasia was guilty of first degree murder. But Anastasia was neither prosecuted, indicted, nor convicted."

"Anastasia played a hand in every murder committed in Brooklyn, and you finally got him, didn't you?" O'Dwyer was asked before the grand jury.

"Yes," he replied, with the first of three monosylabic answers.

"And you could have gotten an indictment against him?"

"Yes."

"And sent him to the electric chair?"

"Yes."

At a later point, O'Dwyer expanded on his testimony. "That thing should have been followed through," he said, referring to the Anastasia case, "but to blame me for it, that is not right."

Thomas Cradock Hughes, acting district attorney during O'Dwyer's absence in the armed forces, summed up what happened with the case after Reles's death and O'Dwyer's leave-taking.

"O'Dwyer went out of office with the Anastasia case safely locked in his breast," Hughes said. "He never spoke to me about it. If he had in mind that it should not be neglected, it seems to me he would have called me in and said, 'I am leaving June 1. This is a most important matter. Follow it up.' "

As for Anastasia, the removal of his wanted card by James Moran in May of 1942 paved the way for his return to the city from his upstate New York hideaway. Within a few weeks, he was drafted into the army where—as a technical sergeant —he spent the next two years training G.I. longshoremen, often relieving the tedium by visiting New York to see the boxing matches. Anastasia, who had jumped ship to enter the United States illegally in 1917, benefited from his military service—using it to obtain his American citizenship. By late 1945, he was re-installed on the Brooklyn waterfront, where his strong-arm tactics continued to insure him control of the rackets. Though he had escaped the consequences of his role in Murder Inc., he retained the underworld accolade, lord high executioner.

4

By the end of 1945, Costello and his longtime Syndicate friends—Siegel, Adonis, and Lansky—were guiding their gambling operations into the exuberant days of postwar expansion.

On the West Coast, Siegel's Trans-America Service, the race wire that he had set up in competition with Chicago's Continental Press, would soon triumph; Continental's owner was first wounded with shotgun blasts, then fatally poisoned with a dose of mercury, while he lay recuperating in the hospital. Trans-America, as a corporate entity, promptly vanished, and the mob took over Continental. But Siegel had greater ambitions. He foresaw the creation of a huge casino-hotel, the glamorous Flamingo, in still-undeveloped Las Vegas, still largely a dusty waystop on Highway 91. With some $1 million in mob money, he was preparing to make his dream a reality—using U.S. Senator Pat McCarran's influence to obtain still-scarce building materials. No expense was to be spared: there would be marble, glass, and chrome gambling rooms, ornate fountains, luxurious bedroom suites, beautiful casino girls, suave maîtres, croupiers, dealers, big-name Hollywood entertainers. In Siegel's eyes, the Flamingo already stood gleaming in the Nevada night, drawing monied patrons from Los Angeles and even from faraway Chicago and New York.

About this time, Siegel and his wife were divorced, enabling him to fully pursue his infatuation with the curvaceous, auburn-haired Virginia Hill, the gangland courtesan who had replaced the Countess DiFrasso as his constant companion.

The Alabama-born Virginia, at seventeen, had migrated to Chicago in 1933, and thereafter she never lacked for money. Gambler-accountant Joe Epstein, a key figure in the Capone mob, was her first benefactor. "I got to know him and we became friends, good friends," Virginia would say, "and then he told me I should take care of my money, and then I told him that when I have it I spend it, so he says, he'll hold it for me, that I had to think about tomorrow and all that stuff."

Epstein used her as a courier, delivering large sums of cash to layoff points in Los Angeles and New York throughout the 1930s, and making pickups as well. "Maybe I just liked to ride on trains," she would later tell investigators. On one of her regular trips to New York, sometime in 1942, she met Joe Adonis, who soon became her lover. The New York *Journal-American*, which heretofore had described Virginia as a Southern "oil heiress," then christened her "a much-photographed Manhattan glamour girl." When she went to Hollywood to try to break into the movies, Adonis frequently visited her there, walking with her hand-in-hand on the Sunset Strip or dining at the Trocadero. By now, the *Journal-American*, noting her free-spending ways, called her "the feminine Diamond Jim Brady," saying that "money is wired to her and she loses no time putting it in circulation."

It was through Adonis that Virginia met Siegel. Over the next few years, she and Bugsy lived in a succession of posh Hollywood hostels—an apartment in the Chateau Marmont, a suite at the Ambassador, a penthouse on Wilshire Boulevard. In these love nests, the stunning Virginia, who usually wore nothing indoors but Chanel No. 5 and silk lingerie, lavished her affections on Siegel. When the couple did go out, Virginia could select her ensemble from among thirty-five-hundred-dollar evening gowns, a hundred pairs of shoes, a dozen fur coats. Her tipping became legendary: fifty dollars to a barman was commonplace. "Fellows give me things," she would say, explaining her seemingly endless supply of cash. "I go out with them, like lots of girls, and they give me presents." She would bet the money at the racetrack. "I win a lot on the horses. I'm just lucky, I guess."

Though Bugsy and Virginia would soon marry, in a private Mexican ceremony, their relationship would be marked by almost as much violence as affection. On one occasion,

Virginia attacked and hospitalized a hatcheck girl she thought had designs on Siegel; on another, she cut a deep gash in Siegel's temple when she struck him, during an argument, with the spiked heel of her shoe. But Virginia Hill was loyal to her friends, sexually faithful in her way, and knowledge-able about the mob. She loved Bugsy, and she worried, as much as she was capable of worry, about his growing obses-sion with the building of the Flamingo. Construction costs were soaring, and the Syndicate was holding Siegel responsi-ble.

On the East Coast, Costello was working, for the most part, with Lansky to develop gambling in Florida and with Adonis to consolidate betting in New Jersey. The Colonial Inn, a lavish casino financed by all three men, opened in Florida in 1945 as a harbinger of things to come: within a few years, the Syndicate would take over the $40-million annual "play" in Miami—using its control of Continental Press as the lever. At the same time, the Costello-Adonis-Moretti-Zwillman group operated out of Duke's restaurant in Cliff-side, New Jersey—just across the Hudson from New York—with what amounted to diplomatic immunity. The prime minister's representative in both camps was porcine Frank Erickson, the so-called King of the Bookmakers. He was the layoff man the country's professionals used to balance their books, the man for whom no bet was too large, and his per-sonal turnover was estimated at some $10 million annually.

The calm, courteous Erickson, then fifty years old, had grown up in orphanages and foster homes. A onetime singing waiter in Coney Island, he parlayed his mathematical skills, during the twenties and thirties, into a seemingly endless supply of cash, countless doublebreasted, pin-striped suits, and a membership in the New York Athletic Club. Along the way, he provided bail money for Dutch Schultz, became the confidante of Luciano, Costello, and Adonis, and cultivated friendships with many members of the New York Police Department. He owned pieces of the action in several gambling resorts, and he had a sizeable interest in Miami's Tropical Park Racetrack, which he had purchased, in 1935, from the aforementioned Bill Dwyer. Under pressure from LaGuardia, Erickson, like Adonis, was forced to shift his activities to New Jersey during the early 1940s. Though he had been arrested a half-dozen times during his career, up to now he had never served a day in jail. Indeed, after being charged with vagrancy in 1939, the gambler showed up in court with six Brink's guards, produced $125,000 worth of securities to prove his solvency, and walked out a free man. It was a classic example of Erickson's modus operandi: he let his money do the talking.

"You don't want to change your mind and give us some information which would be useful, do you?" a recalcitrant Erickson would be asked by an investigator.

"I have no information," he replied.

"There would be a lot of things you could tell us about."

"I am sure I have nothing."

But Erickson, more and more, was finding himself in the headlines. In April of 1941, he and several "business associates" narrowly missed being held up by three gunmen in a nineteenth-floor suite at the New York Athletic Club—with a reported one hundred thousand dollars on the table. They were saved only because Katherine O'Brien, a fifty-five-year-old chambermaid, refused to surrender her passkey to the thugs, screamed at the top of her lungs, and went down under a pistol blow. Erickson rewarded her with one thousand dollars, and a monthly stipend for life. Later, he denied that a police captain had been in his suite at the time of the attempted robbery, and that the officer subsequently had committed suicide. Be that as it may, a police captain did take his own life several days after the incident.

In any case, despite the occassional small setback, the Syndicate groundwork had been laid. Costello, Siegel, Adonis, and Lansky—helped by such colleagues as Phil Kastel, Anastasia, Erickson, Moretti, and Zwillman—had emerged safely from the Dewey years and the Murder Inc. investigation. Now William O'Dwyer was New York's mayor, and all, supposedly, would be right with the world.

PART FOUR

1946-1950:
Mayoralty

1

IN TYPICAL UNPRETENTIOUS FASHION, William O'Dwyer was sworn as the 104th mayor of New York, shortly before midnight on New Year's Eve, 1945, in the modest Belle Harbor, Queens, home of his wife's aunt, Mrs. Mary Lenihan. One of the guests, fittingly, was Thomas Rouse, an old friend of the O'Dwyer family, who in 1910 had met the future mayor at the dock and found the young immigrant his first lodging: a room in a cold-water tenement on Manhattan's West Forty-seventh Street.

Among the elected officials in the new administration were Vincent Impellitteri, president of the city council, and Lazarus Joseph, controller. Impellitteri, running for office for the first time, had polled only four thousand fewer votes than the mayor; he was a Fordham Law School graduate, like O'Dwyer, and he had been a Manhattan assistant district attorney. Joseph, a former state senator, had been the Democratic whip at Albany. Among O'Dwyer's administrators were several holdover commissioners from the LaGuardia years, most notably Arthur Wallander, police; Robert Moses, parks; and Dr. Edward Bernecker, hospitals. New commissioners included Frank Quayle, fire; James Moran, his deputy; and John M. Murtagh, investigations.

Within a few months, it became clear that O'Dwyer would be locked in a drawn-out struggle with Tammany Hall —many of whose leaders had, as we have seen, all too obvious ties with Costello—over who would control the city. High on the mayor's purge list were Tammany's head, Edward Loughlin, as well as the powers behind Loughlin: Bert Stand, the organization's secretary, and Clarence Neal, chairman of its election committee. O'Dwyer drew first blood in the feud when he rammed through the nominations of two State Supreme Court justices without consulting the Hall's leadership. But the victory would not be lasting: throughout his administration, Bill-O would be forced to compromise with Tammany, whipping it when he needed public support for his programs, embracing it when he needed organizational clout.

In the underworld, meanwhile, early 1946 marked a signal event. Governor Thomas E. Dewey, still intent on capturing the presidency, in January granted Lucky Luciano a full pardon, on condition that he leave the United States and return to Italy. "Upon the entry of the United States into the war," Dewey said, giving the reasons for his action, "Luciano's aid was sought by the armed services in inducing others to provide information concerning possible enemy attack. It appears that he cooperated in said efforts. . . ." Later, Dewey elaborated on this enigmatic statement. "Luciano's aid to the navy in the war was extensive and valuable. Ten years is probably as long as anybody served for compulsory prostitution. These factors led the parole board to recommend the commutation."

Costello and Lansky had been working on Luciano's pardon all during the war years. Preying on the fears that enemy agents were sabotaging supplies and shipping on the New York docks (the destruction by fire of the French liner, *Normandie,* while it was being converted to a troopship, had been widely attributed to sabotage), and using their political connections, they convinced the navy that Luciano's good will was essential to insure the loyalty of the Syndicate-dominated waterfront. Simultaneously, if we are to believe the reports, Costello and Lansky induced the prostitute-witnesses against Luciano, in his 1937 trial, to refute their testimony. "All I wanted to do was to let the newspapers know how Dewey got those witnesses to commit perjury," Luciano would say self-righteously. "How he put words in their mouths, how he bribed them broads." Such publicity, of course, would not have helped Dewey's presidential ambitions.

For whatever the reasons, Luciano was transferred from the harshness of Dannemora prison to the country-club atmosphere of Great Meadow—near Albany. There he spent the better part of the war, receiving a constant stream of Syndicate visitors.

In February, a month after his pardon, Luciano sailed for Italy aboard the *Laura Keene.* His going-away party was impressive. "A large crowd of photographers and reporters descended on the Immigration Bureau for passes to board the ship and interview the famous criminal," Attorney George Wolf would say. But when the security man for the bureau tried to lead the press on board, they found their way blocked by 50 stevedores holding lethal-looking bailing hooks. When Luciano arrived, the cheering stevedores let him through, then closed fast once again. The mobster's friends—Costello, Adonis, Lansky, and Anastasia, as well as many judges and politicians, all carrying hampers filled with food and drink—likewise passed through the blockade. All the reporters could do was take notes. The ship-board party, said Wolf, "lasted for hours."

For Costello personally, late 1945 and early 1946 would be ominous dates: the murderous Vito Genovese, whom Dewey had driven into exile and who in years to come would depose Costello as Syndicate leader, was back in New York from Italy, erscorted by army criminal-intelligence division men who had arrested him for extensive blackmarket activities. Don Vitone had prospered—to a large degree through narcotics—both during and after the war. "At one point, I was offered a quarter of a million dollars to let the fellow out of jail," a CID officer later testified. Genovese was handed over to the Brooklyn district attorney's office to stand trail for the 1934-killing of Ferdinand "the Shadow" Boccia. The authorities even had a corroborating witness, Peter La Tempa, a gangland hanger-on who had not participated in the murder but had overheard its planning. Before proceeding could begin against Genovese, however, a fatal accident occured. La Tempa, who was being held in protective custody as a material witness and was taking medication for severe gallstone attacks, one day swallowed what he thought was his regular prescription. He fell to the floor of his cell, poisoned, and quickly died. His murder was never solved, and Genovese, in June of 1946, would walk out of court a free man.

"I am constrained by law to dismiss this indictment and instruct the jury to acquit you," he was told by the irate judge. "Although you have been arrested many times for crimes

ranging from robbery to murder, as far as the law is concerned you have led a charmed life. You are always just one
step ahead of Sing Sing and the electric chair. You have
thwarted justice time and again. . . ."

After his release, Genovese at first sought seclusion, buying an expensive house in Atlantic Highlands, New Jersey, a
quiet resort community. "In those days, when I saw him with
Frank Costello," George Wolf would say, "he was always
friendly to my client." But Genovese deeply resented the
prime minister's power. "He began to undermine Frank in
every way that he could. But he had to move slowly."

Even Genovese had a weakness—in his case, his wife
Anna, whom he had married in 1932 just twelve days after her
first husband was found strangled with a sash cord on a
Greenwich Village rooftop. In the early 1950s, she would sue
Vito for separation and substantial support—an unheard-of
action for a Mafia wife. "My husband has interests in all the
rackets," she would testify. "He's involved in narcotics, gambling, liquor, extortion, and he owns four nightclubs and two
dog tracks. I personally handled twenty or thirty thousand
dollars a week from the Italian lottery he owns in New York.
I ran it myself." According to Anna, Genovese was worth $30
million. "He has safe-deposit boxes in New York and New
Jersey, one in Naples, one in Paris, some in Switzerland, and
another in Monte Carlo." In rebuttal, Genovese, who admitted only to an income of some $125 weekly, would sadly say,
"I don't like the kind of people she's going around with."

The Syndicate could not understand why Vito did not
have Anna silenced. "The word was all around, why didn't
he hit her," Informer Joe Valachi later declared. "But he must
have really cared for her. He would sometimes talk about her,
and I could see the tears rolling down his cheeks. I couldn't
believe it."

2

O'Dwyer's first ninety days in office saw him attending twenty-two public dinners, reviewing two parades, greeting some one thousand nine hundred voters and dignitaries, solving tugboat and transit crises, and learning that the city treasury would have a $6 million deficit by June 30—the fiscal years's end.

"It seems to me that without exception—since January—there's been no relief," he told a reporter. "This job is a job all day long—there are moments when I get scared to death of it. Suddenly I'll realize, 'My God, I'm mayor of the City of New York!' " he said, hitting himself on the side of his head in feigned disbelief. "But I get over it.

"Being mayor doesn't give you much time to think about being mayor. The criticism, the carping—that's all part of the game. If you can't take that, you're in the wrong line of business. I was up at the Waldorf the other night and some lady came over to me and said, 'Oh my, what do I do when I meet the mayor? Do I kiss his ring, or what?' I said, 'In New York, lady, you heave a cuspidor at him.' "

But then O'Dwyer brightened. "In this job, either you make the policy or it isn't made at all. As soon as the new budget is out of the way, we'll be able to get things started. I want to see the public-housing program moving—and I want to fix up the subways, too, one way or another. We'll have plenty of fun yet."

Working ten- and twelve-hour days had left O'Dwyer little time for exercise—he had added twelve pounds since taking office. But he tried to keep up his family ties, lunching as often as possible with his brother Paul. "He's a lawyer," O'Dwyer said, "and we argue. He doesn't like my administration—says it has a lot of weaknesses, says I could do better. He hasn't been specific about policies, though. I'd say his criticism comes under the heading of expert meddling.

"I haven't seen my niece Joan since christmas," he mused, referring to Paul's daughter, "and I'm very fond of her. She can't decide whether to be an actress or a lawyer. She thinks she's thirty and I think she's ten. She's really eighteen."

Some months later, in October of 1946, O'Dwyer suffered a heartfelt loss. His wife, Kitty, who for years had been confined to a wheelchair, finally succumbed to Parkinson's disease. Though her death was not unexpected, it seemed to sharpen O'Dwyer's growing sense of isolation. Kitty Lenihan, the Hotel Vanderbilt telephone operator who had been born in the shadow of the Brooklyn Bridge, and who had married him before he began his climb to success, had been his sweetheart and his friend. Sentimentally, she had always carried in her purse the Canadian dime he had mistakenly given her, to pay for a phone call, when they first met.

"Whoever passed that on you?" Bill-O asked, years later, seeing the coin in her purse.

"You did," she replied. "The first day I ever met you."

Theirs had been a contented life. Before Kitty's illness worsened, the O'Dwyers had seldom been apart. During the 1930s, they had traveled to Ireland together—to visit Bill's birthplace in County Cork; they had journeyed to the seminary at the University of Salamanca; they had cruised to South America aboard the same ship on which he had been a stoker. During the busy months of the Murder Inc. investigation, even during his army years—when his duties kept him from Kitty's side, O'Dwyer would seldom let an evening go by without calling her.

Kitty O'Dwyer's funeral mass was at St. Patrick's Cathedral, with Francis Cardinal Spellman presiding, and the political powers of the city attending. She was buried in the family plot at St. Mary's Cemetery, Staten Island.

Six months later, O'Dwyer still could not speak his wife's name without registering emotion. Appearing at Holy Family Hospital in Brooklyn for the dedication of an ambulance purchased by friends in her memory, he tried to say the appropriate words.

"How I feel I can tell you in a few words," he began. "It is sweet of you to remember Mrs. O'Dwyer—"

Then his eyes filled with tears, his voice broke, he mumbled some words of thanks, turned away from his audience and sat down.

In early November, the city was forcibly reminded of the role the mob played in the election of New York politicians when Joseph Scottoriggio, a Republican district captain in East Harlem, was savagely beaten by hoodlums on the corner of 104th Street and First Avenue. Six days later, he died from his injuries. Scottoriggio had been actively, and effectively, working against the re-election of Vito Marcantonio, the East Harlem boss and its incumbent U.S. Congressman. Decrying the killing, Mayor O'Dwyer ordered Commissioner Wallander to put one thousand policemen on the case. Within days, the notorious Harlem Syndicate leader, Michael "Trigger Mike" Coppola, and his chief aide, Joseph Rao, were arrested and thrown into the Tombs, each held in $250,000 bail. At the time, Coppola controled the district's gambling rackets.

"Seizure of Coppola and Rao," the New York *Daily Mirror* reported, "indicates police belief that the cruel, premeditated assault on Scottoriggio, the anti-Marcantonio campaigner, may have been conceived and directed from the inner circles of the underworld. If they seeded thugs the way they do tennis players, Coppola and Rao would rank in the first ten of any selection."

Coppola's wife, Doris, unfortunately for her, had been present the day the two men discussed the problem of Scottoriggio, just twenty-four hours before the beating, in Mike's home. During the ensuing weeks, on the basis of her evasive testimony before a grand jury, Doris was charged with perjury. With the charge hanging over her, Mrs. Coppola gave birth to a daughter, and the next day died—ostensibly of post-natal complications. Whereupon Coppola, in violation of his Roman Catholic religion, promptly had the body cremated. It was not until years later that additional testimony, by Trigger Mike's second wife, indicated that he had callously had Doris killed, lest she talk.

As far as Scottoriggio was concerned, Coppola got off scot-free. It would not be until fifteen years later that he would pay the law any penalty at all—and then it would be for income-tax evasion.

In late December of 1946, the leaders of the Syndicate gathered in Havana for another summit conference—this time to pay homage to Lucky Luciano, who had journeyed back to Cuba, just ninety miles from Florida, in the hope of ultimately returning to the United States. His visit was arranged by Lansky, who controled the gambling at the Hotel Nacional and who, with Costello, was developing the gambling operation throughout Florida and Louisiana. The meeting would be Lucky's last hurrah.

When the conference opened, Luciano sat at the head of a huge table, flanked by Costello, Lansky, Genovese, and Adonis. Other mobsters present included Anastasia and Moretti,

Steve Magaddino of Buffalo, Tony Accardo and Charley Fischetti of Chicago, Carlos Marcello of New Orleans, Santo Trafficante of Tampa. According to Luciano, his primary concern at that time was the mob's growing tendency, fostered by Genovese, to go heavily into narcotics. "I must've talked for an hour, maybe more," he would say. "On the subject of narcotics, I could see I wasn't gettin' through. Costello had the same feeling and he leaned over and whispered to me, 'Charlie, don't hit your head against the wall. Vito rigged it before the meet started. Someday, they'll all be sorry.'"

Luciano's account may have been self-serving. But regardless of the degree of his personal culpability, there is no doubt the conference drew the close scrutiny of the Federal Narcotics Bureau. "Luciano had become friendly with a number of high Cuban officials through the lavish use of expensive gifts," then Commissioner of Narcotics Harry J. Anslinger would write. "He had developed a full-fledged plan which envisioned the Caribbean as his center of operations. Cuba was to be made the center of all international narcotics operations. We had a number of transcribed calls Lucky had made to Miami, New York, Chicago, and other large American cities, and the names of the hoodlums who called him. He kept himself busy in Havana."

Charley Lucky's secondary concern, and that of the other Syndicate leaders, was Bugsy Siegel. The cost of building the Flamingo, Siegel's hotel-casino in the Nevada desert, had jumped from the original $1 million to more than $6 million, and the end was not in sight. But more importantly, Lansky had produced evidence that Bugsy was depositing large sums of money abroad—in a Swiss bank. The implication was that Siegel was skimming the money from the Flamingo building fund.

With little disagreement, the Syndicate leaders voted that Bugsy should be "hit." Charley Fischetti was given the contract, with the understanding he would work through Jack Dragna, who at the time was Siegel's No. 2 man on the Coast. "Bugsy was as good as dead," Luciano would say.

The decision to assassinate Siegel would not be carried out for several months. Meanwhile, word leaked to the United States press that Luciano was in Cuba and, amid the ensuing clamor, Commissioner of Narcotics Anslinger took direct action. With Washington's approval, he informed the Cuban government that the United States would stop the shipment of medical supplies to the island unless Lucky were deported back to Italy. So heavy-handed was Anslinger's pressure that the Cubans shipped out Luciano in the first boat departing for his homeland. It was a Turkish freighter, much to Lucky's disgust, since Turkey and narcotics were then all but synonomous. Now there was no way, he would claim, he could avoid being labeled "the king of junk."

3

With Luciano's—the King's—second deportation to Italy, Costello's position as the Syndicate's prime minister seemed more inviolable than ever. Even so, starting in 1947, spurred by bouts of depression, Costello began seeing a psychiatrist. His complaint: although powerful, rich, and feared, he was not truly gaining access—as he had hoped—to respectable society. Of course, he would regularly golf with a George Morton Levy, but this friendship—along with others with "respectable" people—was clearly grounded in his under-world connections. Costello's escape from East Harlem poverty, his good manners, his conservative appearance—all these had been calculated to make him acceptable in the American mainstream. Yet the continuing headlines about his Syndicate activities were blocking him from this goal. True, he had run a huge bootlegging operation and, true, he was currently running an even larger gambling network. But, when he could, he had always avoided violence. People wanted to drink, people wanted to gamble—he was simply making it possible for them to do so. In his own eyes, the prime minister was a respectable businessman, and he was depressed that the community at large did not share that image.

Costello's relationship with his psychiatrist, Dr. Richard Hoffman of Manhattan, was not along to remain secret. The newspapers gleefully dug up the story, even quoting Dr. Hoffman to the effect that he had advised his patient to broaden his interests, to seek out new friends in other lines of work. Enraged, Costello reacted predictably: at one and the same time, he denied he was seeing the psychiatrist, and insisted his own friends were of a higher social standing, anyway, than Dr. Hoffman's. The blowing-off of steam dissolved both the doctor-patient relationship and, apparently, Costello's depression.

In the early part of 1947, Frank J. Sampson—acting on orders from Mayor O'Dwyer—announced he was assuming the leadership of the Manhattan Democratic party. Though Sampson had for the past year been the spokesman of the insurgent Tammany district leaders who, more or less, had cast their lot with the mayor rather than Costello, the coup was without parallel in recent Tammany history. Besides the backing of the State Democratic chairman, Sampson had the support of the Truman administration. "It is known that the national leaders of the Democratic party," optimistically reported the *Herald-Tribune,* "are solidly behind the mayor's plan to destroy the underworld influences in Tammany Hall . . . O'Dwyer has set out to eliminate the influence stemming from narcotic dealers, gamblers, and keepers of houses of prostitution."

Within weeks, Sampson, who had been born fifty years before on West Sixteenth Street and still lived there, was officially (and unanimously) elected leader of Tammany, ousting Edward V. Loughlin. "I call upon every district leader," Sampson declared, "to join with me in offering the best possible service to the city. I'll have an announcement to make in the next forty-eight hours." The announcement, of course, would have been that Costello's good friends in Tammany— Bert Stand, its secretary, and Clarence Neal, chairman of its elections committee—were likewise deposed. But the firings did not occur, not in the next two days or the next two years.

"I don't know what I'm going to do," a relaxed Neal told reporters with a laugh. "No one has asked me to resign."

"Are you going to remain at your desk?" one newsman asked Stand.

"I don't know any better desk, the Tammany secretary replied.

The unanimity that attended Sampson's election was misleading. Ostensibly the O'Dwyer insurgents has won a great victory. But the Tammany regulars, knowing that the mayor could withhold federal and state patronage at will, were merely paying lip-service to the idea of reform. Both camps benefited from the charade. O'Dwyer could legitimately claim he was cleaning up Tammany, even while Costello's influence remained strong.

By mid-year, the Syndicate's decision to eliminate Bugsy

Siegel was ready to be implemented. As the Flamingo's patronage increased—thus, in one respect, justifying Siegel's vision—so did the hotel's losses. In the casino, a run of bad luck was going against the house. Room furnishings were often found inadequate, giving rise to angry complaints, and, a final indignity, the huge outdoor swimming pool had developed a sudden crack, draining the water within minutes and leaving bathers more shaken than amused. Financially, Siegel was being pushed to the wall—though he had, with gentlemanly forbearance, turned down the Countess Dorothy Di Frasso's offer of a loan.

In desperation, he hired press agents, raffled cars, prevailed upon Hollywood's Marie "The Body" McDonald to ride the Flamingo float in a Las Vegas parade. Against all Syndicate advice, he called in the top bookmakers in California, Nevada and Arizona and told them he was doubling the price of the racetrack wire-service. His frustration communicated itself, eventually, to Virginia Hill, who one night attempted suicide with barbituates. Soon afterward, she left Las Vegas for Beverly Hills, then Europe, fleeing the fate she saw threatening her paramour.

Siegel was fast losing the charm he had so carefully cultivated since his strong-arm days on the Lower East Side. Typical of his irascibility was the treatment he gave Moe Sedway, his chief odds-maker, during an argument about betting procedures. Instead of just cuffing Little Moe, which would have been bad enough, he turned him around and booted him in the rear—the ultimate sign of mobster disrespect. Sedway was permanently barred from the Flamingo. Meanwhile, the word began circulating—quite openly—that Siegel's days were numbered. Perhaps to reassure his old friend, Meyer Lansky visited him in June, ostensibly to discuss further loans. After a few days, Meyer returned to the East Coast, and Siegel was alone once more.

Bugsy's activities on June 20, 1947, have been carefully chronicled. In the early hours of the morning, he arrived at Virginia Hill's Beverly Hills Home, now vacant, on the night flight from Las Vegas. The next morning, he called on Los Angeles mobster Mickey Cohen.

"Mick, you got any guys with equipment?" Siegel asked him.

"Hooky Rothman's in town," Cohen answered. "Woody may be here, too. They can both handle a rod pretty good."

"Ask Hooky to see me tomorrow."

"What's up, Ben?" Cohen asked.

"Nothing much," Siegel replied. "I'll see you."

That afternoon, Bugsy visited his barber, discussed some Flamingo legal problems with his lawyer, then returned to Virginia Hill's home on Linden Drive.

At one point, the phone rang.

"Hello," said Siegal. "Oh, it's you."

Bugsy listened silently for a moment, his face contorting with rage.

"You son-of-a-bitch!" he exploded, just before banging down the receiver. "Over my dead body you will! You haven't got the guts!"

"Trouble, Ben?" one of his hangers-on asked.

"Just some wise guy who thinks he can take me," Bugsy replied.

Unpleasant as it was, the phone call did not keep Siegel from going out for a quiet dinner with friends. Afterward, he returned to Linden Drive, sat down on a flowered sofa in the living room, and began reading the *Los Angeles Times.* "We have a unique community," the Beverly Hills chief of police later commented. "The streets are patroled every half-hour, and strangers are quickly detected. It is a safe and pleasant place to live."

The time was 10:20 P.M. Outside one of the living room windows, a stranger aimed a thirty-thirty carbine at Bugsy's head. Nine shots rang out in the still night, like so many firecrackers, three of them ripping apart Siegel's face and snuffing out his life. It was the first authorized killing of a major mobster since the Dutch Schultz murder in 1935, when the organization was in embryo.

Twenty minutes later, back in Las Vegas, Little Moe Sedway took posthumous revenge on the man who had humiliated him. Jaunty as a bantam rooster, he walked into the Flamingo and told the staff he and the New York group were taking over.

"How long have you lived at the Flamingo?" Sedway subsequently would be asked by investigators.

"Since 1947"

"What is your business?"

"I am vice-president of the Flamingo."

"Were you ever arrested?"

"In 1919. . . . It was on a Saturday afternoon in New York and we were running a crap game in a loft up in the twenties and it was raided."

"Did you go to prison?"

"I did a little less than a year."

"When were you next arrested?"

"In 1935—it was a bond case."

"Bail bond?"

"Security bonds. I was acquitted by a jury."

"Didn't you stay overnight for assault and robbery in New York in 1928?"

"That was one of those things. In order to hold you in

New York, they put a charge on you regardless of what it is, to keep you overnight."

"Did you go through high school?"

"I didn't finish."

"You gave up working and you became a gambler, is that right?"

"That is right."

Sedway was then questioned about his takeover of the Flamingo after Siegel's death. It seemed that he had been permitted, by the hotel's executors—along with several partners including a Costello representative named Morris Rosen —to buy the Flamingo for a mere $3.9 million, with a down payment of only five-hundred-thousand dollars. After Siegel's assassination, of course, the hotel became a multi-million-dollar property.

"Rosen had an interest in the old Flamingo," Sedway innocently explained, "and when Siegel died he came down to sort of look after the business and see what could be done to salvage it. The place was in bad shape. It was ready to close. . . ."

"Rosen and Siegel had been close in other deals in the past?"

"They were very close. As a matter of fact, Rosen's son just recently married Siegel's daughter, so the families were close."

"How much of the Flamingo do you now own?"

"Seven and eight-tenths percent."

"What is your net worth today? A million dollars or more?"

"I wouldn't know offhand."

"What was your net income last year?"

"I don't know offhand."

"You don't get anything out of the Flamingo?"

"I get my room, I get my board."

Virginia Hill got the news of Siegel's death in Paris, while attending a houseboat party on the Seine, listening to someone sing, "How Are Things in Glocca Morra?"

In New York that July, just one month after Siegel's death, O'Dwyer was having financial problems—municipal ones—of his own. He was putting the finishing touches on the city's 1947–48 budget, which called for an expenditure of $1,031,961,754.73. It was the largest city budget in history—some $166 million more than the one approved the year before. In its printed form, it filled a 1,425-page book, and was easily twice the size of the Manhattan telephone directory. Among the items: $45 for wood-chip bedding for skunks and monkeys that might be taken sick at the Staten Island Zoo; $508,134,356 to pay the salaries of the 157,418 persons who, if all went according to plan, would work for the city during the fiscal period; $10 for two sapphire phonograph needles for radio station WNYC; $96,500 to heat the American Museum of Natural History and $4.80 for cannel coal for the fireplace in the mayor's office; and $1,735,000 for meat to feed the inmates of the city's eight prisons and twenty-five hospitals.

"The Department of Licenses is up $45,000 over last year," Budget Director Thomas Patterson told O'Dwyer at one point during the budget's preparation. "We gave them five new inspectors."

"Have they increased the number of licenses to be inspected?" the mayor asked wearily.

"This department brought in sixty thousand more than last year," Patterson said, pointing out that the Department of Licenses also used police officers to issue its summonses.

"Is that sound?" O'Dwyer mused.

"Didn't you have to help out with license inspections when you were—?" Patterson asked.

"That's right," the mayor said, leaning back in his chair.

"Come to think of it, in the days when I was on the police force, if you failed to report an unlicensed junk wagon or something, and the sergeant came along and spotted it, you were subject to discipline."

Next, O'Dwyer's attention was caught by debt-service. "Before we can buy so much as a lead pencil, we've got to provide the money for debt-service—amortization and interest payments on what the city owes."

Patterson said debt-service came to $201,583,273, the biggest item in the budget.

"And how much does the city owe altogether?" the mayor asked.

"Two billion, eight hundred and fifty-seven million, twenty-three thousand, nine hundred and ninety dollars."

There was a respectful silence. Then Louis Cohen, the assistant to the mayor, volunteered the information that the city's debt was the fault of earlier regimes. Everyone promptly cheered up.

"It's like the time arond 1870, when they went and issued two hundred, seventy-eight thousand dollars worth of seven-percent non-callable bonds to lay some wooden planks on a street in the West Farms section of the Bronx. They're going to cost us nearly fourteen thousand dollars in interest this year."

"You mean we still don't own the Bronx, Louie?" the mayor deadpanned, taking a break from the monotony of the figures.

"Just two hundred more years and it will be ours," Cohen replied. "But for that matter, practically all the bonds the city ever issued were non-callable because the bankers say they won't take any other kind. Why, only back in 1940, when the city took over the subways, it issued more than three hundred million dollars worth of three-percent bonds that won't mature until 1980. Today we could borrow that money at two percent or less, but we can't call those bonds in."

"Most of the subway equipment the city bought with that money has already been discarded," O'Dywer said. "But we'll still be paying for it for the next thirty-three years."

During the days of the public hearings before the Board of Estimate, half the speakers urged O'Dwyer to cut the budget, while half urged him to spend more money. Max Weintraub, a court stenographer, protested that the new budget not only made no provision to increase stenographers' pay, but that there was no opportunity for advancement.

"Firemen can become lieutenants, patrolmen can become sergeants, we can become nothing—so here we are," he said.

"Max, I know you boys work hard," the mayor said. "But the city's too poor to give you a raise this year. Give my regards to the boys at court."

By the fifth day of the hearings, O'Dwyer's weariness was obvious. When a man from the department of sanitation rose to complain about the difficulties of his work and asked the mayor to turn to page 762 of the budget, O'Dwyer sighed resignedly.

"Just tell me what's on the page," he said. "If we go on like this much longer, I'll be wrecking my wrist."

Eventually the proceedings came to an end, and the budget was adopted. With evident relief, O'Dwyer signed the $1,031,961,754.73 certification—the amount of money needed to keep New York running during the next year.

About this time, the mayor's longtime confidante, James J. Moran, may have been involved in his own matters of finance. John P. Crane, the president of the Uniformed Firemen's Association, who later would be called upon to account for $135,000 he had personally withdrawn from his union's treasury, would insist he had given much of this money to Moran.

"During the year 1947, did you cash four checks each in the amount of five thousand dollars?" Crane was asked.

"I had such checks cashed," he replied.

"What did you do with the cash?"

"That money was given in cash to promote the good will of Mr. Moran on behalf of the firemen."

"Where did you deliver it to him?"

"In his office—on the eleventh floor of the Municipal Building."

"Did you hand it to him yourself?"

"Yes, sir."

"Was anyone else present?"

"No one was present."

"Was that money previously withdrawn from the bank account of your union?"

"There was no other place to get it from."

"Did Mr. Moran take any action to aid the firemen in the year 1947?"

"He helped us many times in many small things. But mostly the knowledge in the department, among chief officers in particular, that Mr. Moran was a friend of the firemen, assured them of fair hours and good treatment, and that primarily was my concern."

"Did you, in the year 1947, give any additional money to Mr. Moran?"

"I think there was another ten thousand dollars."

"Was that a contribution or a gift?"

"To me, it's the same."

"You felt you were doing what was necessary in order to get a square deal for the firemen?"

"We were getting a square deal from Mr. Moran and we wanted to make sure it stayed that way."

4

The strain of the mayoralty—to a man who, in his own way, wanted to do well by his city of eight million, was proving an enormous burden to O'Dwyer. In February of 1948, while New York was emerging from one if its severest winters, he was hospitalized with an apparent heart condition. After ten days in Bellevue hospital, no organic weakness was found: the mayor was suffering, instead, from "a marked lowering of metabolism." Treatment called for him "to take it easy, smoke less, and get more sleep." Just before leaving for his brother Frank's produce ranch in El Centro, California—where he usually vacationed—O'Dwyer granted an interview with the *New York Times.* In the course of his remarks, he talked quite candidly about the burden of managing the billion-dollar corporation that New York City had recently become.

"It's something that I can't lay aside." he said. "It's something that is with me every moment of the time that I am awake. It's the last thing that I have in mind when I go to bed and the first thing that I think of in the morning. And often my sleep is broken by dreams about my duties which are so real that they tire me.

"I must see to it that the city's laws are enforced, its streets kept clean, health precautions observed, that our youngsters get a good education, that decent homes be put up for tenement-dwellers, that hospitals are well-run."

It was easy to say that a good executive could delegate

authority, the mayor continued, but this was not always possible.

"Let me give you an example of what I mean," he said. "Last December, when the 'blizzard' broke, I was in California. Do you think I could rest? As soon as I heard about it, I began to stew and fret. I felt it was up to me to be on the job and so I flew back here. I haven't found out yet why nature was so angry at New York this winter. We have had more snow and ice than in years. Yet bad as the weather has been, it wasn't the headache that other things were. The biggest obstacles have been inheritances from the war. We have had a scarity of materials and a spiraling of prices. New housing projects, new schools, and the enlargement of hospitals have all been delayed.

"The trouble is," he summed up, "there seems to be a feeling against the city among some of the upstate legislators. They regard it as their child, but an unwanted one in every particular except to pay taxes. Problems such as New York faces must be approached from the viewpoint of human needs."

Costello and his friends, in their own way, were similarly concerned with human needs—at least those that would yield a profit. During 1948, the New Jersey-based gambling operation was flourishing. Before the year was out, bookmaker Frank Erickson would purchase from Tiffany's some one thousand gold, monogrammed tie-clasps, at a cost of twenty-nine thousand dollars, as gifts for favored customers. The Syndicate chieftains still met regularly at Duke's in Cliffside Park, and they had expanded throughout Bergen County. In layoff betting, and in actual gambling dens ranging from the Aristocrat Baby Carriage Factory in Fort Lee to Costa's Barn in Lodi, the mob held sway—dealing with hundreds of thousands of customers from New York City.

Manhattan District Attorney Frank Hogan pointed up the extent of the New Jersey take that summer, when he focused his attention on the habits of Max Stark, the treasurer of the Costello-Adonis-Erickson combination. Lugging at least two bags filled with currency, Max would daily make the trek across the Hudson, where he would appear at the Canal Street branch of the Merchants Bank of New York. The counting of the money sometimes took five hours. But that was all right with the tellers. Stark owned ten percent of the bank's stock. "Max Stark's cash totaled some two hundred thousand dollars a week," a Hogan aide recalled. "Remember, thirty thousand dollars was a poor day for him, and he often brought in as much as ninety thousand dollars. For this reason, we felt an estimate of a forty thousand dollar average was ultra-conservative. But when we sat down and figured out what this meant, we were truly shocked. Multiply it out. A cash flow of two hundred thousand dollars a week, multiplied by fifty-two weeks in the year, comes to better than ten million dollars. When we hit that figure, we knew we were up against an operation so huge it could only be a major project of the Syndicate." Examining the records of the Merchants Bank, Hogan found that Stark had also deposited some three and a half million dollars in checks in the past year—increasing the Syndicate's take to thirteen and a half million dollars yearly.

Hogan's estimates were based on just one account—the Merchants Bank of New York—where the records were under his jurisdiction. Obviously, Stark's New Jersey bank accounts could swell the Syndicate's profits still more.

Costa's Barn, the name given a Quonset hut located behind a gas station in the rural atmosphere of Lodi, New Jersey, was typical of the gambling dens. From the outside, it appeared drab and nondescript. But inside, Costa's was a

lavish nightspot: the waitresses and cigarette girls were entic-
ing, the dining room offered fine food and wines on the house,
the games were run by suave croupiers and dealers. Once
Adonis felt the pressure from the Hogan investigation, he
quickly converted Costa's to a "sawdust" operation—presumably to give himself more flexibility in shutting it down in
case of a raid. A snack bar replaced the dining room, the
gambling was largely restricted to dice tables. No matter.
Fleets of Cadillacs continued to ferry countless New Yorkers
to and from Lodi all night long.

"Any number of those who played and lost described for
us just how Joey A supervised the operation every night," the
Hogan aide continued. "He didn't actually run any of the
tables himself, but he was always there—the boss, the lord of
the manor."

Hogan's investigation, despite the fact that it had no authority in New Jersey, was making the Syndicate uneasy.
Prudent as ever, Adonis in mid-August closed down Costa's
Barn. Within twenty-four hours, Frank Erickson temporarily
halted all layoff betting, disconnecting the twenty-six hundred phones in the Bergen County bookie network. But the
New Jersey prosecutors did not effectively follow up on
Hogan's evidence, and the pressure on Adonis in that state
soon eased. Almost in desperation, Hogan in mid-September
indicted Max Stark for criminal conspiracy in New York—
citing as evidence the spectacular deposits in the Merchants
Bank. Though Stark was convicted on the charge, the case
was later thrown out on a technicality, the appeals judge
ruling it had not been proven the actual conspiracy occurred
in New York.

Unimpeded, the New Jersey gambling operation started
up again and boomed. Frank Borell, the Cliffside Park police
chief, would later be asked the extent of his bank deposits.

"Approximately fifty, sixty, or seventy thousand dollars," he casually replied. "It could be eighty thousand dollars or so." He had been able to amass such sums on a forty-five-hundred-dollar annual salary, he explained, by running various concessions in Palisades Amusement Park. Yes, he had been a frequent visitor to Duke's, Borell admitted, but not recently, "due to the fact that I can't stand the food. The food is very good, but it is not good for me."

Michael Orecchio, the Bergen County detective chief, would explain his extra income by testifying that the money came from a private real estate business that netted him some thirty thousand dollars yearly.

"Do you keep currency in your safe-deposit box?" the interrogator asked.

"Surely," Orecchio replied.

"How much?"

"I have ten thousand dollars in that box."

"Could you draw that cash quicker than you could draw a check?"

"Not necessarily," the unperturbed Orecchio responded, "it is merely my way of doing business, that is all."

In late June of 1948, O'Dwyer's continuing ostensible feud with Tammany Hall erupted again when the leaders—ignoring the protests of the mayor and Frank Sampson, Tammany's supposed head—designated General Sessions Judge Francis L. Valente for Surrogate. Valente was the nephew of Supreme Court Justice Louis A. Valente, whom the leaders, earlier, had unsuccessfully tried to foist on O'Dwyer for the same post. "More than a Tammany family fracas is on display," the *Herald-Tribune* editorialized. "This is more than Italians and Irish slinging dead cats at one another. By substituting General Sessions Judge Francis Valente for his uncle, Supreme Court Justice Louis Valente, the Tammany bosses make it plain that the candidate means nothing. The point is that the Tammany which takes orders from Frank Costello is determined to move in on the luxuriant Surrogate's Court patronage. O'Dwyer's man, Council President Vincent Impellitteri, took a bad beating from the district leaders. They voted down Mr. Impellitteri, two to one, for the Surrogate's designation. This was their posy for City Hall and gesture to the Bar Association for making an uproar over the elder Valente. What surprises us is that the district leaders bothered to drop the first Valente."

In public at least, O'Dwyer was not long in answering the Tammany challenge. "Leave Tammany Hall in the gutter where it belongs," he asserted when pressed for an answer as to what he would do about the Valente matter.

"Is this something new in politics, Mr. Mayor?"

"It's something new for Tammany. I'll have nothing to do with scavengers planning to get rich on the orphans' money," he continued, referring to the fact the Surrogate deals in millions of dollars annually from estates coming under the court's jurisdiction. Insisting he would form a Democratic organization of his own, O'Dwyer then called for "clean, decent men who are interested in decent public service" to serve as rival leaders to those Tammanyites who had supported the Valentes.

Even as the mayor spoke, he had seen to it that twenty-five Tammany district leaders had been subpoenaed by District Attorney Hogan—to answer charges that bribes had been paid to effect the Francis Valente designation. As the battle lines formed, Manhattan Borough President Hugo Rogers found himself in the middle: a sizeable number of the anti-O'Dwyer leaders held public posts to which they had been recommended by Rogers; obviously, the mayor intended to discipline them by firing them.

By late July, however, the usual truce was struck—through a series of Byzantine maneuvers—between O'Dwyer and Tammany. First, Hugo Rogers, with the tacit approval of the mayor, became Tammany's head, replacing the unfortunate Frank Sampson, who had become too closely identified with O'Dwyer's posturing. Secondly, Francis Valente was dropped from the ticket, in deference to the sensibilities of all concerned, and a compromise candidate agreed upon. Thirdly, Paul O'Dwyer, the mayor's brother, was selected as the Democratic candidate against Republican Jacob Javits in the Twenty-first Congressional District. Fourthly, the dissident leaders who had been forced from their jobs were dutifully restored to the same positions.

The mayor had again succeeded, in the public's eyes at least, at squaring the Tammany circle.

"Those who recall the 1945-election," Tammany hardliner Bert Stand would later testify, "will remember that O'Dwyer won despite the serious charges leveled against him by his opponent. There is no doubt that he assumed office under a certain cloud and that he craftily sought every opportunity to build himself up in the public estimation as a crusader. O'Dwyer's actions were always confusing, contradictory, and irrational. He changed the leadership in Tammany Hall almost as often as he changed his mind. The public, however, was apparently misled by all his artful double-talk into believing that O'Dwyer sought to 'reform' the organization."

When pressed about his own relationship with Costello, Stand would reply: "He never asked me to do anything politically for him. But as an Italian, he probably felt a natural tendency in seeing the candidacy of others of the same racial ancestry advanced."

Amid the seriousness of the Hogan investigations and the

Valente charges and counter-charges, the mayor's more banal duties provided an amusing contrast. "Once I even had to ride on a tallyho," O'Dwyer would reminisce. "They had brewery horses, and Sergeant Burke driving them. I had to climb aboard the damn thing, and the horses started to get out of hand.

"This fellow Whalen—the honorable Grover Whalen— was riding behind in a car, waving and smiling and bowing," the mayor recounted, "and the horses pulling the tallyho were about to break loose and kill the mayor. Luckily, Burke got them under control at last."

But memory does play tricks, as O'Dwyer would be the first to admit.

Frank Zachary, an aide of Whalen's, recalled the incident somewhat differently. "The occasion was the fiftieth anniversary of the consolidation of the five boroughs into the City of New York," Zachary would say. "The Mayor's Reception Committee, of which Mr. Whalen was chairman, had arranged to mark the day with the largest peacetime parade in the history of the city . . . and, at the head of it all, the tallyho in question. It was a magnificent green Brewster—the horse-drawn Cadillac of its day—and it was drawn by four glossy chestnuts.

"The tallyho clattered into the driveway of Gracie Mansion around noon, and as the mayor swung onto the seat alongside the driver, the popping of flash bulbs frightened the horses, and they bolted out of hand. Now, Sergeant Burke was a splendid horseman, but handling a coach-and-four is a tough job. The tallyho spun around the driveway on two wheels, with the mayor clinging to the top for dear life. But Mr. Whalen was a man of action. He threw himself in the path of the charging horses and, grabbing the bridles, brought the tallyho to a shuddering halt. It was a feat of real bravery.

"In deference to Mr. O'Dwyer," Zachary summed up, "I must say that a lesser man would have jumped off the tallyho right then and there, but, after smoothing down his hair, he went through with his role as parade leader. As for me, I was so unnerved that I repaired to a York Avenue bar for a quick one and never did get to see the parade."

5

On January 24, 1949, Frank Costello—who had been appointed a vice-chairman of the Salvation Army's annual fundraising drive by Tiffany's Walter Hoving, the drive's chairman—sponsored a one-hundred-dollar-a-ticket dinner at the Copacabana, the then-lavish nightclub where he was allegedly a silent partner. The ensuing newspaper publicity reddened many faces.

"Loyalty was a way of life with Frank," Attorney George Wolf later recalled, "and it showed with his proposed guest list. It included practically every political leader and judge in the city, then went on to include dozens of top gangsters. I remonstrated with Frank. Nothing I said could change his mind."

Besides underworld associates such as Vito Genovese, Phil Kastel, and Frank Erickson, and Tammany leaders such as Hugo Rogers and Carmine De Sapio, the guests included many New York jurists: Supreme Court Judges S. Samuel DiFalco, Thomas Aurelio, Morris Eder, and Algron Nova, Congressman Arthur Klein (who would subsequently become a Supreme Court judge), Queens County Judge Thomas

Downs, Magistrate Lewis Capozzoli, Special Sessions Justice Joseph Loscalzo. "It was a lovely affair," Mrs. Howard Chandler Christy, wife of the artist, told reporters. "I never met so many judges in my life."

Not everyone fully agreed with Mrs. Christy. "This reporter," wrote Milton Lewis of the *Herald-Tribune*, "was in no position to say it was a lovely affair. I was booted out. I did cadge a couple of free drinks—probably paid for by Frankie himself—at the Copa's upstairs, or streetfloor, bar. But when I tried to go down to the cellar"—the Copa's main room was below street level—"a fat rope in the front and a ham-like hand in the rear belonging to a Neapolitan named Kelly"— John "Jimmy Kelly" Di Salvio—"stopped me. Never having gotten down to the cellar, I was unable to see the pols in action."

The dinner netted ten-thousand dollars for the Salvation Army, which was more than happy to accept the donation. "We will take anybody's backing to further our good work," declared a spokesman. "The money paid by the 150 guests isn't necessarily Costello's." Stated Frank: "For the generous contributions of my many dear friends to this great cause, and for their assistance in making this affair possible, thanks from the bottom of my heart."

Once again, the *Herald-Tribune*'s Lewis put the fund-raising in perspective. "While Frankie had a soft spot for the Salvation Army," he wrote, "he really ran the dinner for another reason: to show Vito Genovese who was boss. Could Vito get himself named a vice-chairman of the Salvation Army's drive and summon—that's the word, all right—150 luminaries to come break 'pommes de terres frites' with him? Of course not. Why, there is some slight question as to whether Vito would know just what 'pommes frites' is. There was a fight for power developing in the underworld—and

Frankie was putting Vito in his place."

Barely had the furor over the Copa affair died down when, two months later, Mayor O'Dwyer revealed he had discovered a plot to wire-tap the phones of some two dozen city officials. The only tap thus far in place, he explained, was on the phone of Tammany's Rogers, who doubled as the Manhattan borough president.

"Hugo, are you standing up or sitting down?" the mayor asked Rogers, calling him in the presence of reporters and neglecting to tell him the wiretappers had not yet had a chance to listen to his conversations. "Well, you had better sit down. Your telephone has been tapped. We have got the man and he has confessed."

Over the next few days, the investigation showed that not one man, but four men, were allegedly involved in the aborted wire-tapping. Paramount among them was Clendenin Ryan, a vociferous reform leader and millionaire grandson of financier Thomas Fortune Ryan. It was Ryan who had engaged the services of Attorney John Broady to gather evidence of municipal corruption. Broady, in turn, apparently without telling Clendenin Ryan, allegedly proceeded to plan a series of illegal wire-taps, assigning Kenneth Ryan (no kin), a former New York City detective, and Edward Jones, a former U.S. Treasury agent, to the task.

At first, even with the arrests of Ryan and Jones, Clendenin Ryan was nothing abashed. According to the *New York Times*, he "lost no time in renewing his charges against the O'Dwyer administration"—telling the press "that District Attorney Hogan was controlled by Tammany Hall; that Mayor O'Dwyer consulted Frank Costello, his 'commissioner in charge of vice and corruption,' at every turn; that he didn't expect a fair hearing from the grand jury; and the ambassadorship to France had been offered to him if he would 'lay off' Mayor O'Dwyer."

Striding into City Hall early one morning with a retinue of reporters, Clendenin Ryan demanded the right to question the mayor, only to be told O'Dwyer was still at Gracie Mansion.

"What's the matter with him?" Ryan shouted. "Is he lazy, or yellow? He knew I was coming."

"It's too bad your father didn't leave you brains instead of money," replied an unimpressed Joseph Boyle, a detective assigned to O'Dwyer's office.

Nothing came of the "Great Wire-tap Confusion," as the newspapers called it. "It is obvious that Mr. Broady got no results," the *Herald-Tribune* editorialized. "We sincerely hope that in the coming campaign the wiretapping hullabaloo will be considered sanely. It is strictly a distraction, and a rather inferior one at that." Asked if he still felt that O'Dwyer should be indicted for corruption, the self-righteous Clendenin Ryan replied, "You know I never change my mind."

About this time, Frank Costello found himself named, by the California Commission on Organized Crime, as the 'slot-machine czar' of the United States, responsible for wholesale bribery of law-enforcement officials. "If the 'gross take' of the national slot-machine racket is in the neighborhood of two billion dollars annually, as it probably is," the commission's report declared, "it is evident that twenty percent of this amount, or four hundred million dollars, is being spent annually by racketeers for bribery of public officers."

Stung by the charge, Costello—whose syntax had obviously been supplied by his attorney—fired off an open letter to California Governor Earl Warren. "Ordinarily," the letter read, "I would have ignored such accusations, as I have in

similar instances in the past. However, my attitude of continued silence has evidently given rise to the belief that I may
be safely used as a target by any individual whose gun is
primed with the powder of political ambition. . . . During
Prohibition, I was a bootlegger, contrary to a law which was
later repealed. I am not particularly proud of it—but not quite
so ashamed as I might be, had not a nation of voters agreed
with me. Also, for several years prior to 1933, and for several
years prior to 1947, I had an interest in a concern that operated
vending machines. . . . Reports of my fabulous wealth and
princely income are—unfortunately—myths, the digits mul-
tiplying with each story-teller."

Understandably, Governor Warren did not reply to Costello's letter.

In late May of 1949, O'Dwyer announced he would not be
a candidate for a second mayoral term, thereby disconcerting
the Democratic bosses of the city, who realized they would be
hard-pressed to agree on a compromise candidate, and raising
the hopes of Republican and Fusion leaders.

It is true that the fifty-eight-year-old O'Dwyer's first four
years in office had been strenuous. He had been forced to
abandon the nickel subway fare—a political shibboleth for
decades—and tell New Yorkers the rides would now cost a
dime. He had presided over a succession of record city budg-
ets, pushed upward by the exigencies of postwar expansion.
Two of the worst snowstorms in the city's history had fallen
in the Decembers of 1947 and 1948. He had co-ordinated the
operations of La Guardia and Idlewild, New York's two giant
airports—Idlewild having opened in June of 1948, and had
fought hard for the city's selection, in August of 1948, as the
permanent home of the United Nations. He had dealt with
potentially paralyzing strikes of tugboat workers, transit
workers, and truckers, developing a highly-praised mediation

technique. And, an immigrant to New York himself, he had been confronted with the post-war influx of some 250,000 Puerto Ricans, with all the resulting racial complications.

Nonetheless, O'Dwyer's real reason for announcing he would not run was strategic: he was gambling that Tammany would be forced to beg him to run, thereby giving him control of the organization. Having dropped his bombshell, he settled back in his mayoral chair, waiting to see what the fallout would bring.

There followed an intricate political scenario. O'Dwyer encouraged Frank Hogan, an exemplary Manhattan district attorney since 1941 and one of Thomas E. Dewey's chief assistants during his racket-busting days, to think he was backing him for the nomination. In reality, O'Dwyer figured Hogan would be black-balled by the organization. Back in 1944, he knew, Hogan—a delegate to the Democratic national convention but a Dewey loyalist—had walked off the floor rather than vote for Franklin Roosevelt for a third term. It was inconceiveable to O'Dwyer that Bronx Boss Edward J. Flynn —first FDR's and now Harry Truman's man in the city— would forgive this transgression. A Hogan candidacy would seemingly divide the party, then an O'Dwyer draft would unite it.

In the end, the plan nearly back-fired. Flynn, along with Brooklyn Boss John Cashmore, did indeed oppose Hogan, but Tammany's Rogers, along with James A. Roe of Queens and Jeremiah Sullivan of Richmond, gave the Manhattan district attorney the nomination—by a vote of three-to-two. A naïve Hogan straightaway informed O'Dwyer of the result. "I phoned the mayor and I told him of the three votes for me, two leaders not voting," Hogan said. "He suggested that I hold out for support from Mr. Flynn and Mr. Cashmore. I replied that I couldn't see how I could do that without embarassing the three leaders who had voted for me. Then the mayor said he thought I shoudl accept, saying it would be worked out later."

For Hogan, "later" was never to come. Within the confines of Gracie Mansion, O'Dwyer's rage was monumental. Ignoring the fact that Hogan's anti-corruption credentials were impeccable, the mayor took his case to the public, accusing the leaders of a "squeeze play" against him, claiming that Tammany's endorsement of the district attorney was forcing him—as the foremost foe of Tammany—back into the race.

"O'Dwyer was boiling mad," Tammany's Rogers would recall. "He was almost inarticulate with rage—lambasting Tammany and carrying on about me as some kind of poison snake. I said, 'Fella, this is your own doing. You've been telling me you're not going to run again. I played it on the level with you. Now if you want to start playing games, you've got the wrong man.'"

But Rogers' firmness, luckily for O'Dwyer, was not matched by Hogan's. The district attorney was a prosecutor, not a politician—he had no wish for an intra-party fight. Within twenty-four hours, he called Rogers to tell him he was declining the nomination. "I don't want to start up a ruckus in the organization," he said. "It would just lead to some nasty primary fights."

Desperately, Rogers tried to change Hogan's mind. "Honestly, Frank, I don't know what the hell's in his mind," the Tammany leader said about O'Dwyer. "He's completely unpredictable. I've heard him get up and make a speech that would charm the ears off a jackass, then turn around and cut a guy's heart out—just for the hell of it. If you hold your ground another eight hours, I'll guarantee it—he'll back away from you. I'm the county leader, dammit. I want to show everybody I can have this thing if I want it."

"I'm sorry to be acting like a reluctant debutante," Hogan replied. "But I suppose I love my job too much to give it up for this kind of hassle."

"You don't have to give it up," Rogers insisted. "Just wait eight more hours. If you stay in the race, you'll have the nomination. You get the nomination and you'll run away with the election."

But Hogan was adamant. "I was double-crossed . . ." he repeated several times.

If Hogan had stayed in the race, and had captured the mayoralty, it is interesting to conjecture how he might have dealt with Costello. In their public confrontations, Hogan would quickly draw the line between Costello and himself. During the grand jury hearings over Frank's role in the Thomas Aurelio Supreme Court nomination, for instance, the district attorney was characteristically outspoken. "I told Costello that if he spoke one word that wasn't the truth," Hogan would recall, "I'd put everything we had into jugging him for perjury. He talked straight, and it was a relief to hear straight talk after listening to some of the yellow politicians who were in that mess squish and squidge all over the place. As soon as it was over, Costello came up to me and said, 'Well, how did I do in there?' I said, 'Pretty well. I notice that every now and then you cut some corners kind of sharp, but it was a lot better than I thought it would be. I'm sorry to say that I don't think we'll have that perjury case after all.' "

"You're right about cutting the corners," Costello said. "I guess I know plenty you'd like to know, but you understand how it is—I'm a legitimate businessman now, but I've still got to protect my boys. They've done a lot for me, and you wouldn't think much of me if I didn't protect them."

"He started telling me," Hogan would remember, "about what a rotten neighborhood he'd lived in, how his family always needed money, what bad associations he'd had. 'Maybe if things had been different,' Costello said, 'I'd have become an honest lawyer and worked this side of the street.' "

With Hogan's withdrawal as a candidate, the Democratic bosses were left with little choice but to offer O'Dwyer the nomination, which he promptly accepted. "After seven weeks of confusion," the *Herald-Tribune* editorialized in late July, "the announcement of the grand retreat from renunciation is out. It is particularly curious that the mayor should go out of his way to tell how he fought for District Attorney Hogan's candidacy, and assumed that all five Democratic leaders saw the same light. Only when the Messrs. Flynn and Cashmore balked was there another of the sudden O'Dwyer changes. It was then that he became convinced of the necessity of rising to smite the resilient Tammany tiger."

Tammany's connections with Costello—with O'Dwyer running for a second term—would remain strong. In deference to the mayor, however, Hugo Rogers was removed from the Tammany leadership, and his place taken by Carmine De Sapio.

"Do I know him?" De Sapio replied slowly, when asked if he knew Frank Costello. "I've met him."

"Will he have any influence at City Hall?"

"Definitely not."

When asked why he had attended Costello's Salvation Army fund-raising at the Copa, De Sapio replied, "I attend many functions. I am not apologizing for being there. It was in a good cause."

During the mayoral campaign that fall, Republican-Liberal-Fusion candidate Newbold Morris tried repeatedly to link O'Dwyer with Costello and the Syndicate—even on the lowest level of organized crime. In mid-October, Morris released a list of 124 purported bookmaking spots in Brooklyn alone, declaring that "the Mayor of the City of New York knows that this corruption exists." Besides the locations, all of which were newstands or small stores, Morris supplied the nicknames of the bookies—"Russ," "Porky," "Micky," and so forth.

Replying to the charge, O'Dwyer—speaking before a Congress of Industrial Organizations Barbers and Beauticians union—told his audience that there were "more serious things for police to do than hunt bookmakers," adding that he wanted "word from the public" before spending "millions to have cops chasing bookmakers all over town." Continued O'Dwyer: "If you had one million cops in this city and there was one barber who said he could not place a bet, I'd like to meet him." As matters now stood, the police department could spare only three hundred of its members for anti-gambling activity. "Let's face it," the mayor said, "we can only keep gambling under control." His opponent would be better off, he asserted, debating the problems of housing, health, and schools.

"We are delighted that Newbold Morris has at last gotten under the mayor's skin," the *Herald-Tribune* editorialized. "Mr. Morris's list of 124 Brooklyn bookmakers is only a sampling, but it does serve to point up that there is corruption in our municipal fabric. The mayor, in effect, admits that the bookies are thriving, and feels that they serve a widespread desire to bet on the horses. But it is not fitting to shrug off the bookies as a social phenomenon about which nothing can be done. We think the mayor should explain himself further, in words and actions that every voter (and the 'cop on the beat,' too) can understand."

Two weeks later, O'Dwyer was embarrassed again, when the *New York Sun* broke a story revealing that Frank Erickson had been conspicuously present, the night before, at a dinner for prominent city Democrats at the National Democratic Club. The *Sun* reported that O'Dwyer had scowled when he saw Erickson at the crowded reception preceeding the dinner, turned his back on the gambler's proffered hand, and quickly squeezed by him to the dais. A detective in the mayor's entourage then moved to Erickson's side, trying to keep the *Sun*'s photographer from snapping pictures.

Newbold Morris took full advantage of the incident. "Time was, just four short years ago, when this racketeer Erickson had to duck a mayor of New York," he said, alluding to the LaGuardia administration. "Shame, I say, that with LaGuardia dead, a mayor of New York has to duck Erickson."

O'Dwyer, highly irate at the *Sun*'s story, immediately called a press conference. His anger was all the greater because—during his fight with the Clarence Neal-Bert Stand faction in Tammany Hall two years before, when he was ousting Edward Loughlin from the leadership—he had labeled the National Democratic Club a "cesspool" of politics. He had boycotted the place since, except for one appearance with Harry Truman during the 1948 presidential campaign.

"It was your own doing, Mr. Mayor," the *Sun* reporter who had broken the story told him.

"I'll go anywhere I like," O'Dwyer retorted. "The *Sun* won't tell me where I can go. That National Association of Manufacturers throwaway [a reference to the *Sun*'s strong Republicanism] did a dirty job cheap, but they're not going to confuse the issues."

Later, the mayor was asked how Erickson happened to be at the dinner.

"How should I know?" he shouted. "I've known frame-ups all my life. I'm a victim of one now."

James E. Brannigan, president of the National Democratic Club, saw nothing wrong in the gambler's presence.

"Frank Erickson has been a member of the club since 1934," he calmly intoned, "and he has all the privileges of a member."

Wrote the vitriolic Hearst columnist Westbrook Pegler about the mayor: "William O'Dwyer is neither bad nor good but just thick. He is a strange character. He is a native of Ireland, but the leading Democratic pols of his blood and faith don't go for him. He seems to be loyal only to himself. His word is not reliable. He never analyzes or discusses issues on an intelligent plane. If he isn't stupid, then he is a magnificent dissembler."

Despite further attacks by Newbold Morris and Vito Marcantonio, the American Labor Party candidate, on everything from O'Dwyer's relationship to Costello to his handling of the Anastasia case, the mayor that November handily won a second term. He received some 1,264,000 votes, compared to Morris' 956,000 and Marcantonio's 356,000.

Seemingly untouched by the New York political turmoil, the Syndicate—during 1949—continued to expand. In Florida, for instance, it moved into the $40-million-a-year Miami bookmaking operation that hitherto had been the exclusive preserve of five local men calling themselves the S & G (the initials had no meaning). Costello, Adonis, and Lansky, together with the Capone group in Chicago, pulled off the coup bloodlessly—simply by cutting off the locals from the nationwide racetrack information supplied by Continental Press's wire service. After eight days of trying to get results via long-distance telephone calls, the S & G capitulated, accepting their new partners philosophically.

Costello and his colleagues had, of course, for some years been running lavish gambling casinos in Miami's Dade County and, to the north of Dade, in Broward County.

Florida's law-enforcement officials looked with forebearance on these activities. Dade County Sheriff James "Whistling Jimmy" Sullivan would admit that his assets increased, during his five-year term, from a few thousand dollars to more than seventy thousand dollars—not including twenty six thousand dollars that he and his wife sent to Mrs. Sullivan's mother for safe-keeping. "Sullivan distrusted banks," an investigator would state, "keeping large amounts of cash in a tin box, an old fishing box, or a blanket." In Broward County, where Costello and his associates ran Boheme and Greenacres, two of the biggest gambling clubs, Sheriff Walter Clark represented the law. A down-to-earth fellow who made a small fortune in a slot-machine supply business, Clark raided the clubs only on complaint, and never seemed to mind when they reopened. "Walter's as comfortable as an old shoe," his admirers would remark.

In late November, shortly after O'Dwyer's re-election, speculation grew that the mayor might marry a dark-haired, violet-eyed model named Sloan Simpson, who had been his constant companion for some time. He was fifty-nine, she was thirty-three. O'Dwyer and Sloan had met the year before at Grand Central Palace, where the city was sponsoring a fashion show celebrating Greater New York's fiftieth birthday. During the course of the show, she asked to be introduced to the mayor, and was led into a small, dimly-lit room off the main hall, where he was having drinks with some cronies.

"My, it looks like a speakeasy in here," she remarked.

"You're much too young to know about speakeasies, young lady," O'Dwyer replied.

When the show was over, the mayor invited all the volunteers to join him for a late supper in Gracie Mansion. The slim and elegant Sloan was asked to ride uptown in his car; he was clearly charmed by her.

O'Dwyer had been living alone in the big executive mansion since Kitty's death. Wrote a journalist: "For the first time in his life, O'Dwyer found himself with a woman who was gay, liked to dress up, go places, be seen. She brought a rush of youthfulness into his life." The couple went arm-in-arm to the Broadway theater, the Sadler's Wells ballet, even the World Series. Increasingly, Sloan was seen with the mayor at official dinners and receptions.

From the beginning of the relationship, however, both Bill and Sloan had doubts about the wisdom of their marrying. "Not only was Bill much older than I," Sloan would say, "but he was not well. Either there would be no children, or if there were—how long would they have a father? Many times I told myself to put him out of my mind, but my heart just wouldn't obey."

One evening, the couple went to see *South Pacific,* the Broadway musical in which Mary Martin, Sloan's age, falls in love with Ezio Pinza, O'Dwyer's age. "At one point in the play,"Sloan would remember, "Mary and Pinza sang a song that was to become our theme. How many times afterward Bill sang 'Some Enchanted Evening' in that baritone of his. Talk about magnetism! Pinza in *South Pacific* was a cardboard cutout compared to Bill."

Sloan Simpson had been born and raised in Dallas, Texas —her father, Colonel John Simpson, had been one of Teddy Roosevelt's rough riders, her mother was a direct descendant of Charles Carroll, a signer of the Declaration of Independence. Though her parents divorced when she was ten, her background was privileged: she lived in a fifteen-room mansion, was catered to by servants, enjoyed a world where riding schools, pretty clothes, and garden parties were taken for granted. While still in her teens, Sloan went to New York, where she settled on a modeling career. Three years later, at the age of twenty-two, she married a polo-playing businessman from Teanneck, New Jersey. Sloan was a Catholic, and he was not, and only a civil ceremony was performed. The marriage lasted five years and, in 1943, she won a divorce on grounds of mental cruelty. In the eyes of the Catholic Church, Sloan had never been married at all. She resumed her career, joining the John Robert Powers Agency.

"Anyone who tells you that modeling is a cinch is crazy," she would recall.

But Sloan persisted, working her rates up to a then-envious twenty-five dollars an hour and becoming perhaps the best millinery model in the city. "She wasn't just a beautiful statue," one fashion photographer would say. "She was always playing a part."

O'Dwyer's romance with Sloan drew the inevitable press attention, with the model being referred to as the mayor's "girl friend"—a casual term whose implication the high-spirited Sloan resented. "You fellows are writing some awful things about me," she challenged a reporter.

The unwelcome attentions of the press reached a high in November of 1949, after the couple flew off in a police department plane for what they hoped would be a quiet weekend in Saratoga Springs—as guests of hotelman Martin Sweeney and his wife. When they entered the lobby of the fashionable Gideon Putnam, they were beseiged by reporters and photographers. "What do you mean by invading our privacy!" O'Dwyer shouted. "It's the end of this circus! We're cutting short our weekend."

Back in the city, the mayor, feeling the pressures of both his public and private lives, only days later was admitted to Bellevue Hospital, suffering from what came to be diagnosed as a heart condition. Announced Dr. Edward Bernecker, his personal physician: "The laboratory tests show the mayor's condition to be somewhat worse than we thought. His metabolic processes are much lowered. An electro-cardiogram shows a very definite heart strain. He must remain in the hospital for at least two weeks."

On December 12, still showing signs of his illness, O'Dwyer departed by train for Florida, ostensibly for a much-needed rest. Seeing him off was Sloan Simpson. But during the mayor's hospitalization, Bill and Sloan had reached a decision: they would marry, and as soon as possible. She flew down soon afterward to Stuart, Florida, the town where O'Dwyer was secluded, and the couple finalized their plans. They would be married in the local Catholic church, St. Joseph's, with members of neither of their families present. The mayor, who sharply disliked his future mother-in-law, flatly refused to invite her; Sloan, miffed by his attitude, insisted on excluding the O'Dwyer clan. On December 20, in a simple, six-minute ceremony preceeded by the singing of "Ave Maria," O'Dwyer—now looking tanned and buoyant—and Sloan—radiant in a navy blue suit—were married by the St. Joseph's pastor. His best man was David Martin, managing director of the New York Athletic Club, her matron of honor was Mrs. Bernecker. Family members, from afar, sent telegrams of congratulation.

The newlyweds went directly to the yacht *Almar II,* which with its crew had been loaned to them by Harry Matthews of Long Island, one of O'Dwyer's friends. Their plan, which seemed an ideal one, was a leisurely cruise of the Florida Keys. But the mayor, whose idea of relaxing was reading or chatting with friends, had to be educated in the ways of the yachting life.

"I know it sounds fantastic," Sloan would reminisce, "but Bill had never set foot on a pleasure boat before. He had never worn a pair of shorts in his life. He had never had a fishing pole in his hands, never even *tried* to swim. This was a man who had known only work."

In the days that followed, a shorts-clad O'Dwyer found himself fishing, swimming, playing deck games. "I was madly in love with him," Sloan would say.

6

O'Dwyer did not bring his bride back to New York until mid-February, but when he did, he was faced with mounting city problems: another possible transit fare increase, municipal pay demands, the balancing of the budget. Of even greater importance, a series of exposés in the Brooklyn *Eagle* had shown that, throughout New York, Syndicate bookmakers was operating flagrantly—paying off the police and city officials with millions of dollars annually. The headlines were revelatory, the details so damning that more and more citizens' groups, blaming O'Dwyer for the corruption, were loudly demanding investigation. As the spring months passed, it became clear that Brooklyn District Attorney Miles McDonald, painstakingly developing his case against the Syndicate bookies, would follow up on the *Eagle's* exposés and deliver further broadsides. Costello was beginning to worry, O'Dwyer was beginning to sweat.

By June of 1950, even Frank Erickson came to grief. Earlier, he had been forced to explain his means of livelihood, while testifying before the newly-formed U.S. Senate Crime Committee, acknowledging that he had been operating a betting network in every state in the nation for years. "Ill-advised" was the way his attorney characterized the admis-

sion. Erickson had probably thought that, because he operated outside of New York, in states like New Jersey and
Florida where the authorities were myopic to his activities, he
was immune to prosecution. During his testimony, he had
mentioned keeping an account at the Pennsylvania Exchange
Bank, forgetting that the main office of the bank was in New
York. Now the ubiquitous District Attorney Hogan, who for
years had been dogging the gambler's trail, closed in on his
prey.

Armed with subpoenas, Hogan's investigators pored over
Erickson's Pennsylvania Exchange account. At first, it appeared legitimate: rent payments, charitable contributions,
the usual overhead expenses. But then the investigators went
further, looking for accounts under the names of the gambler's business associates. Here, under the name of one of his
frontmen, they struck paydirt. The dummy account contained canceled checks identifying Erickson's high-rollers,
who now could be called to testify against him; documents
revealing his partnership with Costello, Adonis, and Lansky
in Florida gambling enterprises; records of myriad business
transactions with Costello and the Syndicate. Erickson's com-
pulsive record-keeping had brought him down.

To protect his Syndicate masters, the fifty-four-year-old
gambler had no choice. On June 26, he pled guilty to sixty
counts of bookmaking and conspiracy. New York Special
Sessions Judge Nathan Perlman sentenced him to two years
in prison and a thirty-thousand-dollar fine. Though the sentence was minimal, it not only served to take the seemingly
untouchable Erickson out of the mainstream of organized
crime, but it sounded a warning—to those who had profited
from his activities—as to what was to come.

"Have you anything to say, Frank?" a reporter asked him.

"Not a word," the gambler replied.

With accusations from newspaper editorialists and good-government groups ringing in his ears, a beleaguered William O'Dwyer, one-hundred-and-fourth mayor of New York, thought it the wiser course to resign his office the end of August. He was the only man in modern times to do so besides the scandal-ridden James J. Walker, who resigned the mayoralty in 1932 while in danger of being removed by then-Governor Franklin D. Roosevelt. Years afterward, thinking about his City Hall days, O'Dwyer would choose to remember the municipal pressures, not the corruption charges. "There were times when I was mayor when I wanted to jump," he would say. "You know, the city's too big for one government. All those reports. You can't rely on them. You have to get your information in person. My Lord, I saw a lot of people in the course of a day!"

But no matter what the pressures, O'Dwyer could usually see the humor in them. Like the time Ed Flynn, the boss of the Bronx, was insisting he appoint a man named Hymie a magistrate. One evening, while O'Dwyer was on the dais at a political banquet at the Concourse Plaza, a somewhat tipsy Hymie decided to take matters in his own hands.

"Are you going to make me a magistrate?" he demanded of O'Dwyer.

"Right now," replied the mayor, "but first you've got to do something for *me*. Stand up straight!"

Though Hymie tried his best to oblige, he ended falling on the seat of his pants.

"*That* was one of the troubles of being mayor," O'Dwyer would recall.

To make his resignation plausible, O'Dwyer announced it was partly for reasons of health (which, to a large degree, was true) and partly to honor President Truman's request that he accept the Ambassadorship to Mexico. His familiarity with the Spanish language and customs, and his friendship with Mexican President Miguel Aleman, he explained, had convinced the President that he was ideally suited for the appointment. Beyond that, he would not elaborate.

"Is there any particular significance in your resigning at this time?" the mayor was pressed by a reporter.

"I am resigning."

"Are you endorsing anyone as your successor?"

"No."

"How do you feel about leaving New York City?"

"I will miss it."

In a last meeting with the Board of Estimate, O'Dwyer made sure that his aides would not suffer from his resignation; he pushed through promotions and pay increases totaling $116,500 annually for his friends. William J. Donoghue, his press secretary at $10,000 yearly, was named executive assistant to the Board of Water Supply at $17,500 yearly. Detective Joseph A. Boyle, his bodyguard, was appointed fourth deputy police commissioner, and Detective Bernard S. Collins, his chauffeur, became seventh deputy police commissioner; the action almost doubled both men's salaries and more than doubled their eventual pensions. "What I do now is in the best interest of the city," said the mayor, asserting it would encourage mayoral aides in future to better perform their duties, knowing that some form of reward was awaiting them. Previously, O'Dwyer had taken care of James J. Moran, his longtime crony, and David Martin, the best man at his wedding. Moran, who had been first deputy fire commissioner in the O'Dwyer administration, was given a lifetime post with the Board of Water Supply. Martin was named to a $15,000-a-year post with the New York Thruway Authority.

Only with a complicated plan to raise the salary and extend the term of City Planning Commission Chairman Jerry

Finklestein, his campaign manager and a guest at his wedding, did the mayor fail. His proposal was blocked by Bronx Borough President James J. Lyons, who pointed out that the Commission, under Mr. Finklestein, had "created more positions than it ever had," and had paid some $350,000 to a consulting firm for a dubious rezoning advice.

"The mayor's last meeting with the Board of Estimate," editorialized the *Herald-Tribune*, "was surrounded by touching sentiment. There were the glistening eye and the husky throat; the tributes of the saddened henchmen; and the last division of the spoils among the faithful. How could there be a dry eye in the house? (Aside, of course, from the serfs, villains, and taxpayers, only casually represented at the ceremonies.) Presumably, Mr. O'Dwyer feels that these didoes are the abdicating lord's perquisites. The taxpayer can only feel that the mayor has grossly confused personal matters with the public interest."

What the mayor may have hated most about departing from New York was the loss of Gracie Mansion. "He seemed to have a genuine feeling for the mansion," a reporter would write, "and on Sundays, especially in mild weather, he would often turn up on the lawn, in his shirtsleeves, and talk with passers-by through the fence. Ocasionally, he would sit outside Carl Schurz Park, on a ledge that runs alongside the park fence on East End Avenue, sunning himself, and chewing the rag with the neighborhood people. After he married Sloan Simpson, he took her on walks in the park; they strolled about, the mayor tipping his hat, and Mrs. O'Dwyer smiling and waving her hand to the burghers. There was an Old World quality to these promenades."

On a hot summer day in August, 1950, O'Dwyer and Sloan left Gracie Mansion for the last time. As their Cadillac rolled them slowly through the gates, the policeman on duty came to attention and saluted. The mayor had the limousine stop briefly outside nearby Doctors' Hospital, where he had often visited sick friends, and he leaned out of the window to say goodbye to the hospital doorman. Then the Cadillac continued on its way. As leave-takings go, O'Dwyer's was quiet, even wistful.

In the weeks that followed, Brooklyn District Attorney Miles McDonald brought his long-awaited investigation of New York City gambling to court—revealing shocking instances of corruption. So closely had Harry Gross, the Syndicate's boss bookie in Brooklyn, worked with the police, for instance, that patrolmen tapped bookie phones, not to gather evidence against them, but to insure that no bookmaking was done except by gamblers who paid for "protection." At a favorite hangout, the Dug-Out Bar and Grill near Ebbets Field, police would listen to betting conversations over the phones and—Gross would reluctantly testify—"when a bookie's name came up they would refer to a list. If the man was not okay, they went out and made a pinch."

The $20-million-a-year Brooklyn operation was itself paying police officials bribes of more than $1 million. Logically, the borough was divided into thirty sections by Gross, one for every police precinct. Most of the payments were made in the Dug-Out, regularly on the first of the month. In the Eighteenth Police Division, Gross explained, "there was $200 for the division office, and I gave the pick-up man a stake of a $20-bill. I paid the lieutenant $50 a location and the inspector $50 a location. I paid the lieutenant in charge of uniformed police $25 a month, the captain $50 a location. I paid the precinct plainclothesmen $20 a man, the cop on the post $2 a day on the 8 to 4, 4 to 12, and 12 to 8 shifts . . . I paid the sector car $45 a month, the sergeant $100 a month, the desk lieutenant $20 a week, and the emergency squad men $10 a man."

"Did you pay any officer higher than division level?" Gross was asked.

"I did. The Borough Squad East got $200 a location. I paid the Borough Super Squad the same and also the chief inspector and the police commissioner's squad. Around Christmas they all got double ice."

Gross's testimony plunged the police department into public disrepute, forcing the resignation of Commissioner William P. O'Brien only eighteen months after he had taken office. Subsequently, the boss bookie would connect O'Brien more directly with the bribe-taking—although the charge was never proven.

Back in 1943, "were you paying in the Nineteenth Division?" Gross was asked.

"I was."

"Who was the inspector?"

"Copeland, but I didn't pay him. I paid his men."

"Then what happened?"

"We had a change. We had an inspector named Mulholland. I had no arrangement with him, but I had one with his squad. Then we got Inspector O'Brien, later police commissioner."

"Did you have an arrangement with him?"

"I did."

"What was the arrangement?"

"The same as the other squads. I used to pay them $200 a location, plus $50 for the lieutenant, and $50 for the boss."

"And the boss?" repeated Gross' questioner, referring to then-Inspector O'Brien.

"That's right."

Such was the extent of the police scandal in New York that Bill O'Dwyer, who had been on vacation in California and was stopping off in the city in mid-October before journeying to Washington to be sworn in as Ambassador, called an impromptu press conference.

"Have you changed your mind about McDonald's investigation being a 'witch-hunt'?" a reporter asked O'Dwyer, referring to his criticism of the investigation while he was still mayor.

"When I made that remark, I'd just come from the funeral of a police captain"—John G. Flynn, whose suicide, subsequent events proved, was in no way connected with the gambling inquiry—"who everyone assured me was an honest man doing a good job," O'Dwyer replied. "I saw his widow at the funeral and his three little children. I was very sorry for her and for them. Then I was called up to the Bronx at 1 A.M. and there was the body of a poor policeman who gave up his life in defense of a citizen who had been set upon by two hoodlums. All this coming at one time was an emotional movement that was most unfortunate."

"Do you now repudiate the statement?"

"Yes," said O'Dwyer. "I'm very sorry I made it in view of the present circumstances."

The former mayor—who went on to say he thought the man replacing O'Brien as police commissioner, Thomas F. Murphy, would be "a very good commissioner"—stated he had never even met Gross.

"Who do you think should be held responsible for the Brooklyn mess?" he was asked.

O'Dwyer's answer was a rambling one. First, he mentioned a proposal he had once made "for every county to have every year an investigation in which peace officers, judges, and district attorneys are brought in to explain how gambling laws have been enforced in the year past." Then, referring to his stand in favor of legal off-track betting, he declared "The problem is that millions of decent citizens want to bet." Finally, he emphasized that "Mine was an honest administration."

Before the McDonald investigation ended, Commissioner Murphy transferred every police inspector in the city to a different command; named a new chief of detectives and a new head of the confidential squad; replaced a handful of other inspectors; demoted dozens of police officers ranging from captain to plainclothesman; and accepted retirement papers from some 110 men. But though Syndicate bookmaker Gross, in late 1950, was acknowledging his payoffs to the police, for the most part he was not actually identifying those men to whom he had paid the annual $1 million in bribes. "I could not hurt these police friends of mine and their families," he said. "It would ruin them. I have been in their homes, at the graduations of their kids. What are you asking me to do?"

While Harry Gross resolved this self-imposed dilemma, he remained in jail—under protective custody.

Down in Mexico, Bill O'Dwyer began to settle into the rounds of parties and public appearances that constituted his Ambassadorship. To all intents and purposes, the corruption charges against him and his administration had been left behind in New York, never to be resurrected. Indeed, many doubted that O'Dwyer was directly involved in the corruption.

"I don't for a moment believe what they say about Bill," Sloan would say. "All that hidden wealth he's supposed to have. Look—I *lived* with Bill. While we were in Mexico, it was I who had control of his checking accounts. If there had been a secret source of income, I would have known it. His savings never amounted to more than five thousand dollars! Maybe some of the men around him were dishonest. But *not* Bill O'Dwyer!"

But already a federal investigation of organized crime, headed by Senator Estes Kefauver of Tennessee, was taking form in Washington, an inquiry that would attract the attention of the American public—like no other before—because of the emerging power of television.

Bill-O would soon be summoned before Kefauver, and so would the prime minister.

PART FIVE

1951:
Investigation

1

ON MONDAY, MARCH 12, 1951, the Senate Crime Investigating
Committee–culminating a ten-month span of hearings in
major cities across the nation—finally came to New York.
There, during eight dramatic days that were witnessed by
some 30 million television viewers, the extent and the insidi-
ousness of Frank Costello's criminal empire was once and for
all exposed. Chairing the committee was Senator Kefauver;
sitting with him were Senators Herbert O'Conor, Democrat
of Maryland, and Charles Tobey, Republican of New Hampshire; the chief counsel, conducting most of the questioning
of witnesses, was Rudolph Halley.

We take television for granted now. It is difficult, a genera-
tion later, to imagine the impact that television in 1951 had on

the hearings. But a crime investigation of this nature—caught live by the video camera for the first time—made an impression on the masses that mere newspaper stories had never achieved. Observed Kefauver subsequently: "Businesses were paralyzed; many movie houses became ghost halls—some even installed television and invited the public to come in free and watch; housewives did their ironing and mending in front of their sets. We became more than a group of officials. We became a national crusade, a great debating forum, an arouser of public opinion."

The proceedings speedily evolved into a morality drama —good versus evil—which Estes Kefauver, a lanky, soft-spoken Southerner, directed with judicial calm, though he rarely questioned witnesses himself. Then forty-seven years old, the six-foot-three Kefauver was a rough-hewn oak of a man, whose strong, homely features personified integrity. Indeed, poor-but-honest was his political image, and he worked it for all it was worth. Coming from Madisonville, a town of some fourteen hundred in the foothills of the Great Smokies, his father a hardware-store owner, Estes went to the University of Tennessee, played tackle on the football team, was elected president of the student body. After graduating from Yale Law School in 1927, he began practicing in Chattanooga, where he developed his own way of handling juries. "He would establish himself as a country boy," a friend remembered, "then recite the facts and lead the jury along. He used language the jurors could understand. He never tried to be eloquent." Legal success, an advantageous marriage, a 1937-citation from the Chattanooga Junior Chamber of Commerce as its Young Man of the Year—all led to a career in politics. Kefauver served nine years in the U.S. House of Representatives and then, in 1947, challenged Boss Ed Crump's Democratic machine for a seat in the U.S. Senate.

Enraged by Kefauver's tireless and effective handshaking in the ensuing campaign, Boss Crump ran full-page ads, in newspapers throughout Tennessee, that sought to ridicule the upstart. "Kefauver," wrote Crump, "reminds me of the pet coon that puts its foot in an open drawer in your room, but turns its head while it is feeling around."

"I may be a pet coon," replied Estes, "but I'll never be Mr. Crump's pet coon." The voters responded to his independence. A coonskin hat became Kefauver's political trademark, and he entered the Senate with a landslide victory.

Already Kefauver and his Crime Committee had uncovered, in city after city, the tell-tale signs and secret partnerships of the Syndicate. Miami, Tampa, New Orleans, Chicago, Detroit, Cleveland, Philadelphia, St. Louis, Las Vegas, Los Angeles—now he and his colleagues were holding public hearings in New York. Though Kefauver's main targets there were Costello and ex-Mayor O'Dwyer, he was intent on showing, through brief interrogations of lead-off witnesses, the close associations that existed in the city among some businessmen, politicians, and mobsters. The first man to be called was George Morton Levy, the wealthy racetrack-owner who admitted he had paid Costello tens of thousands of dollars during the 1940s to keep "bookies" away from his Roosevelt Raceway, then operating at Empire State in Yonkers. There really weren't that many bookmakers at his track, explained Levy—the charge was just a "phobia" on the part of the then chairman of the State Harness Racing Commission. But Levy was afraid that it might result in the loss of his license, so he asked his golfing friend Costello for help. The prime minister passed the word to the right gamblers, and the threat of a license revocation was removed.

"When did you last ask Costello to do anthing for Roosevelt?" Cousel Halley inquired.

"The last time was in 1946," Levy replied.

"But you kept on paying him?" continued the aggressive Halley, referring to the fifteen thousand dollars Costello was receiving yearly.

"I didn't have to ask him to do anything. He knew what I was paying him for."

Next came moon-faced Frank Erickson, who was still serving a jail sentence for his conviction, the year before, on sixty counts of bookmaking and conspiracy.

"Under what circumstances did you join the National Democratic Club?" the gambler was asked—the organization in question being a Tammany stronghold.

"I joined it many years ago as a social club," he said.

"You are a regular attendant?"

"At the beefsteaks and the outings."

"Has Frank Costello ever been your guest at the Club?"

"I refuse to answer on the grounds that it may tend to incriminate me."

To all the questions that followed, Erickson gave the same reason for refusing to reply, citing the Fifth Amendment, and doing so in a scarcely audible voice.

"If you were lost in the woods somewhere out in the country," asked the slightly-built Senator Tobey, elfin-featured behind his spectacles, "and the shades of night were falling fast, and the owls began to hoot, and you wanted a helping hand, would you speak no louder than that?"

"The last time I spoke to you, Senator, I spoke too loud," rejoined Erickson, referring to the burst of candor that had led to his conviction.

"We didn't use you too badly," said Tobey.

"You assured me nothing could happen to me," shot back the mournful Erickson.

"I just want to make an observation," said Tobey. "As I

listened to the testimony of this witness, ninety-nine and one-half percent of which consisted of saying, 'I refuse to answer;' I thought of America and all the liberties under the Constitution. I thought how Frank Erickson—when he goes back to his temporary abiding place—ought to say, 'Thank God, this hearing wasn't held in Soviet Russia.'"

"I do, I do," replied the gambler.

Charles Lipsky, a Queens Republican who was a close friend of William O'Dwyer's, then testified he had gone to the Copacabana in 1946, at O'Dwyer's request, to tell Clarence Neal, a Tammany Hall power, that the new mayor wanted a cleanup. There he found Neal in the company of both Judge Francis Mancuso, a Tammany district leader, and Costello himself.

"Did you receive a reply to your message?"

"Mr. Neal was very indignant. He used language that was very rough."

"He said no, is that right?"

"Correct."

The Committee would have preferred to hear more than it did from Joe Adonis, but the meticulously-groomed Joey A, gruff-voiced but squinting myopically—too vain to wear glasses—had little to say.

"Did you ever have discussions with Mr. Lipsky in connection with primary fights in Brooklyn?"

"I don't recall any."

"Do you remember ever telling Mr. Lipsky you were a sucker, putting so much money into political fights?"

"Not that I recall."

"What is your present business?"

"I don't have any at this time."

"Have you disassociated yourself from the Automotive Conveying Company?"—the company that had monopolized the delivery of Ford cars throughout the Middle Atlantic States and New England, and which Ford had paid some $1 million yearly.

"I decline to answer on the ground that it tends to incriminate me."

So the stage was set, on the second day of the hearings, for the arrival of Frank Costello, the prime minister of the underworld. Conservatively tailored in blue, he at first glance appeared younger than his sixty years—though his barbershop tan was imperfect and his walk somewhat stiff-shouldered. His voice, normally quite gravelly, was now so rough in texture he was said to be suffering from laryngitis. Strangely enough, the millions of television viewers were not to see Costello's face. Geroge Wolf, his attorney, told Kefauver that the intrusion of the cameras would interfere with the privacy of lawyer-client conferences, would make it appear the witness could not reply to questions promptly and forthrightly. Accordingly the chairman, fair to the point of scrupulousness, ruled the cameras should be trained below Costello's face—on his arms and hands. But Wolf's strategem was to backfire. During the hours of questioning that followed, Costello's hands, in their nervousness, revealed more than his face ever could. Under pressure, the hands crumpled a hankerchief; the palms sweatily rubbed together; the fingers interlaced, beat a silent tatoo, rolled a tiny ball of paper. With Costello's hoarse, almost brutal, voice for a soundtrack, the hands became sinister actors in the drama.

The first charge the Crime Committee chose to develop was that the prime minister had lied during his naturalization proceedings in 1925, and therefore was not entitled to United States citizenship. Though Costello has used the name Frank "Saverio," his mother's maiden name, when he was convicted for carrying a concealed weapon, he had failed to note this fact on his naturalization form.

"Were you convicted in the State of New York in 1915 for possession of a revolver?" he was asked.

"I was convicted for a misdemeanor."

"And on that occasion, did you use the name Frank Saverio?"

"I imagine I did."

"Do you remember having been asked, in the course of your naturalization proceedings, whether you ever used any alias?"

"I wouldn't remember that," Costello replied. "Have you got the application in front of you?"

"I do," replied Counsel Halley, handing a copy to the witness and his attorney.

"Now do you remember?" Halley persisted.

"I concede," interjected attorney Wolf. "The name Saverio doesn't appear on the application."

"May we have Mr. Costello's concession?"

"I don't remember," the witness repeated. "I don't remember leaving it out."

Halley then sought to show that Costello was actively engaged in bootlegging—breaking the law—even while he was applying for citizenship.

"You were admitted to citizenship on September 10, 1925, were you not? Prior to that, did you not engage in the business of selling, purchasing, and transporting alcoholic beverages within the United States?"

"I didn't sell no liquor prior to 1925."

"During what period of time were you in the business of buying liquor imported from Canada?"

"I couldn't tell you the exact time. Approximately 1927, 1928. I don't know."

"It could have been as early as 1922?"

"I doubt it."

Costello grudgingly admitted he had been indicted in 1925, along with William "Big Bill" Dwyer and dozens of others, for conspiring to smuggle liquor into the United States.

"Was Harry Sausser one of the people you bought liquor from?" Halley asked, referring to one of Costello's co-defendants in that indictment.

"He might have been."

"How many Harry Saussers do you know?"

"I might have known two or three."

"Do you expect us to believe that story, Mr. Costello?"

The crowd gasped when it heard the prime minister's arrogant reply: "I am not expecting you to believe anything."

For the record, Counsel Halley then pointed out that one of the witnesses to Costello's naturalization application had been Harry Sausser, with both men listing their business as "real estate." Moreover, Halley stated, Costello had previously admitted, in a N.Y. State Liquor Authority hearing, that he had been engaged in bootlegging as early as 1922 or 1923.

"I was covering the blanket years," the prime minister blandly replied. "But now, thinking it over, I know that I didn't sell any liquor prior to 1926 or 1927."

At this point, Senator Tobey broke in. "I am just thinking out loud," he said, "but if there was a conspiracy between the parties here to break the law of this country, and if at a later date the witness was made a citizen, is he not susceptible to deportation?"

"That is my thinking," agreed Halley.

Next the Committee delved into how Costello justified his income. He was, the prime minister admitted, a part-owner of the Beverly Country Club in New Orleans—along with Phil Kastel and Carlos Marcello, the resident Syndicate chieftain. But it was only when the Committee had held its hearings in that city, Costello insisted, that he had learned of Marcello's criminal record, which included convictions for narcotics sales, robbery, and assault.

"What is the business of the Beverly Club?"

"It's a nightclub and restaurant."

"Is there a gambling casino attached?"

"Roulette and dice," Costello conceded. His salary from the club in 1950, he said, had been eighteen thousand dollars.

"What did you do for that salary?"

"I helped to get different acts, and I solicited some business. In other words, if someone was going to Louisiana, I would recommend the place. I was a good-will man. And I would recommend different acts to the club."

"How did you look for acts?"

"If I would hear of a good act, I would go and watch it. If I thought it was good, I would call the Beverly people and tell them."

"What acts did you recommend?"

"Well—Joe E. Lewis, Sophie Tucker, a lot of big ones," replied Costello, triggering a wave of laughter among the spectators.

"Would it take an expert to recommend headliners like that?" asked Halley.

"I don't consider myself an expert. But a good act can go bad. No new material, it could go bad. If the act had new material, I would recommend it."

"For that, you got eighteen thousand dollars a year?"

"That's right."

The shadowy incongruities of Costello's life-style emerged one after the other. Items:

- *Asked about his role in telling bookmakers to lessen their activities at Roosevelt Raceway, thereby helping George Morton*

*Levy keep his license and earing fifteen thousand dollars yearly
for his efforts, Costello tried to explain Levy's wire-tapped appeal, "As boss, you should be able to tell them the way things
stand now." Mumbled the gambler: "There is an error there
somewhere. I was never a boss. I never had any interest in
Roosevelt."*

* *Pressed about his dealings, first with Huey Long and then
with other Louisiana politicans, in his multi-million-dollar slot-
machine business, Costello justified the machines by saying the
governor had been arranging for their legalization. But what,
subsequently, after Long's death, was Costello's connection with
the slots? "I have retired from that business," he replied.*

* *Queried as to how he had raised several hundred thousand
dollars for his purchase in 1943 of three office buildings he re-
named the 79 Wall Street Corporation, Costello explained he had
borrowed much of the down-payment money from Frank Erickson. "You and Mr. Erickson were on pretty good terms, weren't
you?" Halley persisted. "When you wanted money, you could get
it from him, couldn't you?" Answered the prime minister:
"Without hesitation."*

Back on the stand on March 14, Costello vehemently denied any knowledge of an ex-telephone company employee
named James McLaughlin ("Not to my recollection"), or that
he had hired the man to check his phone for wiretaps ("Absolutely not").

Counsel Halley then called on McLaughlin, an expert
technician who had worked for the New York Telephone
Company for twenty-three years, to give his recollection of
events. According to McLaughlin, he had been introduced to
Costello by Irving Sherman, the gambler's garment-center
henchman, in the early 1940s.

"Costello asked me to look over his telephone, and I did. I checked it sometimes two and three times a week."

"How much did he pay you?"

"It varied. He would give me $50, $100, even $150."

"Where did you receive the payments?"

"In the Waldorf-Astoria, just outside of the barber shop. Sherman told me I could see Costello there almost every morning around 10:30 or 11 o'clock."

McLaughlin testified he had arranged a code with Costello, to let him know whether or not his line was safe.

"I would call him at his apartment after making a check and say, 'This is Jim. Everything isn't well,' or words to that effect."

"And he would know from that," interjected Senator Kefauver, "that his line was tapped?"

"That's right."

"And when it wasn't being tapped?"

"I would say, 'I'm feeling fine today.'"

In 1945, McLaughlin went on, he had at Irving Sherman's request checked William O'Dwyer's phone for taps during the mayoral campaign—but had found nothing.

"Where did you do it?"

"At his home in Brooklyn. He was still residing there."

About that time, and again on Sherman's orders, McLaughlin had inspected the phones at the Garment Center Fashion Club—the first floor being occupied by a restaurant, the upper floors by dice layouts and card tables.

"Did you ever see William O'Dwyer in the club?" inquired Halley.

"Yes, in the restaurant part. But not the upstairs part."

"Who was he with?"

"Irving Sherman. It just so happened that I dropped in that night. I sat at another table."

"Were you introduced?"

"No, I wasn't."

Senator Kefauver thereupon announced that Costello's testimony, denying any relationship with McLaughlin, would be referred to the Department of Justice for prosecution. "On the face of it," he said, while the hearing room buzzed excitedly, "someone has committed perjury."

The prime minister's efforts to buy into legitimate businesses next came under scrutiny. A case in point was his attempt, about 1937, to purchase the Whitely Company of London, Scotch whisky distillers whose House of Lords and King's Ransom brands his company, Alliance Distributors, had been selling in the United States since the end of Prohibition. Using ex-bootlegger Irving Haim and wealthy turfman William Helis as frontmen, Costello and Phil Kastel endorsed the Haim-Helis note for the $325,000 down-payment, thereby effectively controlling the venture. Before the Crime Committee, Costello nonetheless maintained he had endorsed the note purely out of friendship for Kastel, expecting no monetary "consideration" in return.

"Are you telling me," said Kefauver, "that signing the three-hundred, twenty-five-thousand-dollar note was purely an accomodation?"

"That's right, Senator," replied Costello.

"Why don't you speak up and say, 'Certainly, I signed the note. I had a deal with Kastel,' " prompted Counsel Halley.

"You ain't gonna put no words in my mouth," said Costello, losing his grammar along with his temper. "I gave you your answer."

When the Whitely people discovered that the notorious Frank Costello was behind the acquisition, they supposedly balked—until he withdrew from the deal. Haim and Helis's family eventually bought the distillery, with Kastel remaining in the picture, but Costello insisted that thereafter he had no further connection with Whitely.

For the record, Halley then quoted Supreme Court Justice Thomas Aurelio's previous testimony that, in 1943, "Costello told me about this distillery, this interest he had in House of Lords or King's Ransom, I don't remember which, when we were drinking it at his home."

"I might have told him that," the gambler admitted. "But I was boasting. The interest was Mr. Kastel's."

Temporarily closing his testimony, Costello was equally evasive, in response to the questioning of Senator O'Conor, about the amount of cash he kept in his house-safe. Yes, he said, there was certainly one thousand dollars in the safe. Might there be as much as one hundred thousand dollars? "I wouldn't know," Costello replied.

"I want to give you the opportunity to change your response—it's palpably false," said O'Conor, warning the witness of further perjury charges.

After huddling with his attorney, Costello amended his statement. He did not know the exact amount of cash in the safe, he said, "I might have forty, fifty or fifty-five thousand dollars."

"How much money do you customarily keep in your bank accounts, Mr. Costello?" Senator Kefauver inquired.

"Oh, from ninety to one hundred thousand dollars or so. I haven't had a chance to look."

"You haven't looked recently?"

"I haven't got my statement."

Before releasing Costello from the stand, Kefauver brought up the 1944 incident, headlined in all the newspapers, in which the Prime Minister forgetfully left $27,200 in cash in a New York taxi. The money had been given to him by Phil Kastel, as part of his regular profits from the New Orleans operation, but Costello would not admit it came from gambling.

"Where did you get that cash?" said Kefauver.

"It was money Mr. Kastel owed me."

"Why would he owe you twenty-seven thousand two hundred dollars?"

"He owed me fifteen thousand dollars—money I had advanced him. He came up to New York and had the cash on him. The other twelve thousand two hundred dollars came from my brother-in-law, Dudley Geigerman. At that time, I was negotiating a real-estate deal."

Summed up Senator Tobey, as much amused as nettled by the now-perspiring Costello's answers: "We're playing ducks and drakes."

More to the point was Brooklyn District Attorney Miles McDonald, whose exposure of the Syndicate's $20 million a year bookmaking network in that borough had rocked the city.

"You have to extend your federal law with respect to wiretapping," he said, "or create a law permitting use of telephone interceptions for the purpose of wiping out organized crime. It is utterly foolish to close our eyes to what is going on, and not take the weapons at hand."

"With regard to horse-race betting, Mr. McDonald, what have you to say?" inquired Senator O'Conor.

"Horseracing is designed for the purpose of gambling. To say it's for the purpose of improving the breed is sheer hypocrisy. As long as you have horse racing, you can't wipe out gambling."

But the Syndicate's control of organized gambling, McDonald continued, could be substantially curtailed "if you cut down on the information that comes to the bookmakers over interstate communications—if you can keep them from getting the weights, the jockeys, the condition of the tracks, all the things that give the bookmakers an advantage."

"Did you ever hear," asked Senator Tobey, going off on another tack, "that this man James Moran, the colossus who is now Water commissioner of New York City by appointment of former Mayor O'Dwyer, demanded cash contributions from many of the gamblers hereabouts to promote the O'Dwyer candidacy? And got them—in large amounts?"

"I have heard stories to that effect," said McDonald, adding that the secrecy imposed on his own grand jury investigation kept him from discussing the allegations before the Committee.

2

On March 15, federal narcotics agent Samuel Levine told Senator Kefauver and his colleagues that the Syndicate, since the end of World War II, had been stepping up its drug-smuggling activities.

"About what time did the Italian ports become important in the narcotics traffic?" he was asked.

"Since the war. From 1947 on, the seizures from Italian ports have become larger and larger."

"That was the year Lucky Luciano was deported to Italy?"

"It was."

Levine's remarks served to introduce the testimony of Virginia Hill, whose restless travels since Bugsy Siegel's assassination indicated her Syndicate courier-work may have envolved from gambling-money to narcotics. Virginia had been her usual histrionic self in the six months following the mobster's death, alternating suicide attempts with lavish spending. In July of 1947, she required hospitalization—in Monte Carlo and Paris—after taking successive doses of sleeping pills. Back at her Miami Beach home in August, she took a third overdose, remaining in a coma for nearly three days. For the rest of the year, she leap-frogged from Biloxi, Mississippi, (to meet with Syndicate gamblers) to Big Sky Lodge in Swan Lake, Montana, (where seaplanes brought her mysterious packages) to Spokane, Washington, (where she bought an extensive new wardrobe) to Phoenix, Arizona, (to meet a friend of Bugsy's who had once served a ten-year narcotics conviction).

From 1948 until mid-1949, Virginia lived in Mexico City, although she spent much of her time in Acapulco. Amid rumors that she maintained a yacht in the seaport city, using it to smuggle dope, she gave glamorous parties, paid in cash for everything, and seemed to have gotten over Siegel's death. Six months in Chicago followed and then, early in 1950, Virginia went to Sun Valley, Idaho, where she spent $11,500 in six weeks, and met and married an Austrian-born ski instructor. She and her husband went on to Spokane, where they bought an expensive home and a Cadillac convertible; New Orleans, as guests of Phil Kastel; and Havana, as guests of Meyer Lansky. Toward the end of the year, she gave birth to a son, at a hospital near Boston, and then returned with her husband and baby to Spokane.

Sweeping into the Crime Committee hearings, thirty-five-year-old Virginia Hill still made a striking appearance: her classic profile and glossy, auburn-colored hair were set off by a black picture hat with a wide straw brim; her blue eyes flashed angrily; her splendid figure was accentuated by a severe black suit and a silver-blue mink stole. Counsel Halley straightaway addressed a series of questions to Virginia, designed to show that she was a Syndicate courier. But she parried them expertly. Yes, she said, she did know Chicago's Charley Fischetti; she also knew Joe Adonis and Frank Costello. But she had never carried gambling cash for any of them. Yes, she was aware of the rumors about her involvement with narcotics. But they were pure fiction.

"In the last few years, you have been earning substantial sums of money," pursued Halley. "You say you have been earning them from wagering?"

"That's right."

"How did you make out in 1947? I see that you say you made sixteen thousand dollars?"

"After Mr. Siegel was killed, I never was around anyone anymore to get betting tips from. I was in Montana, and then I went to Mexico."

"I am trying to establish how you figured your tax."

"I used to give Mr. Epstein"—Chicago bookmaker Joe Epstein, her longtime benefactor—"the money, and he said that was what I made."

"Well, it could not have been a flat sixteen thousand dollars?"

"Maybe it wasn't. I didn't keep any books or anything, but I paid what I thought was right."

"You have lived very well, and you don't seem to have taken the trouble of accounting to Uncle Sam the way the rest of us do," observed Halley.

"Then he'll have to take care of that, won't he?" challenged Virginia.

Senator Kefauver then took up the questioning of Virginia Hill. "You didn't tell us what kind of betting you did with all this money," he said.

"Horses. I used to know some people. When they had good tips, they would give them to me. Some of them were bookmakers. Some of them hung around the tracks. Sometimes Mr. Epstein would make the bets for me."

"How did they get that inside information?"

"I have no idea. I never asked them."

"You were just glad to get the money?"

"Yes."

"Apparently, you were able to win substantial sums every year—from fifteen thousand dollars to thirty thousand dollars. Do you do most of your betting through bookies, or at the track?"

"A lot of times through bookies—here in New York, sometimes in Chicago, sometimes in California."

"Did you ever have any trouble finding bookmakers in New York?"

"I didn't find them. They just seemed to be around."

Neither the blazing camera lights nor the relentless interrogation fazed Virginia Hill. Alternately, she was laconic, indignant, sarcastic, haughty, hurt, and amused. Of gangland matters, she respectfully insisted, she had made it a point not to know "anything about anybody." When she did step down from the stand, the spectators burst into applause, and she rewarded them with an impudent smile. Outside the hearing room, members of the press asking for interviews were treated less graciously. Virginia slapped a woman reporter from the *Journal-American,* knocking her to the ground, and kicked a male reporter for the *Herald-Tribune.* "I hope the atom bomb falls on every one of you!" she shouted at the newspaper people.

Explaining one's income by claiming it came from betting proved to be a favorite mob strategem. Previously, the unflappable Willie Moretti, testifying before the Committee in closed session, declared the bulk of his earnings resulted from racetrack winnings. The money he took in from his linen supply business, for instance, averaged only some $5,000 yearly, but in his tax returns for 1949, 1948 and 1947, respectively, he listed gambling profits of $20,800, $31,200 and $25,000.

"Do you have any breakdown showing what you won and what you lost?" Halley asked the New Jersey mobster.

"This year I didn't lose anything. I won every time I went to the track."

"How many times did you go?"

"Probably twenty—to Aqueduct, Belmont, Monmouth."

But even these earnings did not explain Moretti's standard of living. He cheerfully admitted that he owned two homes, one a six-acre estate on the Jersey shore that was worth four hundred thousand dollars; that his family drove two Cadillacs and a Lincoln; that he had bought waterfront property on Miami's Biscayne Bay; that he stayed in seventy-five dollar-a-day hotel accomodations when vacationing in Florida.

"You have got these automobiles, and two houses, and you pay seventy-five dollars a day in Florida," Halley said to him. "How do you do it?"

"I do it pretty good."

"How does the arithmetic work? How do you manage?"

"I can't tell you. I manage to live on two hundred dollars a week."

"Mr. Moretti," interrupted Senator Kefauver, "when you come home from the track, you put down the amount you have won or lost on a piece of paper, is that it?"

"That's right."

"When you go to your auditor to have him fix up the tax returns, do you show him the piece of paper, or do you just tell him what the amounts are?"

"Just tell him."

"Would you be willing to take a Committee investigator out to your home," resumed Halley, "and hand him this paper?"

"If I can find it," Moretti deadpanned. "I've got grandchildren, you know. They go in all my drawers. Sometimes, I can't even find my shirts and ties."

Midway through the hearings, Frank Costello, pleading laryngitis and fatigue, balked at resuming his testimony. Attorney Wolf asked for a postponement until his client was "physically able to continue." It was clear, said Wolf, that Costello was present before the Committee, not as a witness but as a defendant. "During the entire proceedings, blinding Klieg lights have been on all the time, motion picture cameras have been grinding, hordes of photographers have been roaming the room. With these intolerable conditions, it has become apparent that the witness cannot properly concentrate."

"Mr. Halley," asked Costello, "am I a defendant in this courtroom? Am I under arrest?"

"No," was the reply.

"Then I am walking out," and this the embattled prime minister, his face deeply lined with strain, proceeded to do, while flashbulbs popped and reporters raced to phone in the news to their papers. But Costello's defiance was short-lived: the threat of contempt charges would soon return him to the stand.

Now the Committee turned its attention to William O'Dwyer's Murder Inc. investigation a decade before, and how the November 11, 1941, death of Abe "Kid Twist" Reles —O'Dwyer's star stool pigeon—had dissolved the homicide case against Albert Anastasia, the lord high executioner. The conviction of Anastasia, who was just one level in the Syndicate below Adonis and Costello, might have destroyed the organization.

"I do not think we had enough evidence to indict Anastasia," insisted Frank Bals, the former police captain whom O'Dwyer had brought into the district attorney's office. "We needed corroboration." The case against Anastasia had involved the 1939 murder of union leader Morris Diamond, and the point was, of course, that Reles, a nonparticipant in the crime who heard Anastasia plotting it, could have provided precisely that corroboration. But for eighteen months O'Dwyer and his staff neglected to follow up on the Diamond killing—until Reles's fall, while in protective custody, from the sixth floor of Coney Island's Half Moon Hotel made the matter academic.

"So Reles, at five or six in the morning, fully dressed, is found dead six floors below his room with six policemen of the City of New York on guard," said a sarcastic Senator Tobey to Bals, who had been responsible for the protection. "I asked you how you explained it and you said, 'I imagine the officers all fell asleep about the same time.' Six policemen all feel asleep at the same time. And then Mr. Reles went to the window and killed himself."

"Well, I wouldn't say that was a fair picture," Bals replied. "From all indications, Reles attempted to tie a bedsheet to a radiator with a piece of wire. . . . He only had one sheet. The only place he could have gone was to the window below. . . ."

"He took a sheet and tore it up, and he was fully dressed with his shoes on, and he walked around, and all that might make some noise, and six somnolent policemen slept on. Then he opened the window, lowered himself on the sheet and the wire slipped and down he went. Is that a fair picture?"

"I imagine it is," Bals conceeded, causing a ripple of laughter in the hearing room.

"What disciplinary action was taken against the officers? Were they demoted?" Halley asked.

"Yes, sir. They were tried, and I think most of them were sent back on patrol."

"Was any action taken against you?"

"It was not."

A few years later, Bals even received a promotion. In 1946, Mayor O'Dwyer appointed him to the newly-created office of seventh deputy police commissioner, a post he held only a couple of months, but one which enabled him to retire with a $6,000 yearly pension, compared to the then captain's pension of $2,300.

James J. Moran, the longtime O'Dwyer associate who had been his chief clerk—handling the court calendar and assigning the prosecutors to the various cases—during the Murder Inc. inquiry, echoed Bals's contention that there was no case against Anastasia for the Diamond murder. But why had he ordered the removal of the "wanted cards" on Anastasia and Jack Parisi, the actual gunman, from the files—the cards that instructed the police the men were wanted for questioning?

"There was never a case," Moran said. "There was no sense cluttering up the files with cards. It was purely a clerical move."

A man of great stubborness, Moran had been a city employee since 1930, after the Stock Market crash cost him his legal stenographer's job with a Wall Street law firm. Still in his late twenties, but with a wife and growing children to support, the Brooklyn-born-and-raised Moran turned to civil service, becoming a Kings County court attendant. There he remained nearly a decade, apparently content. "I was born, went to school, married, and still live in the same two-mile area," he would say with satisfaction. Then, about 1938, Moran emerged as the close friend of William O'Dwyer, newly-named to the criminal courts, and his horizons suddenly broadened. Almost overnight, he became O'Dwyer's intimate advisor. "Moran was as close to O'Dwyer as his shirt," an observer would remark. Thereafter, for the next dozen years, the two men's careers advanced in tandem: Moran became O'Dwyer's political confidante, his chief clerk while he was Brooklyn district attorney, his first deputy fire commissioner while he was mayor. Finally, he was rewarded with a lifetime job on the Board of Water Supply just before O'Dwyer left City Hall.

Of all the people caught up in the Crime Committee probe, Moran—supposedly the bagman-designate, supposedly the man who collected bribes for the mayor—was destined to suffer by far the severest legal punishment. His troubles began when Counsel Halley, shifting his interrogation, began to question Moran about Louis Weber, who had been the policy king of Brooklyn until his numbers-bank conviction a couple of years before.

"How long have you known Louis Weber?" Halley inquired.

"Perhaps twenty years."

"He was the big policy man, wasn't he?"

"I don't know how big anybody is, Mr. Halley. Why, I have even gained four inches in stature and sixty pounds in weight, according to my 'colossus' description by Senator Tobey"—in point of fact, Moran was six-feet-four and weighed some 220 pounds—"so there may be the same interpretation of Weber's policy bank."

"At any rate, Weber did visit you, in your fire department office, three or four times over the years?"

"That's right."

"Is it possible he came much more often?"

"No sir, it is not."

Halley thereupon summoned to the stand Gerald Martin, a uniformed fireman who had acted as a receptionist in the fire commissioner's office. Without hesitation, Martin directly contradicted Moran, swearing that Weber had visited him at least fifty times during a thirty-month period. For a long half-minute, the spectators were unnaturally silent, watching in fascination while Moran glared malevolently at the witness: for a moment, it seemed he might rise and strike him.

When it came Weber's turn to testify, the policy man confused the issue further by taking still a third tack, swearing he neither knew Moran nor had he even once visited his office.

Within months, both Moran and Weber, largely on the strength of Martin's testimony, would be found guilty of perjury, each receiving a five-year sentence. But this conviction was only the start of the O'Dwyer loyalist's difficulties. It soon was charged that Moran, sometime in 1947, had set up a special "fuel-oil inspection section" within the fire department. Fireman James F. Smith, a handball partner of Moran's and one of the carefully-chosen inspectors, would admit that the group had regularly extorted cash from fuel-oil suppliers for permits and favorable tank inspections. The bulk of the money, some twenty-five hundred dollars weekly, allegedly was passed on to Moran each Friday night in the Brooklyn Council No. 1, Knights of Columbus, gymnasium. By 1949, Smith asserted, the deputy fire commissioner complained he was "pressed for campaign funds, and asked if I would push payments along a little"—one of the few verbal admissions that the money may have been passed on to O'Dwyer. Corroborated by five other inspectors, Smith's testimony would result, in 1952, in two more convictions for Moran: three years for conspiracy and twelve and one-half to twenty years for extortion.

If Moran did function as a bagman, it seems unlikely he kept much if any of the money for himself. To finance his $25,000-bail on the perjury charge, he had to put up his modest home as security; to help his family meet living expenses during his jail terms, he had to withdraw the $11,500 he had contributed over the years to his city pension fund. "I don't have anything to say to anybody," Moran told his prosecutors, who hoped the stiff sentences would make him talk. He meant it. While continuing to maintain his innocence, he refused to implicate anyone else in the charges.

3

With millions of enthralled TV viewers watching the live proceedings, former Mayor O'Dwyer, temporarily forsaking the Embassy in Mexico City, came before the Crime Committee on March 19. Housewives neglected their marketing— offering their husbands no guarantee dinners would be served on time; public officials, judges, business executives, and secretaries crowded around TV sets in clubs, bars, and offices; merchants ranging from butchers to stockbrokers to theater-owners groused about the lack of interest in their wares. Bill-O was back in New York, and he would be asked some embarassing questions.

Looking fit and tanned, and seeking to establish himself as a misunderstood man, O'Dwyer first read, at some length, a statement detailing his accomplishments in office. He told how he had improved local transportation, built new schools, modernized hospitals, sought able and honest men for the heads of city departments. "I am afraid your voice may give out," Senator Kefauver dryly observed. "It might be well to get on with our inquiry."

Why, the Committee first wanted to know, had O'Dwyer failed to prosecute Anastasia, during the Murder Inc. years, for the Morris Diamond murder? "In this state, you cannot convict any person of a crime on the unsupported evidence of a co-conspirator," he answered. "That's the principle of law that let Anastasia get away." But wasn't Reles, a non-conspirator to that crime, willing to testify against Anastasia, and hadn't O'Dwyer had Reles in custody eighteen months while neglecting to prosecute? "Anastasia was in hiding and so was his co-defendant, Parisi"—the gunman. "While you are waiting to get one murderer, you don't stop prosecuting other murderers." What about the evidence of the teenage grocery-store clerk who had seen Parisi shoot Diamond? With the two suspects at large, retorted O'Dwyer, he had felt he would endanger the young man and his family by revealing his testimony. So the interrogation went—with the former mayor turning aside questions like a clever boxer slipping punches.

Once Reles fell from his room-window while trying to escape the Half Moon Hotel, O'Dwyer stressed—and here he was eminently correct—the case against Anastasia fell apart. But Counsel Halley pointed out that O'Dwyer was down on record as saying Reles had never shown the slightest desire to escape during his stay in protective custody. Indeed, he was in fear of underworld attempts on his life. "That's true," the witness responded.

At this point, Senator Tobey could restrain himself no

longer. "One thought comes to my mind," he said. "Why did those fellows in the room with Reles"—the police guard— "throw him out the window if one witness alone would not be effective in getting an indictment?"

"Do you know they did that, Senator?" said O'Dwyer coldly.

"That is my theory."

"Do you have any facts on which to base it?"

"Only intuition and horse sense—"

"I will not answer a question based on intuition and horse sense," O'Dwyer interrupted.

Counsel Halley reminded the witness that Reles' body had been found more than twenty feet from the wall of the hotel, indicating he had not dropped straight down but had exited from the window with considerable force.

"There is some basis for Senator Tobey's theory," Halley said. "There are those who feel that a man going out that window, unless he took a running jump, could not have landed that far from the building."

"Is that your opinion?" answered O'Dwyer. "Have it that way."

In April of 1942, with Reles dead six months—O'Dwyer was again reminded—Burton Turkus, the assistant district attorney who did most of the Murder Inc. trial work, still publicly insisted that Anastasia should be indicted for the Diamond murder. Moreover, Turkus asked that redoubled efforts be made to find him. Why was nothing done?

"Turkus didn't say we had a good case against him," the former mayor replied. "He said the record of the man was so bad every effort should be made toward developing a case."

"Yet the very next month," said Halley, "James Moran ordered the removal of the wanted cards on Anastasia from the police files."

"That could have been a clerical mistake," O'Dwyer said. "It would not have been fatal to the case. After all, the police had been looking for Anastasia for a couple of years."

Whatever the truth, the Anastasia prosecution, which could have been so damaging to the Syndicate hierarchy, was tidily shelved. On June 1, O'Dwyer went into the army, leaving behind an acting district attorney, Thomas Cradock Hughes, who later testified he had been given no instructions as to how he should proceed regarding the lord high executioner. ("A man takes over, what instructions does he need?" O'Dwyer scoffed.) Nor did Jim Moran or Frank Bals, who obviously could have offered guidance, encourage Hughes to pursue the matter.

"Would you not agree," Halley asked O'Dwyer regarding the failure to indict Anastasia, "that the passage of time seriously affected the chance of success?"

"A lot of things can happen in the passage of time," the witness conceded, removing his hornrim spectacles and rubbing his eyes in the glare of the television lights.

Now the Committee brought up O'Dwyer's 1942 visit to Frank Costello's Central Park West apartment, ostensibly to pursue an army air force investigation of contract fraud at Wright Field in Dayton, Ohio.

"When you went up to Costello's home, were you in uniform?"

"I was," said O'Dwyer.

"Did Costello seem at all surprised that you were taking up army business with him?"

"I didn't notice any surprise. I had half an hour's conversation with him. Then I left."

Asked why Tammany Hall's Mike Kennedy and Bert Stand were present, as was Irving Sherman, O'Dwyer could give no reason. "They were there when I arrived."

"Why did Moran go to the apartment with you, to carry a bag or what?" interjected Senator Tobey. "Was he an errand boy, a companion, an advisor?"

"Senator," said O'Dwyer, "if the question is intended to be other than sarcastic, I will be happy to answer it."

"When you went to see Costello, you were conscious he was a gangster?" said Tobey.

"I was conscious he had a reputation as a very big bookmaker."

"It seems to me you should have said about Costello, 'Unclean, unclean!' and that you should have left him alone, as if he were a leper. But instead you trotted up to his place——"

"I had *business* with him," said O'Dwyer, thoroughly nettled. "You have bookmaking all over the country. They say there is a lot of it in your home state of New Hampshire— thirty million dollars a year."

"I have never seen it proved."

"They say that every New England bookmaker of any account spends his summers at the Breton Woods track in New Hampshire."

"Is that so?" said the reddening Tobey.

"I wonder who the bookmakers in Breton Woods support for public office in New Hampshire?" needled O'Dwyer.

"I will tell you one they do not," Tobey said, "and he is talking to you now."

"And I can tell you that you don't know who supports you," said O'Dwyer. "Because you sent to New York for money to help you in your election, and you don't know where it came from!"

"I never called anybody in New York for contributions!"

"Well, I am under oath, and you aren't."

"I will take the oath now!" shouted an outraged Tobey, while the spectators in the hearing room buzzed over the exchange. "I hate a fourflusher!"

After the chairman's gavel brought the proceedings back to order, the interrogation resumed.

"You were not embarassed [to be visiting Costello's apartment]?" O'Dwyer was asked.

"Nothing embarrasses me that happens in Manhattan."

"Why would Mike Kennedy have been at the meeting?"

"I don't know," said O'Dwyer, volunteering no more information than was necessary.

Irving Sherman, O'Dwyer admitted, subsequently had been of great help to him in his 1945-campaign.

"Did you ask him to help?"

"That was his idea."

"I think you testified before the grand jury that you would not be at all surprised to learn that Sherman had been a collector in the garment center for Costello and Adonis."

"It could be," allowed O'Dwyer.

"Did you ever get any indication that Sherman might be trying, through his friendship, to get you to go easy on bookies?"

"Not at all," the former mayor insisted, temporarily ending his testimony. By now, the strain of the day's interrogation had taken its toll: O'Dwyer's hair, earlier carefully groomed, had become dissheveled; his face was red with anger beneath the tan; the collar of his white shirt was limp with sweat. He was a man facing judgment.

Once again, Frank Costello—now choosing to testify rather than face a contempt charge—took the stand. "We are happy about the recovery of your voice," Senator Tobey told him. "Mr. Costello is happy, too," Attorney Geroge Wolf answered.

"What can you recollect about Major O'Dwyer visiting your home?" the prime minister was asked.

"He was inquiring about a fellow named Joe Baker—on a war fraud. He asked me if I had any knowledge of him— purchasing merchandise, or something. I said, 'I know Baker, but I don't know what business he is in.' Then he asked me if I had any interest in Baker's business. I told him, 'No, absolutely not.' "

"At the time of Michael Kennedy's leadership battle for control of Tammany," said Counsel Halley, establishing Kennedy's indebtedness to Costello, "you helped him subs- tantially?"

"I might have spoken to Jimmy Kelly, Frank Mancuso, Dr. Paul Sarubbi, a few others. I just don't remember."

"So you had this group of district leaders whose votes you were able to bring to bear to help elect Kennedy?"

"Yes," admitted Costello.

Halley's implication was clear to everyone in the hearing room: O'Dwyer in 1942 had paid a ritual call on the prime minister, the Syndicate's gambling boss, asking for his help in getting the 1945 Democratic mayoral nomination. Why else would Kennedy, then the head of Tammany Hall, have been present? Before the evening was over, Halley was implying, the pact with the devil had been made.

4

Back before the Committee for the second day, O'Dwyer was forced to apologize for his earlier charge that Senator Tobey had received campaign contributions from New York book- makers. For the record, Senator Kefauver stated that the money in question came from an unimpeachable source: the National Committee for an Effective Congress. "Is there anything else you have that reflects on my integrity?" a sardonic Tobey asked O'Dwyer. "Nothing anyone else running for office wouldn't admit to gladly, sir," replied the witness. "I am a poor man, and always will be," concluded Tobey, his voice trembling with emotion. "But I am willing that anything I ever did stand in the light of day."

Now O'Dwyer faced a renewed barrage of questions, all aimed at showing his tolerance, during his mayoralty, of Costello's gambling interests.

"Do you believe there was bookmaking on a large scale in New York at the time you resigned?" he was asked.

"After hearing the reports of the Harry Gross investigation in Brooklyn, it seems to me that, over there at least, bookmaking was on a large scale."

"And would you have any doubt that a large part of Frank Erickson's New Jersey operation took place in New York City?"

"I haven't the slightest idea where his operations took place," O'Dwyer demurred. "The man in City Hall, who has a good, honest police commissioner, and a good, honest chief inspector, depends upon *them!* The man in City Hall, who is dealing with hundreds of millions of dollars worth of construction, housing, health—all the things that go into running a city of eight million, cannot himself follow all the details. He depends upon his officials."

"Is it not a fact that, in 1946, you suspected a system of police payoffs by bookies?"

"Anyone who didn't suspect that is born every morning."

"Did you ever check the number of racetrack scratch sheets sold in 1946?"

"I did not."

"Well, sales reached an all-time high for New York of forty-two million five hundred fifty thousand—while in 1941 they were only twenty-three million three hundred thousand."

"We are waiting for that beautiful day," said the former mayor defensively, "when there will be a federal law to prohibit publication of scratch sheets."

O'Dwyer's police commissioner from 1946 until early 1949, it was brought out in testimony, was Arthur Wallander, a holdover from the LaGuardia years. Wallander was appointed to the department in 1914, and rose steadily through the ranks. Square-jawed and direct, he was widely regarded as incorruptible. Yet bookmaking during his police reign was flourishing. After Wallander retired in March of 1949, O'Dwyer replaced him with William P. O'Brien, still another commissioner who came up from the uniformed ranks. It was shortly afterward, through the Harry Gross investigation, that the police scandals came home to roost. O'Brien, who had originally ignored the inquiry, got the entire blame and, in September of 1950, was forced to resign.

To help fight police corruption, O'Dwyer sought to explain, he had assigned John Murtagh, his commissioner of investigation, to conduct a "running inquiry."

"What results came from that inquiry?"

"I think the Senate Committee would not be here today if the authorities in New Jersey had prosecuted on the evidence Murtagh gave to them," O'Dwyer said, begging the question.

"Let's talk about New York. Erickson had an office here. Did Mr. Murtagh ever call him in, or did you ever call him in and ask where he banked?"

"I didn't call him in at all. I took no part in law enforcement, for the reasons that I gave you. The mayor can't do that, he hasn't the time."

Counsel Halley then brought up Frank Bals's brief tenure, in 1946, as seventh deputy police commissioner.

"What did you tell Bals to do?"

"What we talked about when we were still in the district attorney's office years before—to make certain we knew every gangster in the city, his habits, his associates, and where he hung out, and to make lists of this information and have it available for th epolice department."

"He was to do nothing else?"

"That's all," said O'Dwyer, "If he had done that, it would have been splendid."

"Why did you dismiss Bals after two months?"

"Because Commissioner Wallander told me he was crossing lines, that the police inspectors in the various districts were disturbed by his activities—to the point it was affecting morale."

"Did you hear rumors that, as a result of Bals's squad being set up, the usual method of handling gamblers would be abandoned—that anyone who wanted police protection would get it from Bals?"

"This is the first time I heard that, today, from you," said O'Dwyer.

"Isn't the setting up of simple lists of gangsters an ordinary function of every police department?"

"During the Murder Inc. period, we had gangsters shooting each other in the streets for ten years, and you couldn't get a bit of information a mile away from the precinct where it happened. That is what I wanted to correct."

"Bals said he thought he was investigating bookmaking."

"That is why he didn't last. In two months' time, he was out."

When the questioning got back to his relationship with the Costello-controlled Tammany Hall machine, O'Dwyer pointed out—in his defense—that he had frequently been at odds with its leadership during his administration.

"Frank Sampson and his crowd came to me and they said, 'A handful at the Hall [Ed Loughlin, Clarence Neal, Bert Stand] are controlling all the patronage for themselves. They aren't giving us anything and we're fighting in our districts to stay alive.' I listened to Sampson and I said, 'How about getting rid of them?' And he said, 'It's impossible. They keep themselves in power with synthetic votes—nonentities they control.' That was about June of 1946. So I shut off all patronage. And as a result Sampson, that year I think, was elected Tammany's leader."

What O'Dwyer refused to admit was that, while his mayoral confrontations with Tammany often resulted in cosmetic changes in its leadership, the Costello loyalists in the machine remained entrenched, continually resurfacing to dominate the city's political and law-enforcement structure. O'Dwyer had, of course, been in the army when Magistrate Thomas Aurelio made his 1943 (wire-tapped) phone call to Costello, thanking him for getting the jurist a State Supreme Court nomination. But the former mayor did admit knowing that when Aurelio ended that conversation with the remark Costello now "must do something for Joe"—he was referring to Joseph Loscalzo. After he took office, one of O'Dwyer's first acts was his appointment of Loscalzo as a Special Sessions justice.

"Did Costello have any part in that?"

"Nothing whatsoever," O'Dwyer replied. "Mr. Loscalzo

was the first assistant district attorney in Queens for years and years, and highly recommended by the Bar Association."

"I am sure of that," said Counsel Halley. "I was just wondering whether Costello put his touch on the recommendation?"

"He did not."

Among the other mob-connected appointments made by O'Dwyer, however innocently, as revealed by his testimony:

- *Lawrence Austin,* a cousin of Irving Sherman's, was named city marshall.

- *Philip Zichello,* a brother-in-law of Willie Moretti's, became deputy commissioner of hospitals.

- *Abe Rosenthal,* a district-leader crony of Costello's, was tapped as assistant corporation counsel.

- *Frank Quayle,* a longtime friend of Adonis', became fire commissioner.

By the time O'Dwyer left the witness stand, it was obvious he had not adequately refuted the implied charges against him—circumstantial though most of them were. "O'Dwyer Draws Inquiry's Fire—Admits He Placed Gangsters' Friends in City Jobs" read the headlines. From the White House, there was no word as to how the furor would affect his status as ambassador to Mexico. But there was no doubt, in Democratic circles, O'Dwyer was becoming something of a pariah. "President Truman reads the papers every day," volunteered a White House spokesman.

One more bombshell was yet to come. On March 21, the last day of the hearings, John P. Crane, head of the Uniformed Firemen's Association, testified he had paid $55,000 of his organization's money to Moran, and $10,000 more directly to

O'Dwyer. The union leader was being forced to account, overall, for $135,000 he had withdrawn from the UFA's treasury—presumably to win political support for wage increases and work benefits.

The payments to Moran, Crane stated, were in cash. They had been made privately, over a period of time, in the deputy fire commissioner's office: $5,000 in 1946; $30,000 in five payments in 1947; $20,000 in 1949.

"This fifty-five thousand dollars was used to buy Mr. Moran's support for uniformed firemen?" asked Senator Tobey.

"There was never any indication I had to buy Mr. Moran's support," Crane said. "But when I find a man like him, whose influence is such that a word can help or hurt us, I want him on my side. I was getting his help, and I wanted to keep on getting it."

Though the accusation was uncorroborated, its impact moved Vincent Impellitteri, who had succeeded O'Dwyer in the mayoralty, to take prompt action. Within twenty-four hours, he demanded—and got—the silent Moran's resignation from his sinecure post with the Board of Water Supply.

But it was the alleged ten thousand dollar-payment to O'Dwyer, supposedly made in 1949, that caused the loudest stir in the hearing room. The mayor, as Crane related the story, had early in the year reneged on a committment to the firemen for a salary increase and a shorter work-week. As a result, the union had announced it would oppose his candidacy in the upcoming election. By June of 1949, however, with O'Dwyer all but certain of re-election, Crane sought to patch up the quarrel.

This was not easily accomplished. Because of the UFA's previous stand, Crane explained, "at the very mention of firemen's legislation, O'Dwyer would get hysteric. He would not even talk to me." At the yearly ceremony honoring firemen killed in line of duty, "accepting medals out of my hands to pin them on the widows, he wouldn't even look at me." So the union leader went to Moran, asking him to "reinstate the organization in the mayor's good graces."

An appointment with O'Dwyer was arranged, Crane testified, and sometime in August he went up to Gracie Mansion to see him.

"Were you alone with him?"

"Yes, sir. On the porch of the Mansion. I promised the mayor the backing of the firemen, and I offered him some evidence of that support—in the form of ten thousand dollars. It was in cash, in a manila envelope."

"Did he say anything?"

"He thanked me. He didn't look in the envelope, or do anything else."

O'Dwyer was not in the hearing room when Crane made his charges. Reached later by reporters, he said he would not dignify the allegations with a comment. "I was not questioned about them during my testimony," he said frostily, his jaw set in anger. "I won't expand on them now."

PART SIX

1952-1973:
Aftermath

1

IN THE WAKE of the Crime Committee hearings, John Crane's charge that O'Dwyer had accepted ten thousand dollars from his hands was soon forgotten: apparently the necessary corroboration to bring about an indictment was lacking. Crane himself was not so fortunate. A fireman for fifteen years, he had already been dismissed from the department for refusing to waive immunity before the grand jury investigating his activities. Now he was forced to resign the presidency of the Uniformed Firemen's Association and, though the UFA temporarily kept paying him his salary out of union funds, it ceased doing so in 1953. As a final blow, he lost his pension rights.

Unlike the Crane case, the Harry Gross investigation—

Brooklyn's attempt to break the alliance between law-enforcement officials and organized crime—was to stay in the headlines for several years. The first courtroom confrontation, which took place six months after the Kefauver hearings, seemed a victory for the underworld. Brooklyn District Attorney Miles McDonald, who had previously convicted a score of Gross's underlings, thought he had struck a bargain with the chunky, bright-eyed Boss Bookie: Gross, in exchange for a light sentence, would identify the policemen who had taken his bribes. Accordingly, McDonald brought to trial eighteen cops—the first batch of many—against whom Gross would be the star witness. But when the Syndicate gambler took the stand, he surprisingly announced he would not answer "any more questions in this or any other case." Obviously, he felt the mob's penalties would be more severe than the law's.

"Your silence will be deemed a refusal to answer. The court holds you in contempt," ruled the enraged judge, Samuel Leibowitz.

"Why don't you just give me the chair and get it over with?" replied Gross.

"Face around, Mr. Gross," said Leibowitz, pounding his gavel. "You are not at a racetrack now."

"I wish I was."

"Do you want to name them?" said the judge, meaning the persons unknown he presumed had threatened the witness. "If you say no, we will go on to something else."

"Let's go to lunch," deadpanned the gambler.

Gross's change of heart had been induced by his Syndicate masters. Just before the trial began, even though he was in protective custody, he had eluded his police guard for twenty-four hours, eventually turning up at the Atlantic City racetrack. "I just wanted to walk in the sun," he explained. During that period, Gross, a man who spent $6,000 a year for his clothes, had worked out a deal with the Syndicate. He would take the rap, and in turn would be guaranteed a sum of money —perhaps as much as $150,000—for his silence.

Without Gross's testimony, Judge Leibowitz had no choice but to dismiss the indictments against the police defendants. Twenty months of Miles McDonald's efforts apparently had gone for naught. He wept openly in the courtroom, while Gross and the newly-freed defendants, smiling and laughing, gave each other and their attorneys congratulatory handshakes.

The joy was short-lived. A week later, Gross—who had expected a sentence of only four years—was walloped with a penalty of twelve years on Riker's Island. "There is not a shred of legality in this action," screamed his attorney, Michael Kern, meaning it was excessively punitive. In arguing against the sentence, Kern claimed his client had been greatly upset, shortly before giving his testimony, when his six-year-old son, Mickey, had fired a shot from a police revolver at his four-year-old sister. "Gross was visiting his wife and children," Kern said, "and the children had observed the police holstering and unholstering their revolvers. The Grosses asked the policemen to put their revolvers up on something high—out of sight. But Mickey climbed up on some chairs, got one revolver, pointed it at his sister's head and fired. The bullet narrowly missed the little girl.

"Both Gross and his wife were overwrought by this happening," Kern explained.

District Attorney McDonald confirmed that the incident had indeed taken place—which made a number of people, including McDonald, wonder how seriously the police were guarding the star witness. He added that the careless policeman had been promptly dismissed from his staff. Nonetheless, the district attorney was not inclined to reduce Gross' sentence—unless he talked.

With this legal intransigence in mind, a now-worried Gross began to have second thoughts about his defiance. First, he tested the waters by claiming that there had been a "bookie's fund," in 1945 and 1949, that had contributed to Bill O'Dwyer's election campaigns. The "collector," he said, had been James Moran. Then, between May and October of 1952, even as scores of policemen were undergoing departmental trials, Gross began to name names in court—starting at the top. At one point, when identifying a group of 120 officers to whom he had paid protection, he said he had an "arrangement," in 1943 and 1944, with ex-Police Commissioner William P. O'Brien, when the latter was an inspector in the Nineteenth Division. He had paid O'Brien, the gambler said, fifty dollars monthly for each horse-parlor he operated in the division. Subsequently, in 1947, when O'Brien was an assistant chief inspector in charge of Manhattan West, he had paid him similar sums of money.

Reached for comment, O'Brien, who had resigned the police commissioner's post one week after Gross's arrest in 1950, branded the charge "an absolute lie." He had "never laid eyes on Gross," he insisted, until he had seen him in court after the investigation started.

Later Gross testified he had also made regular payoffs to Frank Bals, who in 1946 was in charge of what the gambler referred to as "the mayor's squad," to former Chief of Detectives Richard T. Whalen, to former Chief Inspector August Flath.

"You said you paid Flath two hundred dollars a location?" Gross was asked.

"Yes," the gambler replied. "And I gave him a suit of

clothes, too. And I was under oath when I said that. Any time he wants to come in here and deny it"—under oath—"he can do so."

Few of the scores of policemen named by Gross were willing to challenge his testimony—self-serving though it may have been in many cases—in a criminal courtroom. Most of the officers took early retirement, were dismissed from the force in departmental trials, or were transferred to other commands. Some even served prison sentences. As for the gambler, his belated cooperation did win him one concession: his twelve-year sentence, in October of 1953, was reduced to an eight-year term. Rampant Syndicate bookmaking in New York, temporarily at least, had received a significant setback.

Now Vito Genovese, taking advantage of Costello's weakened authority and beleaguered state after the Crime Committee hearings, became more and more aggressive in his ambitions. In a sense, Vito was a throwback to the old "Mustache Petes"—not for him Costello's use of violence only as a last resort. He had long resented the fact that Thomas E. Dewey's 1937 investigation of the murder of Ferdinand "the Shadow" Boccia had forced him to flee to Europe, thus allowing Costello to become Luciano's heir. What better time, Genovese thought, to begin a campaign to depose the prime minister. Not content with just a share of the Eastern rackets, he was obsessed with dominating the Syndicate. Cautiously, he made his first move against Willie Moretti, Costello's longtime friend.

Since the Kefauver hearings had finally prodded the New Jersey authorities to convict Joe Adonis on a two-to-three-year gambling charge, and since Willie's brother Solly had been similarly convicted, Moretti suddenly became vulnerable. Moreover, Genovese was able to use the argument, with many of the Syndicate bosses, that the talkativeness caused by Willie's syphilitic brain condition was making him too dangerous.

"Vito is like a fox," an informer would comment. "He takes his time. What Vito says is that Frank Costello [Moretti's protector] is right about a lot of things but he is wrong about this. He says he is sad about Willie and that it ain't his fault. Willie is just sick in the head, but if he is allowed to keep talking, he is going to get us all in a jam. . . . This ain't making Frank Costello look any too good."

On October 4, 1951, just six days before he was to appear before a New Jersey grand jury, the fifty-seven-year-old Moretti traveled by cream-colored Packard convertible to Joe's Restaurant in Cliffside Park—opposite the Palisades Amusement Park. He had taken to hanging out there after the law had closed down Duke's Place. It was about 11:30 A.M.— too early for the luncheon crowd, a waitress remembered— but four men, all apparently Italian and in their fifties, had been waiting in the deserted restaurant for some time, dawdling over orange juice and coffee. When Moretti's Packard pulled up outside, one of the men, tentatively identified as John Robilotto, rushed out to the sidewalk and greeted him effusively. Inside the restaurant, more friendly greetings were exchanged, with the group talking in Italian.

Seconds after the waitress went into the kitchen for silverware and menus, shots rang out in the dining room. By the time she and the kitchen staff peered through the swinging doors, the four men had disappeared and the dead Moretti lay on the tiled floor, with two bullets in his skull. His red tie was twisted about his neck, one hand was clutching his chest, a pool of blood spread around his head and shoulders. Detectives later found $1,850 in cash in his pockets, and a newspaper clipping of a radio broadcast he had made in which he said:

"Old gamblers never die—they just fade and fade and fade."

From the outset, the police could not have been more uninterested in solving the crime. October 4 was the opening day of the World Series, with Leo Durocher's New York Giants playing the Yankees at the Stadium, and all afternoon, while Willie's body stayed on the floor, detectives vied with each other to watch the game on a nearby television screen. "Willie was almost ignored," said a reporter. "What I remember most is the police rushing back and forth, telling each other the score of the ball game." Though Robilotto was indicted for the murder in June of 1952, the charge was later dropped for lack of sufficient evidence—when key witnesses became less certain of their identification of him.

But Genovese and the Syndicate made up for the inattention with a lavish funeral. "Moretti had a hell of a funeral, lots and lots of cars and flowers," a mobster commented. "It was sort of, as we put it, a mercy killing, as he was sick."

Costello had little time to mourn the passing of his one-time East Harlem paisan. Post-Kefauver, the authorities were pursuing him on three legal fronts: contempt of the Crime Committee, tax evasion, and deportation.

First came the contempt of the Senate charge, with Attorney Wolf basing his defense of Costello's evasiveness on the argument that his client had been singled out for unfair treatment. The first trial ended in a hung jury, but the second resulted in an eighteen-month sentence and, in August of 1952, Costello—for the first time in thirty-seven years—saw the inside of a jail cell. He was released in October of 1953.

Meanwhile, the Internal Revenue Service was scrutinizing his expenditures, trying to prove that his declared income could not possibly justify his standard of living. The IRS painstakingly toted up the bills he had paid for his suits ($350 custom-made); for his wife's frocks ($600 apiece at Hattie

Carnegie); for nightclubs, restaurants, and hotels ("only the best," commented an admiring agent); for flowers ($2000 yearly); even for a mausoleum (some $23,000). Then, in April of 1954, the government brought the case to trial. Some 144 witnesses were called, some five hundred documents produced. At one point, Costello's attorney, worried about the effect his client's expensive tailoring was having on the jury, suggested he start wearing cheap suits. "I'd rather blow the god-damned case," Frank answered.

Another conviction—this one for five years—quickly resulted. "This is a political thing," Costello told reporters. "A lot of guys trying to get ahead by climbing on my back." Then he added, "I want to give you fellows some advice. When you spend money, spend cash. If your wife has any money, have her declare it right away. Otherwise they will be after you."

For the next two years, the case went through appeals—but to no avail. In May of 1956, Costello began to serve his sentence in the federal penitentiary in Atlanta. Then he hired a new lawyer, the redoubtable Edward Bennett Williams, who temporarily secured his release, after serving eleven months, on the contention most of the evidence against him had been gathered illegally. While the case slowly went up to the Supreme Court, Costello resumed his normal life-style: mornings at the Waldorf barber shop, afternoons with Syndicate cronies, evenings at L'Aiglon. But ultimately Williams' gambit failed and, in October of 1958, he was sent back to Atlanta. He was not released until June of 1961.

The deportation proceedings against Costello, which began in 1956, proved a see-saw battle: Initially the government failed; the Supreme Court ruling the prosecution's case was sullied by illegal wire-tap evidence. On the second go-round, the government won—basing its argument on the grounds that Costello, during his 1925 naturalization hearings, had hidden his bootlegging activities. But Justice William O. Douglas dissented, saying that bootlegging in the 1920s was not sufficient reason to deny a petitioner his citizenship. "If it were, it would be an act of hypocrasy unparalleled in American life . . . the bootlegger in those days came into being because of the demand of the great bulk of the people for his products." Seizing on the dissent, Attorney Williams plied still further legal strategems. Finally, on the third go-round, Costello won, the Supreme Court in 1961 ruling that the deportation order—no matter how valid the facts on which it was based—should not be enforced. The prime minister would live out his remaining years in the United States.

2

Despite the harsh criticism he had received before the Crime Committee, Bill O'Dwyer afterward returned to Mexico City, where he resumed his ambassadorial duties. It was clear he felt he could count on Harry Truman's understanding, and in this supposition he was correct. Indeed, he would resign his ambassadorship only in December of 1952, amid the State Department's general diplomatic house-cleaning to make way for the Republican appointments of newly-elected President Dwight D. Eisenhower. Meanwhile, O'Dwyer threw open the embassy's hitherto-exclusive Fourth of July parties to all away-from-home Americans ("I put ads in the papers. The parties spread good will"); visited every part of Mexico by plane or by car; cemented his friendships with the various members of the diplomatic community.

On a personal level, however, O'Dwyer's marriage was coming apart. Sloan's energy and enthusiasms were becoming too much for a man twenty-six years her senior: she gave gay parties that often lasted until 5 A.M., taught herself to play the guitar and sing Spanish songs, took bull-fighting lessons, sped over the water at Acapulco on water skis. Increasingly, O'Dwyer left parties early, or stayed home altogether, while his wife enjoyed the chic life. Inevitably, he became jealous of her male friends. "If I shook hands with a man at the door," Sloan would say, "Bill would accuse me of holding his hand too long." Whether the suspicions were real or imaginary, O'Dwyer spent more and more time in the embassy in Mexico City, his wife stayed for longer and longer periods in Acapulco.

Just after the sixty-two-year-old O'Dwyer's resignation from the ambassadorship, Sloan left him and returned to New York. Soon afterward, they were divorced. "She couldn't endure the jealous tirades, so she sought escape in swimming and golfing," a friend of Sloan's would say of the break-up. "None of the rumors about Sloan and other men were justified."

Sloan Simpson spent most of 1953 in Spain with her mother, supported by a five-hundred-dollar-monthly-check from O'Dwyer. The next year, back in New York, she began a daily radio-interview show on the Mutual Network—interviewing celebrities ranging from then-Vice President Richard Nixon to Stripper Gypsy Rose Lee. Generously, she waived her right to half of her ex-husband's twelve-thousand-dollar-annual mayoral pension. "There are no children," she explained. "It would be unfair of me to take part of his pension." For the last two decades, she has pursued various successful careers, apparently never looking back. "I think I have been accepted as Sloan Simpson," she once remarked, "and not just as the former Mrs. O'Dwyer." Currently, she again resides in Acapulco, where she is in charge of special promotions for Braniff International Airlines. "Sloan's a beautiful kid," O'Dwyer came to reflect after their divorce, "but she came into my life too late."

For some eight years after leaving diplomatic service, O'Dwyer continued to live in Mexico City—acting as a consultant for O'Dwyer, Bernstein & Correa, the law firm in which his brother Paul was a partner. There he resided in a three-room penthouse atop the small but elegant Prince Hotel, just off the capital's main boulevard and near his office. ("I keep a neat desk down there—no papers. I never kept papers on my desk at City Hall, either.") For much of that time, a non-English-speaking houseman-cook named Pishta tended to his domestic needs.

"Tell my friend your one English sentence," O'Dwyer once said to Pishta while entertaining a friend.

"Shaddup, bay-bee," said the houseman, retreating to the kitchen.

O'Dwyer's health returned to him in Mexico, as did his good humor. A visitor, sharing a Scotch highball with him, would find it hard to believe the Crime Committee hearings had taken place, as the former mayor chuckled over the problems he had encountered in City Hall. On municipal workers: "They wanted a thirty-three-and-a-third-percent raise. The city is more than unions, after all, so the idea was dropped." On taxes: "Whenever the real estate tax is about to be jacked up, someone organizes the homeowners of Queens, a borough of retired Tammany politicians." On political dinners: "I'd eat at home, and have the cops phone me from the Waldorf at the end of the second course, and then I'd zip down."

O'Dwyer's was a comfortable retirement. He would not return to New York permanently until 1960. But the sentiment he felt for the city he had governed remained with him in exile. "Great stuff, that record," he would say, putting an album called "Show Biz" on the phonograph. "Lots of lovely, dirty, naughty New York in that record." And then he would hum, "I'm living . . . up in the clouds . . . chasing . . . a rainbow of a girl. . . ."

For James J. Moran, however, the post-Kefauver years were not nearly so pleasant. Besides the three convictions for perjury (5 years), conspiracy (3 years) and extortion (12 1/2 to 25 years), he found himself accused in 1955, even while serving the extortion sentence, of tax evasion. The federal government declared that he had failed to pay $131,037 on his 1948–49–50 income, which it figured at $297,960. "This is another unholy step in a campaign of persecution," Moran burst out emotionally when he heard the charge. "I'm innocent. I never received that money. I don't owe any taxes. I'm broke." But at his trial he stood mute; he did not take the stand; he called no witnesses. Found guilty, he was sentenced to two more years in prison.

During this last trial, Moran's wife broke down in tears. "I have eaten dirt for three and a half years," she sobbed. But later, as calm and resolute as her husband, she told reporters, "The Moran family accepts its blessings and bears its cross with dignity."

All through his prison years, Moran kept his silence—refusing to name anyone higher-up who might have profited from the huge sums that supposedly passed through his hands. In 1961, while ending one sentence only to begin another, he gave a rare interview to the New York *Herald-Tribune.* "Over nine years in prison, that's a long haul," he said. Now his children were grown—the two boys had even earned their law degrees. "The important thing was to send both boys through college," he said.

"How did they manage?" he was asked.

"I cashed in my insurance, and they worked."

Then he reminisced about a visit he had received from District Attorney Frank Hogan in 1952, while in the Tombs awaiting sentencing on the extortion conviction. Hogan had offered him a lighter sentence, Moran said, if he would name the person or persons to whom he had passed on the money.

"You're breaking the law," Moran remembered telling the district attorney. "I didn't send for you. You can only come and see me when I send for you. I have nothing to say."

"What happened next?" Moran was asked.

"I said to Hogan, 'I came into this world a man, and I'm going out a man.' Hogan turned around and walked out."

"Did you ever hear from O'Dwyer all the time you were away?" the reporter asked.

Moran looked squarely into the eyes of his questioner.

"No," he said, "O'Dwyer had nothing to do with this."

In 1962, the sixty-year-old Moran eventually won parole. "What can an old man with a record do?" he said, when asked about his future plans. "He can't even go to work on the docks any more." But the self-pity did not last long—Moran was made of sterner stuff. He soon enrolled in adult education courses, seeking the college degree he prized so highly, and he took a job as a legal stenographer—ironically, the same sort of work he had been doing more than thirty years before— in the law office of one of his sons. In 1966, while he was riding to work on the subway, accompanied by his wife, he collapsed and died of a heart attack.

"The mystery of Jim Moran's silence remains," the New York *Sunday News* reflected. "You don't know whether to admire him for stubborn loyalty or shake him for being a chump."

3

Of all the years that followed the Kefauver inquiry, 1957 was the watershed—the year the prime minister's leadership of the Syndicate was lost, and temporarily assumed by Vito Genovese. The reasons for the change were many. Not only was the sixty-six-year-old Costello preoccupied with his tax and deportation battles, but he had lost the support of Joe Adonis and Meyer Lansky, his longtime allies.

In early 1956, the fifty-four-year-old Adonis—himself harassed by tax and immigration authorities, had voluntarily agreed to leave the United States for Italy, thus effectively removing him from the day-by-day operations of the Syndicate. He sailed aboard the Conte Biancamano, in the liner's most luxurious suite, and settled in Milan, studiously avoiding all contact with Lucky Luciano in Naples. Soon afterward, when the two men did secretly meet, they were concerned with their own financial well-being, not with Costello: while they both retained great respect in the American underworld, and received regular income from the rackets, they knew they could no longer pull strings and make Genovese hop.

Meyer Lansky, of course, was more of a Syndicate power than ever: he was the Controller—the man who kept the books, deciding which chieftains profited, and to what extent, from gambling, narcotics and the like. But Lansky sensed that the raw vitality of Genovese was dictating a change. Moreover, he was disenchanted with Costello's enforcer, Albert

Anastasia, who was trying to move into the Florida and Cuban gambling that was Meyer's special preserve.

Aware that his power base was eroding, Costello himself initiated the idea that he step down, suggesting to the Syndicate's directors that he be allowed to retire. He asked only that he continue to receive the income from some selected gambling and realty interests. Most of the prime minister's colleagues thought this a reasonable proposal. "Frank should have the right to live in peace after all he's done for everybody," Lansky was reported to have said.

But Genovese, emboldened by his earlier success in eliminating Moretti, wanted blood. Costello alive, even in retirement, in Vito's mind still stood in the way of his boss-of-all bosses ambition. On the night of May 2, 1957, with Costello just a few weeks out of the federal penitentiary on appeal from his tax conviction, Vito set his murder plan in motion.

That evening, Costello, with a group of friends, dined at L'Aiglon. Despite the prison sentence hanging over him, he was in a jovial mood: the previous night, he had won heavily on the Sugar Ray Robinson-Gene Fullmer middleweight fight, which the aging Robinson, a three-to-one underdog, had won by a knockout. He left the table only once, to make a phone call to one of his lawyers. Afterward, the group went on to nearby Monsignore, where they listened to the strolling musicians. About 10:45, Costello excused himself, saying he had to take a call at his home from Edward Bennett Williams regarding his case. Phil Kennedy, a hanger-on, accompanied him. The rest of the party stayed behind.

Some ten minutes later, as Costello's cab stopped outside his Central Park West apartment house, a black Cadillac quickly pulled up behind it. Vincent "the Chin" Gigante, a three hundred-pound, non-too-bright Genovese henchman, managed to get out of the Cadillac so quickly he was able to precede Costello into the lobby. Kennedy, meanwhile, stayed in the cab, giving the driver directions to his own apartment.

As the prime minister approached the elevator, Gigante stepped from behind a pillar, shouted "This is for you, Frank," and pulled the trigger of a .38 caliber revolver. Hearing the words, Costello instinctively turned his head toward his assailant, and the sudden movement probably saved his life. The bullet cut open the right side of his scalp, just above the ear, but did no real damage. Gigante ran back to the Cadillac, thinking his victim dead, while Costello slumped to the lobby floor, bleeding profusely from the flesh wound.

Kennedy was only a block away, the cab stopped for a red light, when he heard the shot. Running back to the apartment house, he found both Costello and the doorman in a state of shock, the gunman gone. He rushed the wounded man to the emergency room at Roosevelt Hospital, where the necessary repairs were quickly made, and the gambler began to recover his composure. Then the police arrived.

"I didn't see no one," Costello maintained, keeping the gangland code. "I don't know who could have done it. I don't have an enemy in the world."

"Whoever this guy was," one detective observed, "he had a very strange way of showing his friendship."

When the police went through Costello's pockets, they found a slip of paper that read, in part: "Gross casino wins as of 4/26/57—$651,284. Casino wins less markers—$434,695. Slot wins—$62,844. Markers—$153,745." Later, they discovered that these totals exactly matched the reported gambling "take" at the Tropicana Hotel in Las Vegas, where—since Nevada law forbade a convicted felon from holding a license —Costello was forced to be a silent partner. For refusing to answer any questions about the paper, or how he came by it, he eventually served fifteen days on Riker's Island.

The case against Gigante, who had been identified by the doorman from police files, did not come to trial until July. By that time, the hulking assailant's appearance had been considerably altered—the result of a crash diet—and the doorman could no longer make a positive identification. More importantly, Costello still maintained his silence, and the jury had no choice but to vote for acquital. After the verdict was announced, Gigante walked over to Costello in the courtroom, stuck out his hand, and incongruously addressed him a second time. "Thanks, Frank," he said.

Costello's attitude about his brush with death was curiously fatalistic: he wished the incident would be forgotten; certainly he had no desire to retaliate. But Genovese did not know this, or could not believe it, and so he moved against Anastasia, with whom he had long quarreled. After all, in underworld circles, Albert's reputation was even more bloodthirsty than Vito's—since Murder Inc. days, he had been the lord high executioner. Sometimes, Anastasia would kill seemingly without reason. So enraged had he been in 1953, for instance, when a young Brooklyn clothing salesman named Arnold Schuster turned bank robber Willie Sutton in to the law, that he had ordered Schuster's murder. "I hate squealers," he is reported to have shouted, as he watched the unlucky Schuster accepting congratulations on TV for his good citizenship.

On the morning of October 25, 1957, Anastasia entered the barber shop of the Park-Sheraton Hotel in Manhattan, took his usual chair number four and settled back for a trim and a shave. While he was relaxing under a hot towel, his bodyguard conveniently left on an errand, and two men with scarfs over their faces and revolvers in their hands walked into the shop, stepped right up to his chair, and fired a volley of shots. Only seconds elapsed from the time they entered the shop to the instant Anastasia staggered out of the chair, pro-pelled forward by the force of the bullets. As more shots hit him, he spun around, crashed backward into the reflecting mirror, and slumped dead to the floor amid a cascade of hair-tonic bottles.

While the barbers still stood transfixed with horror, star-ing at the bullet-riddled Anastasia, the two men were already out the door, striding rapidly to a nearby subway to make their getaway. Later, informers would say the killing had been actually done by Joseph "Crazy Joey" Gallo, whose Greenwich Village mobsters were gaining the reputation, ironically, of the Murder Inc. of the 1950s. Five men including Gallo were supposedly involved—three being back-ups. "You can just call us the Barber Shop Quintet," Joey supposedly had boasted.

Within mere weeks, Genovese attempted to solidify his control of the Syndicate by calling the now-famous gangland meeting in rural Apalachin, New York. On November 24, perhaps a hundred limousines made their stately way up the winding driveway to the hilltop estate of Buffalo mobster Joseph Barbara, the gathering's nominal host. Few of the still-living Syndicate founders attended: Costello was excused for obvious reasons, Luciano and Adonis remained brooding in Italy, the wily Lansky pleaded laryngitis, saying that leav-ing Florida in November "would be too risky for his health." But most of the board members of the late fifties were at Apalachin: Joe Profaci and Joseph "Joe Bananas" Bonanno from New York City; Stefano Magaddino from Buffalo; Joe Ida from Philadelphia; John Scalise from Cleveland; Sam Giancana from Chicago and Frankie Zito from southern Illi-nois; Joe Zerilli from Detroit; Louis Trafficante from Florida; Jimmy Civello from Dallas; Frank DeSimone from Los An-geles; and James Lanza from San Francisco. On the meeting's agenda were serious items: Genovese would be justifying his attacks on Costello and Anastasia; a decision was needed on whether to get out of narcotics, leaving the field to Blacks and Hispanics (the public had accepted bootlegging and gambling, but was drawing the line at heroin); guarantees of loyalty would have to be reaffirmed.

These items were never to be raised. The sixty-year-old Genovese, with final victory in his grasp, saw his boss-of-all-bosses triumph slip away in the midst of an appalling gangland fiasco. A New York State Police sergeant named Edgar Crosswell, who had noted the influx of dark-suited gentlemen and out-of-state limousines into the quiet hamlet, allowed the Syndicate leaders to enter the Barbara estate, then set up roadblocks around it. The meeting had barely begun before the police were noticed, sending the top men in the American underworld into inexplicable panic—for the state troopers, it turned out, had no real grounds on which to arrest them. In pin-stripes and pointed-toed shoes, the mobsters scurried out of back doors and leapt from windows, crashed through underbrush, and attempted to climb fences. Some got away, but more than sixty were rounded up.

Genovese's ambitions did not survive Apalachin. Though he remained a power in the Syndicate, the other leaders felt, resentfully, that he had been to blame for their humiliation. "If soldiers got arrested in a meet like that," a button-man would explain, "you can imagine what the bosses would have done. There they are, running through the woods like rabbits. Who are they kidding when they say we got to respect them?"

But worse was in store for Genovese. Prodded by the Apalachin publicity, the federal government within eighteen months brought a major narcotics case against him and some two dozen others. A minor Puerto Rican criminal, Nelson Cantelops, already in Sing Sing on a drug charge, agreed to testify against Vito in exchange for his freedom. The jury believed Cantelops and, in the spring of 1959, Genovese was convicted, given a fifteen-year sentence, and sent to the federal penitentiary in Atlanta. In his cell, though he continued to direct his "family" interests, he was a killer caged. It was in Atlanta, mob sources say, that he eventually struck a truce with Costello, who had been returned there to finish his tax sentence. The prime minister was released in mid-1961, but Genovese remained in prison, where in 1969 he died.

4

Now the ranks of the players—great and small—in the original Luciano-Costello Syndicate were thinning. Abner "Longy" Zwillman, the last of the Adonis-Moretti-Zwillman axis that for so long dominated New Jersey, was hounded for back taxes through most of the 1950s. So severe was the pressure, and so large the sum of money demanded—perhaps as much as seven hundred thousand dollars—that it was rumored he might make a deal with the law by exposing Syndicate inroads into legitimate businesses. On February 27, 1959, he was found dead in a storage closet in the basement of his West Orange, New Jersey, mansion, a forty-foot electric-light cord twisted about his neck. The police ruled it suicide, a surprising verdict considering that Zwillman, whose hands were tied with wire, would have had to throw one end of the cord around an overhead beam, then hold it taut until he suffocated. There are easier ways of hanging oneself. Among the other passings:

• *Irving Sherman,* Hungarian-born, sixty-two years old in 1959, his health broken and his onetime 220-pound weight down to 140, sobbed openly in a New York court when he was sentenced to thirty days for failing to register as an alien. His lawyer asked for "compassion for this old man."

• *Dandy Phil Kastel,* who in addition to his gambling responsibilities in Louisiana ran the Tropicana Hotel in Las Vegas for Costello, was found in 1962 slumped in a chair in his plush New Orleans apartment, a pistol on the floor beside his dead body and a single bullet in his head. He was sixty-eight years old, and gangland friends explained he had been recently "depressed by ill health."

• *Virginia Hill,* whom the obituary writers termed "once gangland's girl friend," was found dead in 1966, the victim of an apparent drug overdose, on a footpath near the peaceful village of Koppl, Austria. She was forty-nine, and had been living in Austria, with her skiing-instructor husband, for the last dozen years.

• *Frank Erickson* died at seventy two years old in early 1968 of bleeding ulcers, complicated by a heart ailment, as he was about to undergo surgery. Erickson, who in 1954 had paid New York State $327,881 in back taxes, maintained in post-Kefauver years his income was derived from "wise investments."

But still alive, as of early 1980, is seventy-eight-year-old Meyer Lansky, the not-so-grand old man of crime. All through the 1950s, he developed Syndicate gambling operations in Florida, Las Vegas, and Cuba. As the decade drew to a close and Fidel Castro's revolutionaries threw out Fulgencio

Batista, the far-sighted Lansky decided to move his gaming tables into the Bahamas. During the 1960s, he was interested almost exclusively in legal gambling, forming Syndicate connections with relatively younger men whose origins were not in the turbulent Prohibition era. Like Lansky himself, his new financial associates were quiet, astute, almost respectable. By January of 1964, with myriad real estate and construction fortunes already secured by all concerned, the first of Lansky's Bahamian casinos was open and flourishing. From there, it was all but inevitable that legal gambling would spread through the Caribbean.

In 1969, Lansky was back in Florida, where he maintained a home near Gulfstream Park for his second wife, Teddie, a former barber-shop manicurist. There he directed a political campaign for legalizing gambling in Miami Beach, which was defeated in a referendum only by a sixty to forty margin. About this time, amazingly enough, he was also arrested (and soon after acquitted) on an almost-laughable charge of illegal possession of barbiturates (they were phenobarbital pills—prescribed for a persistent ulcer).

In July of 1970, perhaps offended that he, a man who wrote million-dollar drafts on Swiss banks the way ordinary citizens use their checking accounts, should have been inconvenienced by the law, Lansky moved with his wife to Israel. From his Tel Aviv base, in the posh Dan Hotel, he intended to supervise his world-wide hotel-gambling casino empire. Nonetheless, his plans went awry. Pressured by various journalistic exposes, the United States government finally took some meaningful action against Lansky. First, he was subpoenaed to appear before a federal grand jury, in March of 1971, in Miami. When he did not appear, he was cited for contempt. Some weeks later, the IRS indicted him, along with several owners of record, for "skimming" $36 million from the Flamingo Hotel in Las Vegas during the years 1960–67, and evading taxes on the money. This was just one casino: the implication was that hundreds of millions more had been skimmed from other mob-controlled establishments in Nevada and the Caribbean.

In the midst of the controversy, Lansky appeared completely calm. An Israeli journalist, assigned to write about the émigré, reported that his only "regular activity is a daily walk with his dog between 6:30 and 7 A.M." But Israel itself was rent by controversy regarding the visitor. Wrote *Newsweek:* "As some Israeli officials see it, Lansky is a harmless old man whose last criminal conviction was for a Prohibition violation forty years ago. To many critics in the press, however, the government's stance appears to be motivated by self-interest. Each year, Lansky and his underworld associates pour vast sums into Israeli bonds and philanthropies." For months, the government's decision as to what to do with Lansky hung in the balance. Finally, in September of 1972, the Israeli Supreme Court ruled he had to be expelled, and two months later he was deported.

For the remainder of the 1970s, Lansky has lived in Miami, staving off the United States contempt and tax charges against him. In 1975, one federal judge declared that the tax indictment "will lie dormant on the calendar until either the defendant dies or government counsel acts responsibly and dismisses the indictment." Replied an irate justice department official: "The judge refused to dismiss the case. If he didn't bite the bullet, why should we?" So Lansky's storied luck has held—all through his eventful life. "He's out most of the time," an employee at his Miami condominium would later say. "He walks by himself. He does everything by himself."

In Italy, Lucky Luciano's declining years saw a further

ebbing of his power. Though the regular payments of cash continued to arrive from the Syndicate, he no longer had a voice in its operations. Weakened by a series of heart attacks, he died in Naples, at the age of sixty-four, in January of 1962. For his funeral, fellow expatriate Joe Adonis sent a huge wreath with a sentimental farewell: "So Long, Pal." Luciano's body was flown home to New York, where it rests in a Grecian vault in St. John's Cemetery. As for Adonis, he, too, died of a heart attack, but not until November of 1971, in the central Italian town of Ancona, where he had been banished by the authorities for suspected Mafia activity in Milan. He was sixty-nine. "I'm just a poor old man," he had told the Italian police. "I can't understand what you've got against me." His body was flown back to the United States—by friends who refused to give their names.

Frank Costello, after his final release from jail in 1961, lived a monied, leisurely existence. Aside from the deportation proceedings, he had few worries. He would rise early, breakfast alone, go for an undisturbed walk along Central Park West, visit the Waldorf-Astoria, dine with friends at Manhattan's finest restaurants. On weekends, he would go with his wife to their Sands Point, Long Island, home, putter in the garden, entertain old friends.

On February 18, 1973, the eighty-two-year-old Costello, who had been recuperating from a heart seizure in Doctors Hospital, suffered a fatal coronary attack. His wake at the Frank E. Campbell Funeral Home was a quiet one—his wife Bobbie had asked his Syndicate friends to stay away, and the Campbell people shut out the curious. Subsequently, his body was interred at St. Michael's Cemetery in Queens, where it rests, in a marble vault, next to the bodies of his mother and father, whose turn-of-the-century emigration from Calabria had given the Syndicate its prime minister. "He ran the underworld out of respect rather than fear," eulogized a high-ranking policeman. After Costello's death, it came to light the IRS had placed liens for several million dollars on his property. Bobbie, decrying the harassment, insisted she had no money, and left New York for New Orleans—to live with her brother Dudley. Supposedly, her husband's fortune had slipped away as quietly as he had amassed it.

Seventy-four-year-old Bill O'Dwyer, interviewed in his New York apartment on East Fifty-seventh Street in 1964 just a few months before his death, and puffing on a cigar despite doctor's orders, ruminated on the evils of civic corruption. "Scandals will recur all the time," he said. "There is no way of stopping them, except one. That is the legal control of gambling. People will gamble and there will always be a bookmaker to take their bets. No mayor or police commissioner can handle this kind of corruption. When one scandal is straightened out, we'll be getting ready for the next one." Sniffed his housekeeper: "When Mr. O'Dwyer was mayor, we didn't have to be afraid of walking the streets at night. Now I carry a hatpin in my pocketbook."

On November 24, 1964, with his brother Paul and niece Joan at his hospital bedside, William O'Dwyer died of a coronary thrombosis. All the flags in New York were ordered flown at half-staff. Three days later, with former wife Sloan Simpson one of seventeen hundred mourners, a solemn requiem mass was celebrated at St. Patrick's Cathedral, and his body was taken for interment to Arlington National Cemetary. "William O'Dwyer was a warm, gregarious, fallible human being," editorialized the *New York Times.* "His rise was a flamboyant metropolitan success story. His first term at City Hall was marked by substantial accomplishments. His second term was less scintillating.

"There seems little doubt," the *Times* concluded, "that

Mr. O'Dwyer was victimized by men he had trusted. His own excessively tolerant nature enabled grafters to reassert themselves in municipal affairs."

Viscount Morley's remark, almost fifty years before, that "the proper memory for a politician is one that knows what to remember and what to forget," better sums up William O'Dwyer's puzzling public career. On a clear, bright November day, all the flags in New York flying at half-staff . . . the enigmatic O'Dwyer, who himself disliked hearing ill of any man, would *surely* have chosen to remember that honor. . . . If he could, he might have told once more the story of old O'Sheehan, who played the violin and had the big ears, who everybody *said* they remembered, but nobody really did. . . . "And yet we knew he must have played the violin and had big ears, and what *more* do you need to know?" O'Dwyer might have countered, his smile and his brogue his defense to the end.

Bibliographical Note

The following abbreviations are used in the Notes.

FCPMU   Wolf, George, and DiMona, Joseph. *Frank Costello, Prime Minister of the Underworld.* New York: William Morrow, 1974.

LTLL   Gosch, Martin A., and Hammer, Richard. *The Last Testament of Lucky Luciano.* Waltham, Massachusetts: Little Brown, 1975.

MI   Feder, Sid, and Turkus, Burton B. *Murder Inc.* New York: Farrar Straus & Giroux, 1951.

LAN   Messick, Hank. *Lansky.* New York: G.P. Putnam's, 1971.

RSCIOC   U.S. Senate. *Report of the Special Committee to Investigate Organized Crime in Interstate Commerce* (19 vols.) 1951.*
         *Whenever possible, the *Report of the Special Committee to Investigate Organized Crime* (RSCIOC) —when available in the pages of the New York Times—is so cited.

TAU   Dewey, Thomas E. *Twenty Against the Underworld.* Edited by Rodney Campbell. New York: Doubleday, 1974.

UF   Katz, Leonard. *Uncle Frank, the Biography of Frank Costello.* New York: Drake, 1973.

VP   Maas, Peter. *The Valachi Papers.* New York: G.P. Putnam's, 1968.

WOKEO   Jennings, Dean. *We Only Kill Each Other, the Life and Bad Times of Bugsy Siegel.* New Jersey: Prentice-Hall, 1967.

Notes

PART ONE

1942: Friendship

Page 2: "Suddenly there was . . ." and ff., Philip Hamburger, "Friends Talking in the Night," *New Yorker*, Dec. 28, 1946, p. 29. ". . . one of the sweetest . . ." and ff., Ibid., p. 28.
Pages 3–4: "O'Dwyer wanted to know . . ." and ff., *RSCIOC*, vol. 7, p. 630. "You say you . . ." and ff., Ibid., p. 722.
Pages 5–6: "Will your Honor . . ." and ff., N.Y. Criminal Court, April 5, 1915. "I knew I . . ." *FCPMU*, p. 16. "He was a man . . ." Henry Ziegler, *Frank Costello*, Berkley, 1974, p. 25.
Page 7: "I have been prejudged." *N.Y. Times*, March 14, 1951, p. 28. "I know the leaders . . ." Ibid., Oct. 26, 1943, p. 1.
Page 8: "O'Dwyer and I . . ." and ff., Ibid., Aug. 16, 1951, p. 22.
Pages 8–9: "I was at a dinner . . ." and ff., *RSCIOC*, vol. 18, p. 676–77. "I didn't expect . . ." and ff., *N.Y. Times*, March 20, 1951, p. 25.
Page 10: "I have met . . ." and ff., Ibid., March 21, 1951, p. 30.
Page 11: "It's not what we win . . ." Fred J. Cook, *The Secret Rulers: Criminal Syndicates & How They Control the U.S. Underworld* (Des Moines, Iowa: Duell, Sloan & Pearce, 1966), p. 163. "I had no reason . . ." and ff., *NY Times*, March 17, 1951, p. 9.
Page 12: "One of a number . . ." and ff., Ibid., March 14, 1951, p. 28.
Page 15: "Hi-jacked cigarettes . . ." *The Secret Rulers*, p. 122. "I like the climate . . ." and ff., *RSCIOC*, vol. 7, p. 310.
Page 16: "Joey A is . . ." and ff. *The Secret Rulers*, p. 120.
Page 17: "People of character . . ." and ff., *RSCIOC*, vol. 7, p. 336–37.
Page 19: "The Supreme Court held . . ." and ff., Ibid., p. 877 and ff.
Page 20: "One time Huey . . ." *UF*, p. 97.
Page 21: "The people seem . . ." T. Harry Williams, *Huey Long* (New York: Knopf, 1969), p. 824. "Huey Long came to New York . . ." and ff., *NY Times*, March 14, 1951, p. 28.
Pages 22–23: "It knocked a hole . . ." *UF*, p. 98. "I told him . . ." Ibid., p. 99. "Phil Kastel was . . ." Ibid., p. 103. "Tell me, Mr. Costello . . ." and ff., *N.Y. Times*, March 15, 1951, p. 24.
Page 24: "I was about a head taller . . ." and ff. *LTLL*, p. 24.
Page 25: "Meyer Lansky understood . . ." Ibid., p. 145.

Page 26: "There was just . . ." *LAN,* p. 87. "We hadda put up . . ." *LTLL,* p. 169. "When were you . . ." and ff., *RSCIOC,* vol. 7, p. 610 and ff.

Page 28: "These fellows were like . . ." *WOKEO,* p. 29.

Page 29: "You are growing . . ." and ff. *RSCIOC,* vol. 10, p. 87–88.

Page 31: "We drilled . . ." *WOKEO,* p. 57.

Page 32: "Early in August . . ." *MI,* p. 243. "If all the sighs . . ." Ibid., p. 399.

Page 33: "Apparently there were . . ." and ff., *N.Y. Times,* March 20, 1951, p. 24.

Page 34: "Bugsy Siegel . . ." and ff., Ibid., p. 25.

PART TWO

1890–1941: Beginnings

Page 36: "My God, the past takes me . . ." and ff., Philip Hamburger, "That Great Big New York Up There," *New Yorker,* Sept. 28, 1957, p. 77.

Page 37: "When we took . . ." Ibid., p. 80. "I wish you could . . ." and ff., "Friends Talking in the Night" p. 30.

Page 38: "Only by the intercession . . ." Milton MacKaye, "The Ex-Cop Who Runs New York," *Saturday Evening Post,* May 31, 1947, p. 79. "Amos and Andy . . ." Ibid., p. 19. "I became a member . . ." and ff., *N.Y. Times,* March 20, 1951, p. 24. ". . . was not so good . . ." and ff., "Friends Talking in the Night," p. 29.

Page 39: "I remember one Saturday . . ." "That Great Big New York Up There," p. 76.

Page 41: "Did you know . . ." and ff., *N.Y. Times,* March 21, 1951, p. 29. "Judge, I don't think . . ." and ff., "The Ex-Cop Who Runs New York," p. 81.

Page 43: "Say, do you remember . . ." "Friends Talking in the Night," p. 34.

Page 44: "She always swore . . ." *UF,* p. 22. "All we took . . ." Ibid., p. 22.

Page 46: "We liked to go . . ." *LTLL,* p. 11. "I had to lean over . . ." Ibid., p. 11. According to Luciano, Costello's voice sounded like he had a "permanent sore throat" when they first met. According to several later-day journalists, the voice rasp was caused, or at least accentuated, by radiation therapy in 1933 to counteract either throat cancer or polyps on the vocal chords. Costello was a heavy smoker. "When I met . . ." *FCPMU,* p. 14.

Page 47: "This young man . . ." and ff., N.Y. Criminal Court, April 5, 1915.

Pages 47–48: "We was the best . . ." *LTLL,* p. 25. "Why should the Jews . . ." and ff., Ibid., p. 25. "We always knew . . ." Ibid., p. 81.

Page 48: "All I know . . ." *UF*, p. 62.

Page 50: "Costello was one . . ." *FCPMU*, p. 23.

Page 52: ". . . a square deal . . ." and ff., Martin Mayer, *Emory Buckner* (New York: Harper & Row, 1968), p. 205. "What happened . . ." and ff., *FCPMU*, p. 59.

Page 53: "If a guy named Hershey . . ." *Frank Costello*, p. 53. "You used the office . . ." and ff., *N.Y. Times*, Oct. 26, 1943, p. 1.

Page 55: "We got to put ourselves . . ." *FCPMU*, p. 79. "Tell me when . . ." Ibid., p. 80.

Page 56: "They came from . . ." *LTLL*, p. 100–101. "It's your district . . ." and ff., Ibid., p. 112–15.

Page 58: "Masseria's luck . . ." Ibid., p. 129. "Whether you like it . . ." Ibid., p. 130.

Page 59: "The cops asked me . . ." Ibid., p. 132.

Page 60: "As Frank once said . . ." *FCPMU*, p. 83. "I can't get along . . ." *VP*, p. 108.

Page 61: ". . . were all sitting . . ." Ibid., p. 113. "I explained to them . . ." *LTLL*, p. 145.

Page 62: "Why should you . . ." Ibid., p. 147.

Page 63: "When Jimmy Hines . . ." Craig Thompson and Allen Raymond, *Gang Rule in New York* (New York: Dial Press, 1940), p. 138. "In politics . . ." Ibid., p. 139. "You stuffed in . . ." Ibid., p. 141. "You are a millstone . . ." Jack Alexander "District Leader" (third of three parts), *New Yorker*, Aug. 8, 1936, p. 23.

Pages 64–65: "I have met Fay . . ." Ibid. (second of three parts), *New Yorker*, Aug. 1, 1936, p. 21. "I know Jimmy . . ." Ibid., p. 23.

Page 66: "It was a Helis note . . ." and ff., *N.Y. Times*, March 15, 1951, p. 24.

Page 69: "Who sold the beer barrels . . ." *TAU*, p. 118. "In 1928, you filed . . ." and ff., Federal Court, Southern District of N.Y., Nov. 20, 1933 and ff.

Page 71: "Before I discharge you . . ." *TAU*, p. 272.

Page 72: "It was worth . . ." Ibid., p. 273.

Pages 72–73: "Dewey was bound . . ." *MI*, p. 118. "I say . . ." Ibid., p. 119. "They could not risk . . ." *TAU*, p. 275.

Pages 73–74: "Was it the boss . . ." and ff., *N.Y. Journal American*, Oct. 26, 1935, p. 1. "The arrested women . . ." *TAU*, p. 193. "Frank Costello told me . . ." *FCPMU*, p. 108. ". . . told us that Luciano . . ." *TAU*, p. 203.

Pages 74–75: ". . . with Frederico . . ." Ibid., p. 214. "I said to him . . ." Ibid., p. 202. "A decent, hard-working . . ." Ibid., p. 216. "What are your duties . . ." and ff., N.Y. State Supreme Court, May 15, 1936 and ff.

Page 76: "There has not been . . ." and ff., Ibid. "How can I . . ." *TAU*, p. 253.

Pages 76–77: "The top Mafia leader . . ." Ibid., p. 264. "The Dutchman was right . . ." and ff., *LTLL,* p. 199. "I was sure . . ." Ibid., p. 200. "Lepke was the brains . . ." and ff., *TAU,* p. 297.

Page 78: "The machine-controlled . . ." Ibid., p. 298. "There is an alliance . . ." Ibid., p. 325.

Page 79: "He wasn't in narcotics . . ." *FCPMU,* p. 111.

Page 80: ". . . he had to have . . ." *TAU,* p. 384. ". . . testified that thousands . . ." Ibid., p. 386. ". . . testified that Hines . . ." Ibid., p. 387. "picked up Hines . . ." Ibid., ". . . testified that Hines had telephoned . . ." Ibid.

Page 81: "How would you . . ." Ibid., p. 473. "I had no notion . . ." *N.Y. Times,* March 20, 1951, p. 24.

Page 82: "In a ten-year period . . ." *MI,* p. 1.

Pages 82–83: "We knew there were mobs . . ." Ibid., p. 18. "When I was twenty . . ." and ff., Ibid., p. 29.

Page 84: "Why should I keep . . ." Ibid., p. 30. "You were in on . . ." Ibid., p. 51.

Pages 84–85: "I can make you . . ." Ibid., p. 52. "I can tell you . . ." Ibid., p. 53. "Me and my partners . . ." Ibid., p. 57.

Pages 85–86: "I will become . . ." Ibid., p. 152. "I went out social . . ." Ibid., p. 156. "Me and Pretty . . ." Kings County Criminal Court, May 13, 1940 and ff. "I walk in . . ." and ff., Ibid.

Page 87: "Albert gave me . . ." and ff., Ibid. "What happened next . . ." and ff., Ibid.

Page 89: "What did Bugsy Goldstein say?" and ff., Ibid.

Pages 89–90: "Phil was saying . . ." and ff., Ibid. "What's the hurry . . ." *MI,* p. 312. "Mr. Hoover, this is Lepke . . ." and ff., Richard Hammer, *Playboy's Illustrated History of Organized Crime,* (Chicago: Playboy Press, 1975), p. 192.

Pages 90–91: "I wanted to get out . . ." *MI,* p. 313. "I stood enough . . ." Kings County Criminal Court, Sept. 15, 1941 and ff. "On the Friday before . . ." and ff., Ibid.

Page 91: "I asked Capone . . ." and ff., Ibid.

Page 92–93: "There are detectives working . . ." and ff., Kings County district attorney's office report by assistant District Attorney Edward A. Heffernan, Nov. 11, 1941. "Here was a veteran . . ." *MI,* p. 388.

Pages 93–94: "When I saw him . . ." and ff., *RSCIOC,* vol. 7, p. 587–96. "Reles would have had . . ." *MI,* p. 397–99.

Page 95: "I come over . . ." Ibid., p. 405.

Page 96: "Referring to the Anastasia case . . ." and ff., *N.Y. Times,* March 20, 1951, p. 24.

Page 97: The fact that the "little boy" was both sturdy and a teenager comes from several primary sources, including *MI,* p. 407. "Now, in May of 1942 . . ." and ff., *N.Y. Times,* March 20, 1951, p. 24.

Page 98: "There never was a case . . ." and ff., *RSCIOC,* vol. 7, p. 623–24. "Hello, cabbage-head . . ." and ff., *N.Y. Times,* Nov. 5, 1941, p. 1.

PART THREE

1943–1945: Interregnum

Page 101: "Good morning, Francesco . . ." and ff., *N.Y. Times,* Oct. 26, 1943, p. 1.

Page 102: "What business . . ." and ff., Ibid. "The meeting was for . . ." and ff., Ibid.

Page 103: "Have you in the last . . ." and ff., Ibid. "Everyone believes . . ." and ff., Ibid., Oct. 27, 1943, p. 1.

Pages 104–105: "Early in Aurelio's career . . ." *FCPMU,* p. 144. "Have you got a minute . . ." and ff., *N.Y. Times,* March 14, 1951, p. 28.

Pages 105–106: "That is just a saying . . ." and ff., Ibid. "He told me . . ." and ff., Ibid.

Page 106: "I said, 'I will want . . .' " and ff., *N.Y. Times,* March 13, 1951, p. 26.

Page 107: "Where did you get . . ." and ff., *N.Y. Times,* March 14, 1951, p. 28.

Page 109: "He never let you know . . ." *UF,* p. 242. "Of course, there's a Mafia . . ." and ff., Ed Reid, *Mafia* (New York: Random House, 1952), p. 35.

Page 110: "You just can't . . ." and ff., *FCPMU,* p. 149.

Page 112: "Bill O'Dwyer has done more . . ." "The Ex-Cop Who Runs New York," p. 82. "I shall never forget . . ." S.J. Woolf, "It's a Friendly Town," *N.Y. Times* Magazine, April 6, 1947, p. 15.

Page 113: "I am a judge . . ." and ff., *N.Y. Times,* Oct. 28, 1945, p. 1.

Page 116: "Let us talk about a man . . ." and ff., Ibid., Oct. 31, 1945, p. 1.

Page 120: "When I took over . . ." and ff., Ibid.

Pages 122–123: "Their opinion ammounted . . ." Alva Johnston, "The Great Expurgator," *New Yorker,* March 29, 1947, p. 40. "The undisputed proof . . ." and ff., *N.Y. Times,* Dec. 21, 1945, p. 1.

Page 124: "O'Dwyer went out of office . . ." Ibid.

Pages 125–126: "I got to know . . ." Hank Messick, *Secret File* (New York: G. P. Putnam's, 1969), p. 203. "Maybe I just . . ." *The Secret Rulers,* p. 180. "Fellows give me . . ." Ibid., p. 182.

Page 128: "You don't want . . ." and ff., *N.Y. Times,* Nov. 16, 1950, p. 1.

PART FOUR

1946–1950: Mayoralty

Page 132: "Upon the entry . . ." and ff., *LTLL,* p. 277.

Page 133: "All I wanted . . ." Ibid., p. 267. "A large crowd . . ." *FCPMU,* p. 166.

Page 134: "At one point . . ." *The Secret Rulers,* p. 280.

Page 135: "In those days . . ." *FCPMU,* p. 164. "My husband has . . ." *N.Y. Herald-Tribune,* March 3, 1953. "I don't like . . ." Ibid., March 4, 1953. "The word was . . ." *VP,* p. 149.

Page 136: "It seems to me . . ." and ff., "Talk of the Town," *New Yorker,* April 13, 1946, p. 24.

Page 137: "Whoever passed that . . ." *N.Y. Herald-Tribune,* Oct. 13, 1946, p. 1.

Page 138: "How I feel . . ." Ibid., April 8, 1947. "Seizure of Coppola . . ." *N.Y. Daily Mirror,* Nov. 18, 1946.

Page 140: "I must've talked . . ." and ff., *LTLL,* p. 314–15

Page 141: "Bugsy was . . ." Ibid., p. 317.

Page 143: "It is known . . ." *N.Y. Herald-Tribune,* Jan. 15, 1947. "I call upon . . ." Ibid., March 6, 1947. "I don't know . . ." Ibid. "Are you going . . ." and ff., Ibid.

Pages 144–145: Meyer Lansky's visit to Siegel, *WOKEO,* p. 191. "Mick, you got . . ." and ff., Ibid., p. 194.

Pages 145–146: "We have a unique . . ." Ibid., p. 203. "How long have you . . ." and ff., *RSCIOC,* vol. 10, p. 64.

Page 147: "Rosen had an interest . . ." and ff., Ibid., p. 86.

Page 148: How Virginia Hill got the news of Siegel's death, *WOKEO,* p. 9. "The Department of Licenses . . ." and ff., Lillian Ross, "A Reporter at Large," *New Yorker,* July 12, 1947, p. 32.

Page 150: "Firemen can become . . ." and ff., Ibid., p. 35.

Page 151: "During the year . . ." and ff., *N.Y. Times,* March 22, 1951, p. 26.

Page 152: ". . . a marked lowering . . ." and ff., Ibid., Feb. 29, 1948, p. 1. "It's something that . . ." and ff., S.J. Woolf, "O'Dwyer Tells Why It's Tough," *N.Y. Times Magazine,* March 21, 1948, p. 14.

Page 154: "Max Stark's cash . . ." *The Secret Rulers,* p. 237.

Page 155: "Any number . . ." Ibid., p. 240.

Page 156: "Approximately fifty . . ." and ff., Ibid., p. 251. "Do you keep . . ." and ff., Ibid.

Pages 156–157: "This is more than . . ." *N.Y. Herald-Tribune,* June 25, 1948. "Leave Tammany Hall . . ." and ff., Ibid., July 2, 1948, p. 1.

Page 158: "Those who recall . . ." and ff., *N.Y. Times,* March 22, 1951, p. 26.

Page 159: "Once I even had . . ." "That Great Big New York Up There," p. 68. "The occasion was . . ." "Department of Amplication," *New Yorker*, Oct. 10, 1957, p. 139.
Pages 160–161: "Loyalty was a way . . ." *FCPMU*, p. 184. "It was a lovely . . ." *N.Y. Herald-Tribune*, Jan. 26, 1949. "This reporter . . ." Ibid. "We will take . . ." and ff., *N.Y. Times*, Jan. 26, 1949. "While Frankie had . . ." *N.Y. Herald-Tribune*, Jan. 26, 1949.
Page 162–163: "Hugo, are you . . ." *N.Y. Times* March 12, 1949, p. 1. " . . .lost no time . . ." and ff., Ibid., March 15, 1949, p. 1. "What's the matter . . ." and ff., Ibid. "It is obvious . . ." *N.Y. Herald-Tribune*, April 14, 1949. "If the 'gross take.' . . ." *N.Y. Times*, March 12, 1949, p. 1. "Ordinarily, I would have . . ." *N.Y. Herald-Tribune*, March 15, 1949, p. 1.
Pages 165–166: "I phoned the mayor . . ." Ibid., July 14, 1949, p. 1. "O'Dwyer was boiling . . ." and ff., Barry Cunningham with Mike Pearl, *Mr. District Attorney*, (New York: Mason/Charter, 1977), p. 119–20.
Pages 167–168: "I told Costello . . ." and ff., Richard H. Rovere, "Father Hogan's Place," *New Yorker*, Aug. 16, 1947 p. 55. "After seven weeks . . ." *N.Y. Herald-Tribune*, July 22, 1949.
Pages 168–169: "Do I know . . ." and ff., Ibid., p. 1. ". . . the Mayor of the City . . ." Ibid., Oct. 19, 1949. p. 1. ". . . more serious things . . ." Ibid.
Pages 169–170: "We are delighted . . ." Ibid., Oct. 20, 1949. "Time was . . ." Ibid., Oct. 29, 1949, p. 1.
Page 170–171: "It was your own . . ." and ff., Ibid. "Frank Erickson has been . . ." Ibid. "William O'Dwyer is neither . . ." *N.Y. Journal-American*, Nov. 7, 1949.
Page 172: "Sullivan distrusted . . ." *RSCIOC*, vol. 6, p. 36. "Walter's as comfortable . . ." Pat Frank and Luther Voltz, "Florida's Struggle With the Hoodlums," *Collier's*, March 25, 1950, p. 78.
Pages 172–173: "My, it looks . . ." and ff., A.E. Hotchner, "She Married the Mayor," *Redbook*, October 1954, p. 92. "For the first time . . ." Ibid. "Not only was . . ." and ff., Ibid. p. 92.
Pages 173–174: "At one point . . ." Ibid. "Anyone who tells . . ." and ff., Ibid. "You fellows . . ." Ibid., "What do you mean . . ." Ibid., p. 93. "The laboratory tests . . ." *N.Y. Herald-Tribune*, Dec. 1, 1949, p. 1.
Page 175: "I know it sounds . . ." and ff., "She Married the Mayor," p. 93.
Page 176: ". . . ill-advised . . ." *N.Y. Times*, June 27, 1950, p. 1.
Page 177: "Have you anything . . ." Ibid.
Page 178: "There were times . . ." "That Great Big New York Up There," p. 82. "Are you going . . ." Ibid.
Page 179: "Is there any . . ." and ff., *N.Y. Times*, Sept. 1, 1950, p. 1. "What I do now . . ." *N.Y. Herald-Tribune*, Aug. 26, 1950, p. 1.

Page 180: "... created more positions ..." Ibid., Aug. 18, 1950, p. 1. "The mayor's last ..." Ibid., Aug. 19, 1950. "He seemed to have ..." Philip Hamburger, "Some People Watch Birds," *New Yorker,* Dec. 26, 1953, p. 18.

Page 181: "... when a bookie's name ..." *N.Y. Herald-Tribune,* Oct. 17, 1950, p. 1. "... there was two hundred dollars ..." and ff., Ibid.

Pages 182–183: "... were you paying ..." and ff., Ibid., May 8, 1952, p. 1. "Have you changed ..." and ff., Ibid., Oct. 10, 1950, p. 1.

Page 184: "I could not hurt..." Ed Reid, *The Shame of New York* (New York: Random House, 1953), p. 29. "I don't for a moment ..." "She Married the Mayor," p. 92.

PART FIVE

1951: Investigation

Page 188: "Businesses were paralyzed..." Estes Kefauver, *Crime in America* (New York: Doubleday, 1951), p. 283. "He would establish ..." *Time Magazine,* March 24, 1952, p. 22.

Page 189: "Kefauver reminds me ..." and ff., Ibid. "When did you last ..." and ff., *N.Y. Times,* March 13, 1951, p. 26.

Page 190: "Under what circumstances ..." and ff., Ibid. "If you were lost ..." and ff., Ibid.

Page 191: "Did you receive ..." and ff., Ibid. "Did you ever have ..." and ff., Ibid.

Page 193: "Were you convicted ..." and ff., Ibid., March 14, 1951, p. 28.

Pages 193–194: "You were admitted to ..." and ff., Ibid. "Was Harry Sausser ..." and ff., Ibid.

Pages 194–195: "I was covering ..." and ff., Ibid. "What is the business ..." and ff., Ibid.

Page 196: "As boss, you should ..." Ibid.

Pages 196–197: "I have retired ..." Ibid. "You and Mr. Erickson ..." and ff., Ibid. "Costello asked me ..." and ff., Ibid., March 15, 1951, p. 25.

Page 197–198: "Did you ever see ..." and ff., Ibid. "On the face of it ..." Ibid. "Are you telling me ..." and ff., Ibid., p. 24.

Pages 199–200: "I wouldn't know ..." and ff., Ibid. "Where did you get ..." and ff., Ibid.

Page 200: "You have to extend ..." and ff., Ibid.

Page 201: "About what time ..." and ff., Ibid., March 16, 1951, p. 24.

Page 203: "In the last few years ..." and ff., Ibid.You didn't tell us ..." and ff., Ibid.

Page 204–205: "I hope the atom bomb . . ." Ibid. "Do you have any . . ." and ff., *RSCIOC,* vol. 7, p. 360–61.

Page 205: "You have got . . ." and ff., Ibid., p. 367–70.

Pages 206–207: "Mr. Halley . . ." and ff., *N.Y. Times,* March 16, 1951, p. 24. "I do not think . . ." and ff., Ibid.

Pages 208–209: "There was never . . ." Ibid., March 17, 1951, p. 9. "I was born . . ." Ibid. "Moran was as close . . ." *N.Y. Journal-American,* May 26, 1952, p. 9. "How long have you . . ." and ff., *N.Y. Times,* March 17, 1951, p. 9.

Pages 210–211: ". . . pressed for campaign funds . . ." *N.Y. Sunday News,* July 31, 1955, p. 68. "I don't have . . ." Ibid., p. 69.

Page 212: "I am afraid . . ." *N.Y. Times,* March 20, 1951, p. 21. "In this state . . ." and ff., Ibid., p. 24.

Pages 212–213: "That's true . . ." Ibid. "One thought . . ." and ff., Ibid., March 21, 1951, p. 27.

Pages 213–214: "Turkus didn't say . . ." and ff., Ibid. March 20, 1951, p. 25. "Would you not agree . . ." and ff., Ibid. p. 24. "When you went . . ." and ff., Ibid. p. 25.

Page 215: "Why did Moran . . ." and ff., Ibid. pp. 21, 25.

Page 216: "You were not embarassed . . ." and ff., Ibid. p. 25. "Did you ask . . ." and ff., Ibid. "We are happy . . ." and ff., Ibid. p. 1. "What can you recollect . . ." Ibid., p. 25.

Page 218: "Is there anything else . . ." Ibid., March 21, 1951, p. 29. "Do you believe . . ." and ff., Ibid. p. 28.

Page 219: "What results came . . ." and ff., Ibid.

Page 220: "What did you . . ." and ff., Ibid.

Page 221: "Frank Sampson and his crowd . . ." Ibid.

Pages 221–222: "Did Costello have . . ." and ff., Ibid., p. 29. "O'Dwyer Draws . . ." Ibid., p. 1. "President Truman . . ." Ibid., p. 30.

Page 223: "This fifty-five thousand dollars was used . . ." and ff., Ibid., March 22, 1951. p. 26. ". . . at the very mention . . ." and ff., Ibid., p. 27.

Page 224: "Were you alone . . ." and ff., Ibid. "I was not questioned . . ." Ibid. p. 24.

Part Six

1952–1973: Aftermath

Page 226: "Your silence . . ." and ff., "A Big Laugh on the Law," *Life Magazine,* Oct. 1, 1951, p. 21. "I just wanted . . ." Ibid. p. 20.

Page 227: "There is not . . ." *N.Y. Times,* Sept. 28, 1951, p. 1. "Gross was visiting . . ." Ibid.

Page 228: Moran identified as "collector," Ibid., Sept. 29, 1951, p. 1. Gross' claim of an "arrangement," Ibid., May 8, 1952, p. 1. O'Brien's denial, Ibid. Gross' charge against Bals, Ibid. Gross' charges against Whalen and Flath, Ibid., Oct. 28, 1952, p. 1.

Page 230: "Vito is like . . ." *VP,* p. 210.

Page 231: "Old gamblers . . ." *N.Y. Herald-Tribune,* Oct. 5, 1951, p. 1. "Willie was almost . . ." *The Secret Rulers,* p. 290. "Moretti had . . ." *VP,* p. 213.

Page 232: "I'd rather blow . . ." *UF,* p. 212. "This is a political . . ." Ibid. p. 216.

Page 233: "I put ads . . ." "That Great Big New York Up There," p. 50.

Page 234–235: "If I shook . . ." "She Married the Mayor," p. 94. "She couldn't endure . . ." Ibid., p. 95. "There are no . . ." *N.Y. World-Telegram & Sun,* March 14, 1956, p. "I think I have . . ." Brooklyn Eagle, March 25, 1954 "Sloan's a beautiful . . ." "She Married the Mayor," p. 96.

Pages 235–236: "I keep a neat . . ." "That Great Big New York Up There," p. 56. "Tell my friend . . ." Ibid. "They wanted . . ." Ibid. p. 68. "Whenever the real estate . . ." Ibid. "I'd eat . . ." Ibid. "Great stuff . . ." Ibid., p. 62. "This is another . . ." *N.Y. Sunday News,* July 31, 1955, p. 69. "I have eaten . . ." and ff., Ibid. "Over nine years . . ." and ff., *N.Y. Herald-Tribune,* June 20, 1961, p. 1.

Page 237: "You're breaking the law . . ." and ff., Ibid. "What can an old . . ." Ibid. "The mystery of . . ." *N.Y. Sunday News,* July 31, 1955, p. 69.

Page 239: "Frank should have . . ." *LTLL,* p. 385.

Page 240: "This is for . . ." *N.Y. Times,* May 3, 1957, p. 1. "I didn't see . . ." Ibid.

Page 242: "You can just . . ." *The Secret Rulers,* p. 325. ". . . would be too . . ." *LTLL,* p. 398.

Page 243: "If soldiers got arrested . . ." *VP,* p. 249.

Page 245: ". . . compassion for this . . ." *N.Y. Herald-Tribune,* Jan. 13, 1959 ". . . depressed by . . ." Ibid., Aug. 17, 1962.

Page 247: ". . . regular activity . . ." *LAN,* p. 284. ". . . will lie dormant . . ." and ff., *N.Y. Times,* April 20, 19755

Page 249: "Scandals will recur . . ." and ff., Ibid., July 11, 1964 "William O'Dwyer was . . ." Ibid., Nov. 28, 1964

Index

Abbandando, Frank "Dasher," 82–83, 85–86, 89
Abrams, Hyman "Hymie," 23, 62
Accardo, Tony, 140
Adonis, Joe "Joey A" (Joseph Doto), 6, 23, 47, 57, 114, 117, 128–29, 134, 139, 222
  Amen's charges against, 16–17
  automobile businesses of, 15, 191–92
  Brooklyn territory of, 10, 12–15, 40, 54, 79, 115
  Buchalter's arrest and, 89–90
  Carfano and, 24
  casino operations of, 11–12, 127, 155
  cigarette business of, 14–15
  conviction of, 229
  death of, 248
  early mob activities of, 12
  election fixing by, 13–14, 191
  in extortion rackets, 14
  gambling enterprises of, 11–12, 18, 34, 124, 171–72, 177, 229
  Hill and, 126, 203
  home life of, 14
  Joyce and, 40–41
  in Kefauver hearings, 191–92
  LaGuardia and, 15–16
  in legitimate businesses, 14–15
  Masseria assassination and, 11, 59
  murder charges against, 16
  as murder target, 60
  in narcotics traffic, 14
  New Jersey territory of, 15, 17–18, 109
  Reles's testimony and, 32, 87, 92
  retirement of, in Italy, 238
  union breaking by, 14
  violence engineered by, 12–13
Ahearn, Walter, 11–12

Aleman, Miguel, 179
Ambro, Jerome, 12–13
Amen, John Harlan, 117–19
  Adonis charged by, 16–17
Anastasia, Albert, 12, 32, 129, 134, 139, 171
  attempt to invade Lansky's territory by, 238–39
  Buchalter's arrest and, 89–90
  citizenship obtained by, 124
  death of, 241–43
  Masseria assassination and, 11, 58–59
  as Murder Inc. head, 13–14, 34, 76, 78, 87, 117, 206–7, 241
  O'Dwyer's failure to prosecute, 95–98, 121–24, 206–8, 212–14
Anastasia, Anthony, 11, 14
Anslinger, Harry J., 140, 141
Aurelio, Thomas, 110, 160, 199
  Costello's backing of, 101–4, 221
  hearings over nomination of, 102–4, 167
  wiretaps and, 101–2, 221
Austin, Lawrence, 222

Baker, Joe, 3, 9, 217
Balitzer, Mildred, 74–75
Balitzer, Pete, 74–75
Bals, Frank:
  in Anastasia investigation, 121, 207–8, 214
  bookmaking investigated by, 220–21
  payoffs to, 220, 228
  promotion of, 208, 220
  Rele's death and, 93–94, 96
Barbara, Joseph, 242
Batista, Fulgencio, 26, 246
Beldock, George J., 116–20, 122

Bello, Marino, 30
Berman, Otto "Abadaba," 73
Bernecker, Edward, 132, 174–75
Bernecker, Mrs. Edward, 175
Bernstein, Sholem, 85, 92
Betillo, "Little Davie," 75–76
Blank, Benjamin, 30, 33
Blumenfield, Isadore "Kid Cann," 23, 62
Boccia, Ferdinand "the Shadow," 79, 134, 229
Bonnanno, Joseph "Joe Bananas," 59, 242
bookmaking, 6, 12, 18, 53–54
    by Erickson, 18, 53, 127, 176–77, 218–19
    Gross's payoffs for, 181–84, 218–19, 226–29
    Kefauver investigation and, 189–91, 195–96, 200–201, 215–20
    Lansky's activities in, 25–26
    layoff betting in, 53, 127, 155
    McDonald investigation of, 181–84, 200–201, 226–27
    payoffs for, 7, 12, 17, 104–7, 155–56, 171–72, 176, 181–82, 189–90, 195–96, 218–19, 226–29
    at racetracks, 104–7, 189–90, 195–97
    wire services for, 26, 28–29, 125, 200–201
    see also gambling
bootlegging, 6, 12
    procedures of, 49–51, 71–72
    profits of, 50–51
    Schultz and, 68–72
Borell, Frank, 155–56
Boyle, Joseph A., 163, 179
Brady, Diamond Jim, 37
Brannigan, James E., 170–71
bribery:
    for bookmaking, 7, 12, 17, 104–7, 155–56, 171–72, 176, 181–82, 189–90, 195–96, 218–19, 226–29
    in O'Dwyer's campaigns, 201, 209–11
    Rothstein's activity in, 48–49

slot-machine income used for, 163
Broady, John, 162–63
Brooklyn *Eagle*, 176
Brown, Florence "Cokey Flo," 74
Brown, Marjorie, 75–76
Buchalter, Louis "Lepke," 23, 27, 62, 114
    arrests of, 14, 89–90
    conviction of, 90–92
    Dewey's prosecution of, 77–79, 90–92
    extortion racket of, 14, 77–78
    in Murder Inc. investigation, 31–32, 72, 77–79, 92
    Rosen murder and, 90–92
Buckner, Emory, 52
Bugs & Meyer mob, 24–25, 49–51, 78, 82
    see also Lansky, Meyer; Siegel, Benjamin "Bugsy"

California Commission on Organized Crime, 163–64
Camarda, Emil, 116–17, 118–19
Camarda family, 117
Cantelops, Nelson, 243–44
Capone, Al, 24, 29, 54–55, 125, 171
    jail agreement of, 55, 62
Capone, Louis, 13, 82, 90–92
Capozzoli, Lewis, 161
Carfano, Anthony "Little Augie" (Anthony Pisano), 12, 24
Carroll, Charles, 173
Cashmore, John, 165, 168
casinos:
    Adonis's operations in, 11–12, 127, 155
    Costello's operations in, 127, 194–95, 240
    Florida police and, 171–72
    mob control of, 11–12, 125, 127, 141, 144, 146–47, 155, 171–72, 194–95, 240
    see also gambling
Castellammarese War, 56, 58

Castiglia, Francesco, see Costello, Frank
Castiglia, Luigi, 44–45
Castiglia, Maria, 44
Castro, Fidel, 245
Catalano, Julie, 85, 86, 95
Christy, Mrs. Howard Chandler, 161
Citron, Anna, see Lansky, Anna Citron
Civello, Jimmy, 242
Clark, Walter, 172
Cohen, Louis, 149
Cohen, Mickey, 145
Coll, Vincent "Mad Dog," 60–61, 72
Collins, Bernard S., 179
Considine, Bob, 108
Copeland, Royal S., 16
Coppola, Doris, 139
Coppola, Michael "Trigger Mike," 138–39
Corbett, Jim, 2
Costello, Edward, 51, 52
Costello, Frank (Francesco Castiglia), 17, 18, 28, 30, 33–34, 65, 87, 89
  assassination attempt on, 239–40
  Aurelio's Supreme Court nomination and, 101–4, 114, 167
  in bootlegging, 49–53, 164, 193–94, 232–33
  bribery and, 48–49
  Buchalter arrest and, 14, 89–90
  businessman appearance of, 7, 51, 142
  casino operations of, 127, 194–95, 240
  citizenship questioned, 192–94, 232–33
  contempt conviction of, 231
  death of, 248–49
  as Democratic party power, 3–5, 7, 10, 49, 62, 65–66, 101–4, 107, 132, 143, 158, 191, 217, 221–22
  deportation proceedings against, 232–33, 248

Dewey's jurisdiction and, 79–80
Dewey as murder target of, 72–74, 76–77
Dwyer and, 49–52
early arrests of, 5–6, 45, 47
early life of, 5, 44–47
first meeting of O'Dwyer with, 3–5, 7–10, 111–12, 114, 214–17
"Frank Saverio" name used by, 47, 192–93
gambling enterprises of, 6–7, 10, 12, 53–54, 153–54, 177
Genovese and, 79, 134–35, 229–31, 238–43
gunman reputation of, 5–6
Haim-Helis distributorship and, 66–68, 198–99
Hogan and, 167–68
Kastel partnership of, 19–23, 110, 194–95, 198–200
in Kefauver hearings, 185, 187, 189–90, 192–200, 206, 216–17
LaGuardia and, 15
Levy and, 104–7
liquor suit against, 52–53
Long and, 20–22, 196
Luciano release and, 27, 132–34
Luciano's friendship with, 45–48, 139–40
Maranzano assassination and, 25, 59–61
Marcello's partnership with, 194–95
marriage of, 46–47, 108–9
Masseria assassination and, 11, 25, 56–59
mistress of, 109
Moretti protected by, 109–10
National Crime Syndicate leader, 6–7, 23–24, 33–34, 54–62, 77, 107–11, 141, 171
police payoffs made by, 7
Prohibition career of, 6, 49–53
psychiatric treatment of, 141–42
racetrack bookmakers and, 104–7, 189–90, 196–97

Costello, Frank *(Continued)*
  Salvation Army fundraising by,
    160–62, 168
  Sherman and, 114–15
  slot-machine enterprises of, 6, 15,
    19–23, 53–54, 79, 102, 107, 163–64,
    196
  tax evasion conviction of, 231–
    32
  taxi driver's find as embarrass-
    ment to, 110–11, 199–200
  television coverage of, 192
  Wall Street property of, 107–8, 196
  wiretapping and, 196–97
  Wright Field fraud and, 9–10, 111–
    12, 217
Costello, Loretta "Bobbie" Geiger-
  man, 46–47, 51, 67–68, 108–9,
  248–49
Crane, John P., 150–51, 222–25
Crime Investigating Committee,
  U.S. Senate (Kefauver hear-
  ings), 176, 185
  Adonis's testimony to, 191–92
  Bals's testimony to, 207–8
  betting income claimed by de-
    fendants in, 203–6
  Costello's testimony to, 192–200,
    206, 216–17
  Erickson's testimony to, 190–91
  Hill's narcotics testimony to,
    201–3
  importance of television to, 187–
    88, 192
  Levy's bookmaking testimony to,
    189–90
  McDonald's bookmaking testi-
    mony to, 200–201
  McLaughlin's wiretapping testi-
    mony to, 196–98
  Moran's testimony to, 208–10
  Moretti's testimony to, 204–6
  O'Dwyer implicated in corrup-
    tion during, 185, 189, 191, 197–
    98, 201, 208–11
  O'Dwyer's testimony to, 211–24

  Tobey accused of bookmakers'
    support during, 215–18
Crump, Ed, 188–89
Culhane, Matty, 2, 38–39

Dalitz, Moe, 23, 54, 62
Daly, Arnold, 2
Davis, Dixie, 80
Democratic party, New York:
  LaGuardia's control of, 15–16
  mob connections of, 3–5, 7, 15–16,
    49, 62, 65–66, 101–4, 107, 132, 143,
    190–91
  Sampson's control of, 142–43,
    156
  see also Tammany Hall
Dennis, Margie, *see* Kastel, Margie
  Dennis
DeNoia, Johnny "Duke," 17
De Sapio, Carmine, 160, 168
DeSimone, Frank, 242
Dewey, Thomas E., 116, 129, 165, 229
  bootlegging investigations by,
    68–71
  Buchalter prosecuted by, 77–79,
    89–91
  Costello outside jurisdiction of,
    79–80
  Genovese prosecuted by, 79
  gubernatorial candidacy of, 81
  Hines prosecuted by, 80–81
  Luciano pardoned by, 132–33
  Luciano prosecuted by, 24
  plot against life of, 72–73
  Schultz prosecuted by, 68–73
  Shapiro prosecuted by, 77–79
  Wexler prosecuted by, 68–71
Diamond, Jack "Legs," 51, 54
Diamond, Morris, 95–98, 121, 207–8,
  212–13
DiFalco, S. Samuel, 160
DiFrasso, Countess Dorothy, 30–31,
  33, 125, 144
Di Salvio, John "Jimmy Kelly," 161
Dolly Sisters, 37
Donoghue, William J., 179

Doto, Joseph, *see* Adonis, Joe
Doto, Mary, 14
Douglas, William O., 233
Downs, Thomas, 160–61
Dragna, Jack I., 29, 141
Dwyer, William "Big Bill," 64, 128
  as bootlegger, 49–52
  tax suit against, 52

Eder, Morris, 160
Eisenhower, Dwight D., 233
Epstein, Joe, 125–26, 203–4
Erickson, Frank, 26, 109, 153, 155, 160
  bookmaking by, 18, 53, 127, 176–77, 218–19
  conviction of, 176–77
  death of, 245
  in Democratic Club gatherings, 169–71, 190
  in Kefauver hearings, 190–91
  money controlled by, 18, 127–28, 153, 196
  in National Crime Syndicate, 127–29, 177

Fay, Larry, 51, 64
Federal Narcotics Bureau, U.S., 140–41
Finestein, Irv "Puggy," 83–84, 87–89
Finklestein, Jerry, 179–80
Fischetti, Charley, 140, 141, 203
Flaherty, Big Nell, 38–39
Flath, August, 228–29
Flegenheimer, Arthur "Dutch Schultz," 51, 54, 76, 79, 127
  as bootlegger, 49, 64, 68–69, 71–72
  death of, 73, 146
  Dewey's prosecution of, 68–72
  Hines and, 80
  plans to kill Dewey by, 72–73
  tax evasion charges against, 71
Flynn, Edward J., 165, 168, 178
Flynn, John G., 183
Frederico, Jimmy, 74, 75–76
Fullmer, Gene, 239

Gable, Clark, 30
Gallo, Joseph "Crazy Joey," 242
gambling:
  Hogan investigation of, 154–56
  national organization of, 10
  in New Jersey, 18, 153–56
  profits from, 154
  see also bookmaking; casinos; slot-machines
Gasberg, Sam, 16
Geigerman, Dudley, 23, 200, 249
Geigerman, Harold, 23
Geigerman, Jerome, 23
Geigerman, Loretta, *see* Costello, Loretta "Bobbie" Geigerman
Geigerman, William, 23
Genovese, Anna Vernotico, 79, 135
Genovese, Vito "Don Vitone," 58–59, 60–61, 160, 161–62
  Anastasia ' assassination and, 241–42
  Apalachin meeting called by, 242–43
  Boccia murder and, 7–9, 134–35
  Costello assassination attempt and, 239–40
  as Costello rival, 79, 134–35, 229–31, 238–43
  death of, 244
  escape to Italy of, 79, 134
  marriage of, 79, 135
  Masseria assassination and, 11
  Moretti's death and, 230–31, 239
  narcotics conviction of, 243–44
  narcotics operations of, 140, 243–44
  violence of, 79, 241
Giancana, Sam, 242
Gigante, Vincent "the Chin," 239–41
Goldstein, Betty, 88
Goldstein, Bugsy, 82–84, 87–89
Goldstein, Jonah T., 123
  O'Dwyer accused of mob connections by, 113–15, 120
Gordon, Waxey, *see* Wexler, Irving "Waxey Gordon"

Gorman, Jack, 8
Greenberg, Harry "Big Greenie," 27, 31, 33
Gross, Harry, 181–84, 218–19, 225–29
Gross, Mickey, 227
Grosswell, Edgar, 243
Guinan, Texas, 51
Guistra, Anthony, 118, 119
Gully, Richard, 30
Guzik, Jacob "Greasy Thumb," 54

Haim, Irving, 66–68, 198
Halley, Rudolph, 187, 189–90, 193–99, 203, 205–6, 208–10, 212–14, 217, 222
Hand, Peter, 20–21
Hanley, Joseph, 116, 118, 121
Hearst, Mrs. William Randolph, 40
Heffernan, Edward, 116, 118–19, 121, 123
Helis, William, 66–67, 198
hi-jacking, 12, 14–15, 16, 38, 50–51
Hill, Virginia, 125–27, 144–45, 148
    death of, 245
    in Kefauver hearings, 201–4
Hines, James J., 62–65, 80–81
Hoff, Max "Boo-Boo," 54
Hoffman, Richard, 142
Hogan, Frank, 102, 162, 237
    Erickson prosecuted by, 177
    gambling investigation by, 154–55
    mayoral candidacy of, 165–68
    Valente investigation of, 157–59
Holtz, Hyman "Curley," 27
Hoover, J. Edgar, 89–90
Hoving, Walter, 160
Hughes, Thomas Cradock, 123–24, 214

Ida, Joe, 242
Impellitteri, Vincent, 131–32, 157, 223

Javits, Jacob, 158
Jones, Edward, 162
Joseph, Lazarus, 131–32
Joyce, George, 40–41
Juffe, Isidore, 16

Kastel, Margie Dennis, 22
Kastel, Phillip "Dandy Phil," 10, 53, 129, 160, 202
    death of, 245
    Haim-Helis distributorship and, 66–67, 198–99
    Louisiana operations of, 20–23, 110, 194, 199–200
    slot-machines and, 19–23, 53
Kefauver, Estes, 192, 197–200, 201, 203–5, 212, 217–18, 226, 229
    as Crime Investigation Committee chairman, 185, 187
    as Crump challenger, 188–89
Kefauver hearings, *see* Crime Investigating Committee, U.S. Senate
Kelly, Frank, 13
Kelly, Jimmy, 217
Kennedy, Michael, 3–5, 9, 102–3, 214, 216–17
Kennedy, Phil, 239–40
Kern, Michael, 227
Kid Cheese gang, 2
Klein, Arthur, 160
Kovalick, Philip "Little Farvel," 27

LaGuardia, Fiorello, 3, 123, 132, 170, 219
    Adonis and, 15–16, 128
    Buchalter and, 71
    Erickson and, 128
    O'Dwyer's campaign against (1941), 98–99
    retirement of, 112
    slot-machines banned by, 19
Landau, Abe, 73
L & G gang (Lepke and Gurrah), 77–78
Lansky, Anna Citron, 25, 54
Lansky, Jake, 25
Lansky, Meyer, 6, 10, 18, 28, 30, 34, 54, 79–80, 124, 129, 133–34, 144–45, 202
    casino operation of, 127, 245–47

Costello retirement and, 238–39
Cuban territory of, 26–27, 139,
    245–46
early crime career of, 24–25, 47–49
gambling enterprises of, 25–27, 139,
    171–72, 177, 245–47
Israeli home of, 246–47
jukebox enterprises of, 27
Luciano release and, 27, 133–34
Maranzano assassination and,
    60–61
marriage and divorce of, 25
role in Syndicate organization of,
    23
second marriage of, 246
stolen car operations of, 24
tax evasion charges against,
    246–47
Lansky, Teddie, 246
Lanza, James, 242
La Tempa, Peter, 134
Lee, Gypsy Rose, 234
Lehman, Herbert, 16, 43, 71, 81, 117
Leibowitz, Samuel, 226–27
Lenihan, Catharine, *see* O'Dwyer,
    Catharine Lenihan
Lenihan, Mary, 131
Lepke, Louis, *see* Buchalter, Louis
    "Lepke"
Levine, Pretty, 83–84, 86
Levine, Sam "Red," 25, 61
Levine, Samuel, 201
Levy, George Morton, 141
    appeal to Costello by, 104–7,
        195–96
    Luciano prosecuted by, 76–77
    testimony to Kefauver of, 189–90
Lewis, Joe E., 195
Lewis, Milton, 161
Lipsky, Charles, 191
Long, Huey P., 20–22, 196
Longano, Arthur, 17
Loscalzo, Joseph, 161, 221–22
Loughlin, Edward V., 132, 143, 170, 221
Lucchese, Thomas "Three-Finger
    Brown," 17

Luciano, Charles "Lucky" (Sal-
    vatore Lucania), 6, 14, 30, 34, 54
    bootlegging by, 49, 56–57
    "Charles Ross" alias of, 75–76
    Costello's friendship with, 45–48
    in Cuba, 139–41
    death of, 248
    Dewey prosecution of, 73–77
    exiles in Italy of, 132–34, 140, 247–
        48
    Lansky and, 23–27, 47–49
    Maranzano assassination and, 25,
        60–61
    Maranzano meetings with, 57–58
    Masseria assassination and, 11, 25,
        56–59
    narcotics plans of, 140–41
    National Crime Syndicate orga-
        nization role of, 49
    prostitution charges against,
        74–77
    release of, 27, 132–34
    sentence of, 76, 133
    Siegel and, 24–25, 47–49, 140–41
Lyons, James J., 180

McCarran, Pat, 125
McCooey, John H., 40
McDonald, Marie "The Body," 144
McDonald, Miles, 176, 183–84, 226–27
    bookmaking testimony of, 200–201
McGraw, John, 2
McKee, Joseph V., 13, 40
McLaughlin, James, 196–98
McNicholas, Bridget, *see* O'Dwyer,
    Bridget McNicholas
Madden, Owen "Owney," 49, 64
Maffetore, Dukey, 83–84, 86, 88–89
Magaddino, Stefano "Steve," 140,
    242
Magoon, Blue Jaw, 85, 89, 91–92
Maione, Happy, 82–86, 89
Mancuso, Francis "Frank," 191, 217
Maranzano, Salvatore, 25, 33, 55–61
Marcantonio, Vito, 138, 171
Marcello, Carlos, 25, 140, 194–95

Marinelli, Albert, 62, 65–66
Martin, David, 175, 179
Martin, Gerald, 210
Masseria, Giuseppe "Joe the Boss," 11, 25, 33, 49, 54, 55–59
Matthews, Harry, 175
Medalie, George, 68
Moran, George "Bugs," 54, 55
Moran, James J., 3–4, 8, 9, 111, 115, 116, 215
    Anastasia and Parisi "wanted" cards removed by, 97–98, 124, 208, 213–14
    bookmaking payoffs to, 201, 209–10
    death of, 237
    Firemen's Association payoffs to, 150–51, 210–11, 222–23
    in Kefauver hearings, 208–11
    prison term of, 236–37
    sentencing of, 210–11, 236
    in union investigation, 119
    Water Supply Board appointment of, 179, 209
Moretti, Solly, 17, 229
Moretti, Willie, 127, 129, 139, 222
    Costello's protection of, 109–10
    death of, 229–31, 239
    in Kefauver hearings, 204–6
    statements about mob by, 17–18, 109–10
Morley, Viscount, 250
Morris, Newbold, 123, 168–71
Murder Inc., 16, 17, 43, 72, 76
    Anastasia as head of, 13–14, 34, 78, 87, 117
    Anastasia never prosecuted for, 95–98, 120–24, 206–8
    Buchalter and, 89–92
    Bugs & Meyer mob and, 24–25, 49, 78
    Finestein killing and, 83–84, 87–89
    Jewish hitmen of, 24–25, 49, 78
    O'Dwyer investigation of, 3, 14, 32–33, 43, 78, 81–99, 112, 114, 116–22, 129, 220
    Parisi never prosecuted for, 95–98

    Reles's death and, 32–34, 92–95, 121, 206–8, 212–13
    Reles's testimony on, 32–33, 82–85, 92, 95
    Rudnick killing and, 83, 84–86
    Siegel and, 31–34
    Tannenbaum's testimony on, 32–33
Murphy, Charles F., 63
Murphy, Thomas F., 183–84
Murtagh, John M., 132, 219–20
Mussolini, Benito, 31, 79
"Mustache Petes," 23, 55–56, 61, 229

narcotics traffic, 14, 140–41, 201–3, 243
National Crime Syndicate, 82
    Anna Genovese's testimony on, 135
    Apalachin meeting of, 242–43
    Brooklyn bookmaking payoffs by, 181–84, 218–19, 226–29
    Costello's leadership of, 33–34, 77, 107–11, 141, 171
    Costello takeover of, 6–7, 23–24, 54–62
    Erickson's records and, 177
    expansion of, in Florida, 171–72
    founding of, 6–7, 23–24, 54–55, 61–62
    killings prior to, 25, 54–61, 146
    New Jersey meeting places of, 17–18, 153
    organization plans for, 61–62
    post-Kefauver years of, 238–49
    in Siegel assassination, 140–41, 143–48
Neal, Clarence, 132, 143, 170, 191, 221
Newsweek, 108, 247
New York *Daily Mirror*, 138–39
New York *Herald-Tribune*, 143, 156, 161, 163, 168, 169, 180, 204, 236
New York *Journal-American*, 108, 126, 204
New York Sun, 169–70
New York *Sunday News*, 237
New York Times, 52, 152, 162, 249–50

"Night of the Sicilian Vespers," 61
Nitti, Frank "the Enforcer," 54
Nixon, Richard, 234
Nova, Algron, 160

O'Bannion, Dion, 54
O'Brien, Katherine, 128
O'Brien, William P., 182, 219, 228
O'Conor, Herbert, 187, 199, 200
O'Dwyer, Bridget McNicholas, 35–36
O'Dwyer, Catharine Lenihan "Kitty," 37–38, 39, 113, 137–38, 172
O'Dwyer, Frank, 42, 152
O'Dwyer, Jack, 42
O'Dwyer, Jim, 42
O'Dwyer, Joan, 137, 249
O'Dwyer, Patrick, 35–36, 42
O'Dwyer, Paul, 42–43, 137, 158, 235, 249
O'Dwyer, Sloan Simpson, 172–76, 180, 184, 234–35, 249
O'Dwyer, Tommy, 42
O'Dwyer, William "Bill-O":
  accused of associations with mob, 113–22, 162–63, 168–71
  Adonis and, 12
  Amen union investigation and, 117–19
  Anastasia not prosecuted by, 95–98, 120–24, 206–8, 212–14
  army career of, 3, 99, 111–12
  Bals's promotion by, 208
  bookmaking ignored by, 168–70, 176, 218–20
  as Brooklyn district attorney, 3, 43
  brothers of, 42–43
  budget problems of, 136, 148–50
  campaign bribes to Moran for, 201, 209–11
  Catharine's illness and, 113, 137–38
  charged with investigation irregularities, 116–22
  corruption imputed to, in Kefauver hearings, 185, 189, 191, 197–98, 201, 208–11

  death of, 249
  as district attorney, 78–79, 81
  divorce of, 234–35
  education of, 36, 39
  elected mayor, 123
  Firemen's Association payoffs to, 222–25
  first mayoral candidacy of (1941), 98–99
  first meeting with Costello of, 3–5, 7–10, 111–12, 114, 214–17
  first New York years of, 1–3, 36–37
  Hogan mayoral candidacy and, 165–68
  Irish background of, 35–37, 42
  Kefauver testimony of, 211–24
  as lawyer, 40
  Loughlin and, 132, 143
  McDonald bookmaking investigation and, 182–84
  as magistrate, 13, 37, 40–43
  marriage to Catharine Lenihan of, 37–38
  marriage to Sloan Simpson of, 172–76
  as mayor, 131–32, 136–38, 152–53, 159–60, 164–65, 176, 178–81, 211–12, 235, 249–50
  Mexico Ambassadorship of, 178–79, 183, 184, 211, 222, 233–35
  mob-connected appointments made by, 221–22
  Murder Inc. investigation of, 3, 14, 32–34, 43, 78, 81–99, 114, 116–22, 129, 206–8, 220
  newspaper embarrassments of, 169–71
  Parisi not prosecuted by, 95–98
  police career of, 2–3, 38–40, 112–13
  political appeal of, 112–13
  Reles's death and, 32–33, 92–94, 121, 206–8, 212–13
  resignation of, 178–81
  retirement of, 235–36
  Rosen's backing of, 122–23

O'Dwyer, William *(Continued)*
  second mayoral candidacy of
    (1945), 112–13, 122–23, 164–68
  Sherman and, 114–15, 197–98
  Stand and, 132, 143, 158
  in Tammany struggle, 132, 142–43,
    156–58, 165–68, 191, 221–22
  testimony of Costello meeting
    with, 3–5, 8–10, 214–17
  Tobey accused of bookmaking
    support by, 215–18
  Valente nomination and, 156–59
  wiretapping and, 162–63, 197–98
One hundred and Fourth Street
  gang, 46
Orecchio, Michael, 156
Organized crime, *see* National
  Crime Syndicate
Orgen, Jacob "Little Augie," 77

Panto, Peter, 116–21, 123
Parisi, Dandy Jack, 95–98, 208, 212
Parkowitz, Louis, 70
Patterson, Robert L., 112
Patterson, Thomas, 148–49
Pegler, Westbrook, 171
Perlman, Nathan, 177
Perry, Harry C., 65–66
Pinza, Ezio, 173
Piping Rock Casino, 11–12
Pisano, Anthony, *see* Carfano, An-
  thony
police payoffs, 7, 12, 17, 155–56, 171–72,
  176, 181–82, 218–19, 226–29
Presser, Nancy, 74
Profaci, Joe, 59, 242
Prohibition, 62, 66
  bootlegging after, 26
  bootlegging in, 6, 12, 24, 49–
    53
  criminals' reputations in, 38
prostitution, 74–77
Purple Gang (Detroit), 54, 85
Putnam, Gideon, 174

Quayle, Frank, 13, 132, 222

Raft, George, 28
Rao, Joseph, 138–39
Red Hook, 117
Reles, Abe "Kid Twist," 82–89, 92–
  98, 120, 124
  death of, 32–33, 92–94, 121, 206–8,
    212–13
  Finestein killing and, 83–84, 87–89
  Rudnick killing and, 86
Ricca, Paul "the Waiter," 24
Robilotto, John, 230–31
Robinson, Sugar Ray, 239
Roe, James A., 165
Rogers, Hugo, 157–58, 160, 162, 165–67,
  168
Romeo, Tony, 117, 118
Romero, Anthony, 14
Roosevelt, Franklin Delano, 62, 65,
  103, 112, 165, 178
Roosevelt, Theodore "Teddy," 173
Roosevelt Raceway, bookmakers at,
  104–7, 189–90, 195–97
Rosen, Al, 122–23
Rosen, Joseph, 90–92, 117
Rosen, Morris, 147
Rosen, Nig, *see* Stromberg, Harry
Rosenkrantz, Bernard "Lulu," 73
Rosenthal, Abe, 222
Ross, Charles, *see* Luciano, Charles
  "Lucky"
Rothman, Hooky, 145
Rothstein, Arnold, 6, 48–49, 53
Rouse, Thomas, 131
Rubin, Max, 91
Rudnick, George "Whitey," 83–86
Ryan, Clendenin, 162–63
Ryan, Kenneth, 162
Ryan, Thomas Fortune, 162

Saietta, Ignazio "Lupo the Wolf,"
  45, 49
St. Valentine's Day Massacre, 54
Sampson, Frank J., 142–43, 156, 158,
  221
Sarubbi, Paul, 217
Sausser, Harry, 194

Saverio, Frank, *see* Costello, Frank
Scalise, John, 242
Scannavino, Gus, 117, 119–20
Schoenhaus, "Big Harry," 80
Schultz, Dutch, *see* Flegenheimer, Arthur "Dutch Schultz"
Schuster, Arnold, 241
Scottoriggio, Joseph, 138–39
Seabury, Samuel, 65
Sears, Charles B., 104
Sedway, Moe "Little Moe," 29–30, 144–48
Segal, Harry "Champ," 30
Shalleck, Joseph, 64
Shapiro, Irv, 82
Shapiro, Jacob "Gurrah," 27
    Dewey's prosecution of, 77–79
    extortion racket of, 14, 77–78
Shapiro, Meyer, 82
Shapiro, Willie, 82
Sherman, Irving, 8–9, 114–15, 196–97, 214, 216, 222, 245
Shor, Toots, 51, 109
Siegel, Benjamin "Bugsy," 6, 10, 18, 23, 47–49, 51, 60, 85, 92, 114, 129
    assassination plans for, 140–41, 143–45
    death of, 143–48
    divorce of, 125
    Flamingo construction of, 125, 127, 141, 144, 146–47
    Greenberg killing and, 31–33
    investigation of crimes of, 31–33
    as Jewish mob leader, 27–28
    Lansky and, 24–25
    life style of, 28, 30–31
    Luciano and, 24–25
    Maranzano assassination and, 60–61
    Masseria assassination and, 11, 25, 57–59
    mistresses of, 30–31, 125–27, 144, 148, 201–3
    second marriage of, 126–27
    West Coast territory of, 28–30

    wire service operation of, 28–29, 125
Simpson, John, 173
Simpson, Sloan, *see* O'Dwyer, Sloan Simpson
slot-machines:
    bribery from profits of, 163
    Costello and, 6, 15, 19–23, 53–54, 79, 102, 107, 163–64, 196
    in Louisiana, 20–23, 79
    as mint machines, 19–20
    profit from, 19, 22, 163–64
Smith, Alfred E., 62, 65
Smith, James F., 210–11
Solomon, Charles "King," 54
Spellman, Francis Cardinal, 138
Stand, Bert, 170, 214
    at O'Dwyer-Costello meeting, 4, 9, 221
    as Tammany Hall secretary, 4–5, 103, 132, 143, 158
Stark, Max, 154
Steingut, Irwin, 12
Strauss, Harry "Pittsburgh Phil," 82–83, 86–89, 90
Stromberg, Harry (Nig Rosen), 23, 54, 60, 62
Sullivan, Christopher "Christy," 65–66
Sullivan, James "Whistling Jimmy," 172
Sullivan, Jeremiah, 165
Sullivan, Timothy "Big Tim," 65
Sutherland, Kenneth, 13
Sutton, Willie, 241
Swann, Edward, 47
Sweeney, Martin, 174

Tammany Hall, 40, 142–43, 168
    Aurelio Supreme Court appointment and, 102–4, 221
    Costello and, 3–5, 7, 49, 62, 65–66, 101–4, 107, 132, 143, 158, 191, 217, 221–22
    federal positions controlled by, 65

Tammany Hall *(Continued)*
  Francis Valente nomination and, 156–59
  Hines's mob connections and, 62–65
  Kennedy leadership of, 3–5, 102–3, 217
  Marinelli's mob connections and, 65–66
  mayoral nominations and, 4–5, 217
  O'Dwyer's accusation of criminal influence on, 78–79
  O'Dwyer's fight with, 132, 142–43, 156–58, 164–68, 191, 221–22
  Rothstein as mob liaison for, 48–49
  Stand as secretary of, 4–5, 103, 132, 158
Tannenbaum, Allie, 31–32, 91–92, 95
Terranova, Ciro, 45
Tobey, Charles, 187, 190–91, 194, 201, 207, 209, 212–16, 215–18, 223
Torrio, Johnny, 24
Trafficante, Louis, 242
Trafficante, Santo, 140
Truman, Harry S., 38, 143, 165, 170, 178, 222, 233
Tucker, Sophie, 195
Turkus, Burton, 32, 72, 82–85, 91, 92–93, 117, 121, 213

Uniformed Firemen's Association, 150–51, 210–11, 222–25
union takeovers, 78–79
  Amen's investigations of, 117–19
  Panto's death and, 116–19

Valachi, Joe, 135
Valente, Francis L., 156–59

Valente, Louis A., 156–57
Vernotico, Anna, *see* Genovese, Anna Vernotico

Wahrman, Abe, 75–76
Walker, James J., 2, 40, 178
Wallander, Arthur, 132, 138, 219, 220
Wapinski, Isidor, 16
Warren, Earl, 163–64
Weber, Louis, 209–10
Weinberg, Abraham "Bo," 56–57
Weinberg, George, 80
Weintraub, Max, 150
Weiss, Carl A., 22
Weiss, Mendy, 90–92, 117
Wexler, Irving "Waxey Gordon," 49, 54, 68–71, 79
Whalen, Grover, 159
Whalen, Richard T., 228
Williams, Edward Bennett, 232–33, 239
Winchell, Walter, 89–90, 108
Winslow, Francis A., 53
Wolf, George, 50, 51, 52–53, 55, 60, 74, 79, 104, 110–11, 133–34, 135, 160, 192–93, 206, 216, 231
Workman, Charley "the Bug," 56–57, 73
Wright Field fraud, 3, 9–10, 111–12, 217

Yale, Frankie, 12, 49, 54

Zachary, Frank, 159–60
Zerilli, Joe, 242
Zichello, Philip, 222
Zito, Frankie, 242
Zwillman, Abner "Longy," 17, 18, 23, 49, 54, 62, 109, 127, 129, 244